W9-BDU-784

Eric Bentley is Brander Matthews Professor of Dramatic Literature at Columbia University, and author of several books, including *What Is Theatre?* and *The Playwright as Thinker*. He is also well known as a stage director and has directed several Shaw plays.

Here are some of the comments that his *Bernard Shaw* gave rise to:

". . . the best critical description of my public activities I have yet come across."   BERNARD SHAW.

"Mr. Shaw has scored another victory. He has conquered Mr. Bentley. This is no trivial feat."

MARGARET WEBSTER, *Accent.*

". . . its author's best critical performance to date."

GEORGE JEAN NATHAN,
The New York Herald Tribune.

". . . the best book on Bernard Shaw in the language."
Theatre Arts.

". . . the fairest, most illuminating, and the best analysis so far to have been written of (Shaw's) beliefs, his methods, and his meaning."

JOHN MASON BROWN, *The Saturday Review.*

". . . a splendid book which I regard as quite the best study of Shaw available in insight and scope. It is an essential item for the student."

EDMUND FULLER, *George Bernard Shaw: Critic of Western Morale.*

While, except for a few corrections, the original text (1947) has been left as it was, the 1957 edition contains a new appendix on "Shaw and the Actors."

BERNARD SHAW

BERNARD SHAW

1856 - 1950

BY ERIC BENTLEY

Amended Edition

A New Directions Paperbook

First Published as New Directions Paperbook No. 59, 1957.

Manufactured in the United States of America.
New Directions Books are published for James Laughlin
by New Directions Publishing Corporation,
333 Sixth Avenue, New York 10014.

FIFTH PRINTING

TO

JACQUES BARZUN and LIONEL TRILLING

". . . it would seem that what is called wit is a certain "dramatic" way of thinking. Instead of treating his ideas as mere symbols, the witty man sees them, he hears them, and above all makes them converse with one another like persons. He puts them on the stage, and himself, to some extent, into the bargain. . . . But if wit consists, for the most part, in seeing things "sub specie theatri," it is evidently capable of being specially directed to one variety of dramatic art, namely, comedy."

—*Henri Bergson*

> "Real culture lives by sympathies and admirations, not by dislikes and disdains; under all misleading wrappings it pounces unerringly upon the human core."
>
> —William James

The books in this series * are introductions to modern authors who are insufficiently or incorrectly known. But what is unfamiliar or difficult about Bernard Shaw? Who has not already formed his opinion of Shaw? Who has not published it? "Every habitual writer now before the public from William Archer and James Huneker to 'Vox Populi' and 'An Old Subscriber' has had his say about Shaw." These are words that get truer all the time; and they were written—by H. L. Mencken—in 1905.

I should not pretend that I wrote this book to Fill a Gap of the kind often mentioned in favorable book reviews. I wrote it because I wanted to. I had written two books in which Shaw came to occupy a central and yet—to me at least—problematic position. I say "came to" because in the earlier drafts of my first book Shaw's place was both inconspicuous and, so to say, disgraceful. He was a villain in a gallery of villains. When the manuscript was revised for the press, however, he looked like the solitary hero of the collection. In the second book my interest was in the theatre, especially in the so-called drama of ideas. In this realm too Shaw rose in my estimation from being one of a

* The book was written for the Makers of Modern Literature Series.

crowd to being the chief one in the crowd. I went on reading him, and seeing him in the theatre, after finishing both books. Although with the passage of time I was less and less able to understand him, in the sense of being able to explain him with a formula, I became more and more aware of the inadequacy of the formulae which I and others had up to now made shift with.

When a publisher asked me to collect the opinions of the best critics and make up a book from essays and excerpts, on the lines of current critical volumes on Henry James and Franz Kafka, I took the opportunity of reading a lot of things on Shaw. It was a gruelling experience. Although infinitely more had been written about Shaw than about James or any other modern writer, it was impossible to find a couple of dozen essays and excerpts on the level of the James and Kafka volumes. Instead of making the anthology I asked myself: if Shaw is a simple author, why did so many people feel obliged to give their opinion of him, why did their opinions differ so widely from each other, and why were so many of them complacently shallow? I found praise, but most of it naive or invidious. I found blame, but most of it incoherent and scurrilous. Everyone had certainly had his say on Shaw, but the say was casual without being tentative and vehement without being solid. Léon Daudet had called Shaw a "fool," Ezra Pound had called him "an intellectual cheesemite," "a ninth-rate artist" and the like. Everyone had a clever phrase for Shaw. George Moore's was: "the funny man in the boarding house," Winston Churchill's the same thing in Churchillese: "the World's most famous intellectual

Clown and Pantaloon in one, and the charming Columbine of the capitalist pantomime." "John the Baptist pretending to be Karl Marx," said St. John Ervine. "Red rags and white corpuscles," said Edward Arlington Robinson. "The unspeakable Irishman," was Henry James' contribution. W. B. Yeats said: "a barbarian of the barricades." W. H. Auden was more flattering but no less pertly alliterative with: "Fabian Figaro." Lesser fry spawned: "A fifth carbon copy of Voltaire," "a second-hand Brummagem Ibsen." . . .

Shaw's work is most conveniently considered under the three heads: politics, religion, and drama. In reading through the endless comments on Shaw one is aware of opposition in each of these three fields, opposition coming from a few easily identified sources. The opposition to his politics has come from conservatives, from Marxists, and from liberals. The conservatives dismissed Shaw as an ass or denounced him (1914–1918) as a traitor. The Marxists (Lenin, Trotsky, Lunacharsky, Mirsky, Caudwell) stamp him as a *petit bourgeois* mind. The British communist R. Palme Dutt once wrote of "the open and blatant counter-revolutionism of Shaw . . . distrust of the proletariat . . . the last pitiful bleat of the rentier or *petit bourgeois* faced with the conditions of capitalism which he cannot understand." Many liberals, especially anticommunist liberals, share Dutt's view. Sidney Hook writes:

> Shaw has a passion for anaesthetic efficiency at any cost to human life and freedom. He does not see the masses as individuals but as material to be

sawed and planed to fit a fixed pattern. He would have no objection to an efficient Hitlerism without heroics or race nonsense.

Shaw's "religion" has also been attacked from opposite wings. Huxleyan agnostics like H. G. Wells, J. M. Robertson, and Joseph McCabe have thought him soft-headed and fundamentally friendly to traditional religion. Prince Kropotkin said that Shaw's case against science was the old Catholic line. On the other hand, Catholics and Anglo-Catholics have thought of Shaw as a neo-pagan or at least a Calvinist. G. K. Chesterton said (referring to the last speech of *Back to Methuselah*):

> It is *not* enough that there is always a beyond. Intelligent people want to know what it is that is beyond and how it can really be shown to be better than what is behind.

The Catholic view is that Shaw's philosophy is home-made and eclectic. It accrues, says J. P. Hackett, from "taking over the parts of Christianity that attract, combining them with the latest scientific news, and calling the result the religion of the twentieth century." T. S. Eliot says: "The potent ju-ju of the Life Force is a gross superstition." This sentence is one on which probably all Shaw's hostile critics agree. But they not only speak from different convictions of their own. Their diagnosis of the Shavian outlook is also different. To some, Shaw, the champion of will and feeling, is an arch-irrationalist. Perhaps this is what Mr. Eliot means by "potent ju-ju." To others, Shaw, the champion and incarnation of intellect, is the arch-rationalist. W. J.

FOREWORD

Turner says: "Mr. Bernard Shaw is the last and the purest of the rationalists." This view has spread in ever-growing circles, reaching the readers of *Life* in August 1946 when an editorial declared that, according to Shaw, the human race can "add cubits to its stature and centuries to its span merely by taking thought." Questioned about this, *Life's* editors wrote to me: "Shaw believed in the Guiding Force of pure thought and pure reason rather than any faith behind it."

T. S. Eliot distinguishes between Shaw's religion of Life and the artist's interest in life. "Mr. Shaw never was really interested in life." A writer in Middleton Murry's *Adelphi* once said of Shaw: "he is in love with life but only *interested* in human beings" and added a comparison with Nietzsche:

> Both have that great longing which is a great contempt and both use prevalent biological ideas to express it: to Shaw Evolution is the path of Godhead, and to Nietzsche Man is a bridge to the Superman. But here similarity ceases. To Shaw Godhead is omniscience and omnipotence: To Nietzsche it is innocence. To Shaw the Superman is an Ancient who aspires to become Force without Form: to Nietzsche the Superman is a Child. Shaw's Ancient seeks a heaven where contemplation shall be his only joy: Nietzsche's Child seeks nothing but to stand as man upon the natural earth and be a man with men. But there is a still deeper difference. Shaw sees a moment only as a point on an infinite straight line, and imagines the

only Life Eternal to be Everlasting Life; but Nietzsche, knowing otherwise, cancelled the Dogma of the Superman by the equal and opposite Dogma of the Eternal Return so that every moment's living should be Eternal Life.

The gist of this seems to be that Shaw is a rationalist even in his irrationalism. He may talk about life, but he is somehow apart from it, abstract and cold. From this position it is but a step to the view—of H. G. Wells, Frank Harris, and D. H. Lawrence—that Shaw is a kind of eunuch.

"A pure ratiocinator, a manipulator of ideas" says Mr. Turner. The characterization leads us to the critique of Shaw's theatre. "The talky, sexless type of play" was Frank Harris's phrase. At the outset of Shaw's theatrical career the best newspaper critic in London said Shaw's pieces were NOT PLAYS and later the next best compared Shaw to a ventriloquist and also a jelly-fish. A leitmotif of Victorian and Edwardian criticism is that Shaw's plays are impossibly new-fangled. The next generation changed the tune: they found Shaw *passé*. Edmund Wilson in *The New Republic* and George Jean Nathan in *The American Mercury* wrote of Shaw as of a man who had had his day. "Dramatically precocious and poetically less than immature," says one of the speakers in a dialogue by T. S. Eliot: no speaker puts a case *for* Shaw. Like James and Conrad among novelists, like Synge, Apollinaire, and Cocteau among playwrights, Mr. Eliot is highly critical of the "literature of ideas" which Shaw's generation had given vogue to. Mr. Eliot once praised James for his

xvi

"mastery over, his baffling escape from, ideas; a mastery and an escape which are perhaps the last test of a superior intelligence. He had a mind so fine that no idea could violate it. . . ." That Shaw's mind has been so violated is a general assumption. "He has sacrificed emotion to intellect, intuition to the syllogism. . . . In all his plays, even in *Saint Joan,* he is the chief character and he always gets the best of the argument." This is not Mr. Eliot speaking but Harold J. Laski. The view was a commonplace years before either Mr. Eliot or Mr. Laski advanced it. Here is one of the earlier versions:

> Just as the persons of his drama are logical abstractions to whom, to aid in their acceptance, a surface humanity is added, so is his drama itself a secondary image of his picture of the world. He sees men as ideas walking. He sees art as a conflict of ideas. A thousand lovable, intimate, humorous, ridiculous traits he sees, and he makes a pastiche of them for his purposes. They do not result in the comic vision. . . . They do not result in the tragic vision. . . . It is a publicist's vision.

Such are the opinions of Shaw's critics. And there is one critic who has probably been more damaging than all the rest: Shaw himself. Some people think him chiefly a self-advertiser. After all, he once wrote:

> With the single exception of Homer there is no eminent writer, not even Sir Walter Scott, whom

I despise so entirely as I despise Shakespeare
when I measure my mind against his.

And even if we see that Shaw here means something very
special by *mind,* can we forget the self-praise which Shaw
has fed to the press over the last fifty years and more?
Well, we need not forget it. For it is precisely the pose of
arrogance that has harmed Shaw. He hoodwinked the
public all too well, and they decided to forget that Shaw
had called his plays "petty tentatives" and himself "a
comparatively insignificant Irish journalist," that he wrote,
coolly surveying his career as a playwright:

> I dare not claim to be the best playwright in the
> English language; but I believe myself to be one
> of the best ten and may therefore be classed as
> one of the best hundred.

From such a sentence as this we learn that Shaw has dam-
aged his own reputation, first, by his supposed vanity, by
pretending to be "better than Shakespeare," and, second,
by precisely the opposite method, by excessive modesty.
The critics accordingly attack him for his "vain" remarks,
using his "modest" remarks as ammunition. Shaw the
thinker and sociologist has never been more ruthlessly
debunked than in the following passage:

> As both he [Sidney Webb] and Beatrice con-
> scientiously refrained from forming their conclu-
> sions until they had with inexhaustible industry
> investigated all the available evidence, they had
> furious disputes with me at almost every step. I

am not a complete apriorist, because I always start from a single fact or incident which strikes me as significant. But one is enough. I never collect authorities nor investigate conditions. I just deduce what happened and why it happened from my flair for human nature, knowing that if necessary I can find plenty of documents and witnesses to bear me out in any possible conclusion. This is a shorter method than that of the Webbs. . . .

Shaw's greatness as an artist has never been more authoritatively denied than in the following passage where Shaw speaks of the obtrusion of "funny business" in his plays:

This has prevented me from becoming a really great author. I have unfortunately this desperate temptation that suddenly comes on me. Just when I am really rising to the height of my power that I may become really tragic and great, some absurd joke occurs and the anti-climax is irresistible. . . . I cannot deny that I have got the tragedian and I have got the clown in me; and the clown trips me up in the most dreadful way.

These "modest" remarks of Shaw's are really no truer than the "vain" remarks. He exaggerates both the vanity and the modesty and thus produces what he is most famous for among the critical—Contradictions. It is remarkable how large an amount of Shaw criticism is taken up with refutation. Even admiring critics from Chesterton to Edmund Wilson might have called their books and essays: Shaw Found Out. Perhaps the critic who called his book *Bernard Shaw: the Man and the Mask* meant only that Shaw assumed a pose before the world. But gradually the pet notions of modern literary psychology—the split and multiple personality—became clichés of Shaw criticism. A Catholic critic wrote *Shaw: George versus Bernard*, simply dividing Shaw into the part he liked and the part he disliked, and assigning one name to each. Lenin's "a good man fallen among Fabians" expresses the same like-and-dislike. Shaw has diverse gifts and diverse opinions. One cannot sympathise or agree with them all. One therefore separates the sheep from the goats and talks about Shaw's Contradictions.

"A chaos of clear opinions"—this is the latest summary of Shaw's work. Not surprisingly, the author of it observed that Shaw was an indifferent artist. In this book, it will be assumed that most of Shaw's opinions *are* clear and that those who are not already acquainted with them would prefer Shaw's own summary (in *Everybody's Political What's What*) to anything second-hand. One need not try to do Shaw's work for him. This book asks, not: what does Shaw think? but: to what end does he think? what kind of a thinker is he? Not: what plays has he written? nor yet, primarily: just how good are they? but: what kind of plays? what sort of an artist have we in Shaw? Not: what are the facts of his life? what anecdotes are told by him and about him? but: what kind of a man is he? what is the nature and upshot of his career?

Obviously I am presuming to save Shaw both from his friends and his foes. And from himself too. Anyone who admires Shaw and sees beneath his surface has to undertake this triple defence. I do not mean that I in my turn am penning a logical refutation. Such opinions as I have been stating are not all of them such as one can refute with any finality. What I shall do is to compare what Shaw is generally thought to be with what I have found him to be. Though there is no formula for the understanding of Shaw —the more one reads him the more one discovers—there is a formula for this book about him. It claims to present, not *A*, which is said to be so, but *B*, which, if you look freshly at Shaw, you will find to be so.

The book is polemical. It is a defence, and cannot but be limited in its usefulness and validity by the tactics of defence. I can only say (defending *myself* now) that the time has not yet come to write unpolemically of Bernard Shaw. Our greatest contemporary polemicist, he is immersed in our liveliest—that is to say, most unsettled —problems. Not being detached from Shaw's world, we cannot be detached about Shaw. It is precisely the people who pretend to be impartial about him who are suspect. The rest can confess their partiality and reduce it to a minimum by being aware of it and on guard against it.

When a critic sets down the merits of a writer he admires, he tends to make of him something all too complete. You would gather from certain biographies and critical monographs that their subject—X, Y, or Z—is a liberal education in himself. Conversely, there are critics these days who make it a complete condemnation of an author if he is *not* an education in himself, if he is not as great as the very greatest, if he lacks any one splendid quality. Let me state at the beginning that I am not setting up Shaw as the Complete Genius who renders other writers unnecessary by uniting every great attribute in his single person, but neither can I hold it legitimate to dismiss Shaw because he lacks such and such a fine attribute of another writer. In Shakespeare there is much that is not to be found in Dante, and *vice versa*. There are realms which Shaw never enters (though he does not deny their existence) and we cannot find in him what we go to Dostoevsky, Proust, or Kafka for.

This book is about what we *can* find in him. Since Bernard Shaw has made so much of the writer as thinker, since he himself is so full of doctrine, and is accused of being doctrinaire, it is advisable to begin by examining Shavian thinking. Chapter 1 deals with politics: Shaw's "clear opinions" do not seem so chaotic if we see them in their historical context and if we see the "contradictions" as a synthesis of different political traditions. Chapter 2 deals with Shaw's religion: his famous "naturalistic mysticism" does not seem so arbitrary if we see it too in an historical context and if we see that Shaw is trying to salvage as much as possible both in orthodox and free-thinking attitudes to life. Both/And: such is the Shavian inclusiveness. The phrase will recur like a leitmotif throughout this book. Shaw has tried to balance individualism and collectivism, freedom and authority, diversity and unity, not in the interests of mechanical symmetry, ostentatious broadmindedness, or naive eclecticism, but in an intelligent effort to lay hold of that which is good in each philosophy of life. He has done this as a concrete moralist with a feeling for the simplicities, the basic human facts. He has therefore been brought into conflict with the portentous orthodoxies of our time. He has defended socialism against the socialists, liberty against the liberals, science against the scientists, religion against the religionists. Naturally he is accused of being anti-socialist, anti-liberal, anti-scientific, and anti-religious.

One of the advantages of looking at Shaw's thinking before looking at his art is that the conclusion is at once thrust upon us that his thinking is at all points the thinking of an artist. Nor is this to discredit it. The thinking of an artist is not necessarily the thinking of a dilettante. Shaw has his contribution to make in politics, in science, and in religion. That he thinks as an artist is a peculiarity and not a handicap. In Chapters 1 and 2, nothing, perhaps, emerges more clearly than the fact that in the realm of the general and the abstract Shaw is always gravitating towards the particular and the concrete. The peculiar intensity with which he sees human beings and the peculiar intensity with which he feels life as he lives it—these things are at the bottom of his politics and his philosophy.

It is not likely that such a thinker would, in his art, suddenly turn abstract and statistical. It is not likely, and it does not occur. Shaw's plays have been thought abstract by simple and absurd inference from the fact that they are full of discussion of general topics. Shaw tells us that the whole universe, insofar as he can comprehend it, is his workshop. He tells us that economics are to him what anatomy was to Michelangelo. The *treatment* of such topics, however, is not abstract. Abstract thought becomes the material for non-abstract thinking as much in Shaw as in the famous—and otherwise absolutely different—John Donne. In the end, then, Shaw's mind is *not* "violated by ideas." Shaw not only *preaches* feeling as a philosopher of "irrationalism," he objectifies feeling as an artist. And one of the deepest feelings he objectifies is a sense of the failure of those very "ideas" which are commonly supposed to be the whole Shaw.

Chapter 3—"The Theatre"—is the center of this book. The gist of it is that terms like "drama of ideas" and "problem play"—suggesting as they do that Shavian drama is abstract and propagandist—are not adequate descriptions of the plays Shaw has written. Shaw is primarily an artist. His plays are worth analysis both for what is original in them and for what is in the tradition of high comedy. They cannot be divorced from Shaw's thinking, because Shaw, like every literary artist, is what Flaubert called a "triple thinker," one who thinks with his imagination and on several planes at once.

The fourth and last chapter offers an interpretation of Shaw's career, a success story that is all the better for its failures. Shaw has lived out the "tragedy of greatness" that is depicted in more than one of his plays: he has achieved a kind of prestige but has not in the least been understood. He has failed, moreover, in his big propagandist purposes. On the other hand, having succeeded as an artist, he may also enjoy some success as a teacher. Is it not good Shavian doctrine that art is the great educator? Shaw has often said that in the past century or two our artist-thinkers have given us a body of literature that constitutes a sort of new Bible. To this Bible—along with Voltaire, Goethe, Ibsen, Tolstoy and others—Bernard Shaw has been a liberal contributor.

"What is unfamiliar or difficult about Bernard Shaw?"

FOREWORD

The question is not rhetorical. Despite appearances, an interpretation of Shaw is twice called for: to disentangle a credible man and artist from the mass of myth that surrounds him, and to discover the complex component parts of his "simplicity." Such are the aims of this book.

C O N T E N T S

FOREWORD   xi

1. POLITICAL ECONOMY   1

2. VITAL ECONOMY   44

3. THE THEATRE   93

4. THE FOOL IN CHRIST   183

APPENDIX TO THE SECOND EDITION (1957):
SHAW AND THE ACTORS   220

BIBLIOGRAPHICAL NOTES   233

KEY TO QUOTATIONS   244

INDEX   248

1. POLITICAL ECONOMY

1

"The love of economy is the root of all virtue."
—JOHN TANNER, M.I.R.C.

OF THE FIFTEEN REPUTATIONS WHICH SHAW HAS LAID CLAIM to, his reputation as a socialist is perhaps the most familiar. Shaw has been expounding socialism for over sixty years, and there would be no excuse for expounding it for him, were it not that ignorance of it is displayed in nearly everything that is said on the subject. Before giving Shaw a careful reading I myself had heard only two things about his politics: that when he was young he belonged to a dreary group of half-hearted socialists who imagined that capitalism could be overthrown by wire-pulling and talk; and that when he grew old he came to admire tyranny and condone violence. I was not the only one to hear things of that sort. Most of Shaw's biographers re-affirm the cliché about the Fabian Society. Perhaps the biographers have read H. G. Wells, who, when the Fabians threw him out, wrote: "If they had the universe in hand, I know they would take down all the trees and put up stamped tin green shades and sunlight accumulators." Shaw's political philosophy is buried as deep as, say, William Godwin's. Digging Shaw up again, as if he were one of those writers whose chief glory is to be rediscovered in academic theses, I propose to discuss three questions: first, what is Shaw's "Fabianism"? second, what are Shaw's views on the prime problems of political philosophy, the problems of the state and revolution, authority and liberty? third, what is the pedigree and status of Shaw's political philosophy? where does he stand in the tradition of European socialism?

The attack on Shaw's politics has taken several different lines: that he has betrayed his earlier Fabianism, that Fabianism was not worth betraying, and even that he never was a real Fabian. Evidently we need light on Fabianism as well as on Shaw. The Fabian Society, founded in 1884, and after a few months opening its doors to Sidney Webb and Bernard Shaw, was a club of Victorian intellectuals whose plan was never either more or less than to influence the public life of their country as much as a club of intellectuals can. Even today, when the Society is larger than ever before, it has not more than 5000 members. It is idle, then, to complain that it is not a proletarian party and it is impossible to sneer at it as a group of intellectuals unless one thinks groups of intellectuals have no right to exist. The Fabian Society differed from a political party not only in its sheer lack of party organization but also in not being bound to have

2

a 'party line.' [1] There was in fact wide divergence of opinion on many things. Agreement limited itself to the socialist goal and to certain attitudes concerning ways and means, attitudes which gradually defined themselves in the struggle against capitalism and, perhaps even more, in the struggle with other kinds of socialism, especially Marxism. Not that Shaw, for one, ever concealed his debt to Marx. His socialism began with Marx and Henry George in 1882. The economic basis of history "dawned on" Shaw when he heard George speak; it was clinched by his reading of the first volume of *Kapital.* In later years Shaw would call himself an "old Marxist." Nevertheless, when he declares (*Fabian Quarterly,* April 1944) that "Socialists who are not essentially Marxist are not Socialists at all" he apparently understands by Marxism solely the economic interpretation of history and the uncompromising collectivist stand. It does not appear that Shaw read anything in Marxist literature except the *Communist Manifesto* and *Kapital* I and II. For their part the Marxists denounced Shaw and the Fabians. It is to them even more perhaps than to reactionaries that we owe the legend that Fabianism was academic and futile. Even so moderate a liberal as Mr. Edmund Wilson confesses to having derived his damaging critique of Bernard Shaw's Fabianism from a Marxist source.

Marxist socialism claims to be, not a sentiment of indignation at injustice, but a scientific demonstration that

[1] See *Fabian Tract No. 70* (1896): "It [the Society] has no distinctive opinions on the Marriage Question, Religion, Art, abstract Economics, historic Evolution, Currency, or any other subject than its own special business of practical Democracy and Socialism."

capitalism will give way to socialism. Fabianism begins and ends as an appeal—emotionally based—for social justice. Negatively stated, it is a protest against social inequality. Though the Fabians were far from knowing it their attitude reached its most highly articulated expression in Shaw's *Intelligent Woman's Guide* in which exact economic equality is called for to provide a basis for the natural diversity—or inequality—of men. How such conceptions differ from Marxism became clear in lengthy disputes between the two schools of thought.

The Fabian quarrel with the early Marxists was over two closely connected parts of Marxist doctrine: the labor theory of value and the class struggle. Shaw himself led the Fabians in both disputes. The technical side of his critique of the labor theory of value he derived from the British economist Stanley Jevons who advanced a theory of "marginal utility" identical with that which was independently advanced on the continent in the 'seventies and 'eighties. Following Jevons, Shaw denied that the exchange value of a commodity depended primarily on the amount of socially necessary labor put into it and argued that the value of any commodity is a function of the quantity available. Fearing that this argument would take the teeth out of socialism by denying that the capitalist's profits were stolen from the workmen's earnings, in the sense that the product of labor is in excess of its price, the Marxists clung to Ricardo's labor theory of value. Shaw was more impressed by another side of the Ricardian economics: its description of rent. In rent he finds the diagnostic of capitalism. And in *Fabian Essays* (1889), written before the advent of inductive, historical

4

economics (it was Beatrice Webb who would lead the Fabians into this path later), Shaw proceeds on time-honored Ricardian lines. His account of rent may be read as a parable.

Mr. A seizes the best piece of land in a virgin region and makes $1000 with its products. Mr. B, the next man to turn up, gets inferior land which yields, say, $500. Mr. A may now rent his land to Mr. B for $500, for the latter could not make a higher rate of profit anyway. Mr. A can now retire and live as an idler on rent. So much for the parable. Shaw now extends the use of the term "rent" to the whole area of private profit making. The remedy for the injustice it involves is socialism:

> What the achievement of socialism involves economically is the transfer of rent from the class which now appropriates it to the whole people. Rent being that part of the produce which is individually unearned, this is the only equitable method of disposing of it.

In other words Shaw agrees with Proudhon that "property is theft." Shaw's "rent" is much the same as Marx's "surplus value," but the injustice of the capitalist system is to Shaw all the greater because commodities do *not* exchange according to the labor that has gone into them:

> Commodities produced in the most favorable situations, well inside the margin of cultivation, with the minimum of labor, will fetch as high a price as commodities produced at the margin

5

with the maximum of labor. And all the difference between the two goes to the landlord.

Thus from the Ricardian parable follows the Jevonian
principle that "the exchange of the least useful part of
the supply fixes the exchange value of all the rest." From
this principle follows the Shavian definition of humanity
under capitalism.

In a society of buying and selling the vast mass of the
population has nothing to sell but itself. If there were
only one workman in their settlement, Mr. A and Mr. B
would have to pay a good deal for his services. But, the
supply of workmen being in excess of the need, their value
falls to nothing. To nothing, not to their wage level. For
a wage is only the feeding and stabling of the animal.
Wherever horses are to be had for the asking, at no cost
save their maintenance, their value is not the cost of
maintenance: it is nil. Capitalism ought thus, says Shaw,
to be called proletarianism, which again is but a polite
word for prostitution. Mrs. Warren's profession is only the
most dramatic example of proletarianism. That is why
Shaw, the dramatist, chose it to illustrate the nature of
modern society.

Shaw's theory of value, then, was, like Marx's, the hub
of an analysis of capitalism. Where it differed from Marx,
other than verbally, it differed in being less of a "scientific" demonstration on the one hand and less of a metaphysic on the other. And this meant not only that Shaw's
economic essays are infinitely smaller things in intention
and effect than Marx's but that Shaw is much less of a believer in fixed laws both in economics and nature. He

6

seized on Jevons because the latter seemed to leave a loophole for human will and effort. In Jevons there was no "law of motion of capitalism," no historical inevitability. Shaw fought the Marxists whenever, like the Darwinists, they seemed to be determinists.

The discussion of value was opened and closed in the 'eighties. The matter of the class struggle needed a lengthier airing. (Again Shaw's chief antagonist was the contemporary English champion of Marx, H. M. Hyndman.) Shaw's argument in this battle was not in the least the argument of classical economy—that there is a harmony of interests as between capital and labor. He fully agreed with Marx that there was no such harmony. He fully shared Marx's wish for a classless society. He did not agree however that present antagonisms of interest would automatically induce the proletariat to struggle for power. Again it is the law of history, the historical necessity, the inevitability, that Shaw objects to. He fears that reliance on them is as futile as reliance on God and that to wait for History to produce socialism is to wait forever. When the Marxist replies that if the workers are not class-conscious they must be made so he is of course appealing from historical necessity to the will of a minority. Shaw is not averse to this. He merely concludes that, so prompted, the struggle for socialism will have lower and upper class people on both sides and is therefore not accurately described as a *class* struggle.

The present absence of class consciousness is not the only thing. There always will be an absence of proletarian class consciousness on the part of those whose customers are the rich:

The line that separates those who live on rich customers from those who live on poor customers: in other words, which separates those interested in the maintenance of Capitalism from those interested in its replacement by Socialism, is a line drawn not between rich and poor, capitalist and proletarian, but right down the middle of the proletariat to the bottom of the very poorest section.

Thus the class struggle of the Marxists—the struggle between those who pay and receive wages—is cut across by another struggle—the struggle between those whose customers live on interest and those whose customers live on wages.

To the Marxist all this is ineffably bourgeois: the Fabians fail to see the historic mission of the working class. Naturally. For the Fabians deny that such things as historic missions exist. And—it is true—they are unique as post-Marxist socialists in putting no more faith in the proletariat as such than in any other group. Less, if anything. Shaw has always held that if the poor were already wiser and better than anybody else that would be a reason for keeping them poor. His socialism resembles D. H. Lawrence's in that he wishes to do nothing with the proletariat except abolish it. At this point the Marxist abandons his argument of necessity and appeals to pure sentiment, to that praise of the poor as poor which is the essence of demagogy. Theoretically the Marxist should not believe in the superiority of the poor or in the villainy of the rich. Actually very much Marxist propaganda does

8

posit these things. The Fabians offered a much less dramatic program: that of permeating the liberals, of using parliamentary methods, of gradualness. What could be more disgusting to the political salvationist? To this day our scorn for the Fabians unconsciously echoes the indignation of the outraged revolutionaries. The defense of the Fabian position should be two-fold. First, sanity is often less exciting than insanity. Second, permeation and gradualness were the beginning, not the end, of Fabian policy.

That Fabian policy was sane is shown by the astonishing measure of success which attended it. No group of *philosophes* since the Benthamites had known so well how to get results. It would be impossible to account for the social legislation of England in the twentieth century without the work of preparation performed by such people as the Webbs. That most of it was enacted by Liberal and Conservative regimes is a tribute to the policy of permeation. Meanwhile the Fabians themselves had taken a new stand. They were one of the most solid bodies of informed support that went to the making of the Labour Party (1900–1906). The reconstitution of the Labour Party in 1918 was the work of Sidney Webb as much as any one man. At this date the kind of people who earlier mocked at the Fabians for their academicism and remoteness from the political struggle began to shift their ground. They noted with glee how the purities of theory are contaminated by the impurities of practice. They pointed to the number of Fabians in the Labour governments of 1924 and 1929 not to show the success but the failure of Fabianism. But can the vacillation and pusillanimity of

Ramsay MacDonald's cabinets be blamed upon the doctrines of Fabianism? One should recall that Sidney Webb was the first to denounce MacDonald's treachery, that Beatrice Webb was at this time proposing a new Reform Act more revolutionary than that of a century earlier, that Shaw was suggesting a new set of Fabian Essays to bring Fabianism up to date with schemes for a new kind of government.

Mention the Fabians and someone will bring up "the inevitability of gradualness." It can be brought up here, however, only to be dismissed. Coined as late as 1923 by Sidney Webb, deplored by Beatrice as early as 1932, the phrase was never a summary of the Fabian mentality and never meant what it is generally supposed to mean. It meant, not that gradual socialism possessed the same kind of historic inevitability as is claimed by Marxist communism, but only that deep social changes take time. In the first flush of youth the Fabians had believed that socialism could take effect in a fortnight. Later, as Shaw put it, they realized that though you may nationalize the railways in an afternoon, it will be a long time before all your first-class and third-class carriages become second-class carriages. Thus in reviewing Russian history between 1917 and 1924 Shaw rebukes Lenin for being insufficiently Fabian: the latter, trying to introduce communism at a stroke, had subsequently to acknowledge the "inevitability of gradualness," and beat a retreat. Webb's famous phrase is therefore no blanket endorsement of parliamentary methods.

In fact, the anti-parliamentary animus was nothing new to British collectivism, as readers of Carlyle and Dickens can testify. If the Fabians were willing to make use of parliament it was never because they were all parliamentarians on principle but because they could see no other practical path to reform. They were not pacifists. Their difference with the advocates of violent revolution was based on the conviction, not that violence was wrong, but that it was inappropriate at the time. Fabius was chosen as their patron not because he waited but because he waited *before he struck*. H. G. Wells's taunting observation that Fabius waited and *never* struck may have been pertinent as applied to some of the Fabians—but it was especially inapplicable to the socialism of his chief antagonist, Bernard Shaw, who in *The Clarion* (21 October 1904) had already protested against the idea

> that there are two courses open to us: parliamentary action and physical force, each of which excludes the other. That is not so: Parliamentary action is usually the first stage of civil war. It brings the issues before the man in the street; it works up public feeling; and when the reactionary party is not prepared to fight, and the advancing party is, it settles the question without bloodshed. It is of course possible that Capitalism will go under without a fight; but I confess I should regard any statesman who calculated on that as an extremely sanguine man. The mistake made by our wildcat barricaders is not in believing that the revolution will be effected by force, but in putting the fighting at the wrong end of the process. It will take many more years to make

the questions burning ones; and it will take more years still before the burning works up a single Englishman to the point of firing on any other Englishman—if necessary—sooner than tolerate the status quo. The Marxists believe that the whole thing will be done by 'historical development,' which the Liberals (Marxism being only an intellectually pretentious form of proletarian Liberalism) call Progress with a large P.

Passages like this have been forgotten by those who think that Shaw began to talk this way only under the influence of Stalin. But we must not pretend that Shaw and Fabianism never changed with the times. They would have been stupid not to. The changes, however, were adaptations and adjustments, not betrayals and conversions. The major adjustment concerned this very question of violence. The First World War and the Russian Revolution opened Shaw's eyes to many things. Perhaps now he fully realized what Engels had meant by describing war as the midwife of social change. In 1904 he had said that the situation was not yet revolutionary. From the 'twenties on he was not so sure. He began to think it high time the Englishman *was* ready to shoot:

> I am afraid our property system will not be settled without violence unless you make up your minds that, if it is defended by violence, it will be overthrown by violence.

These words were spoken a few months before the Nazis defended property by violence and were met, not by counter-violence, but by a disunited left weakened by years of propaganda against the use of force—weakened, many Marxists said, by the German equivalent of Fabianism, recalling how Eduard Bernstein had Fabianised the Social Democrats after his association with the Fabians in London. But I hope I have shown with what doubtful propriety one equates Fabianism with the perennial wishy-washiness of labor's right wing.

"Shaw, then, began by attacking the non-Fabian socialists for their bellicosity and ended by attacking them for their pacifism"—so say his critics. There is no inconsistency in Shaw's two positions. In each case he was opposing a strategy that could not succeed. An armed insurrection led by Hyndman would simply have shocked the British gentleman without doing socialism any good. Was it not preferable, so long as no more drastic action was feasible, to win the sympathies of as many British gentlemen as possible? After 1919, however, came a change. A peaceful Social Democracy led by Ramsay MacDonald would inveigh against capitalism in vain. The time for drastic action had come. In the earlier situation Shaw believed that a "showdown" would be premature: the socialists would get more by asking for less. In the later situation Shaw believed the avoidance of a "showdown" would be missing a chance of socialist victory and giving capitalism a new lease of life: asking for a little at this stage would be to get nothing at all. As for militarism and pacifism they are abstractions and superstitions. In politics there are only ends and the means—now "militaristic," now "pacifistic"—by which ends are reached.

Probably few of the Fabians were as clear-headed as

Shaw about all this. The Webbs seem to have harbored for a long time the un-Shavian illusion that capitalists can be talked into socialism. But we should not imagine that the Webbs always led the way in Fabian thinking. In this matter of violence it was Shaw who led, and the Webbs who came to his conclusion much later. It is the same in the related question of leadership. The Webbs had always believed in the expert but they had imagined him wholly as servant (the servant, they said, is our noblest functionary) and not as leader. Shaw did not leave it to Lenin or Stalin to give him a belief in the active leader who does much more than merely carry out the expressed will of the masses. One need hardly cite his *Caesar and Cleopatra,* his prefatorial praise of the Bismarckian man of action who will sweep away all humbug, or his doctrine of Superman. The most acute analyst of Shaw's socialism in the early days, Max Beer, saw in it all the things that would later offend the liberals. Writing in 1904 from the Marxist standpoint, Beer said Shaw was the victim of relativism:

> Having no objective guide, no leading principle to go by, Shaw necessarily arrives at hero-worship—at the hankering after a Superman to guide mankind. I have noticed the same mental development in several continental critics like Harden, Bahr, Ernst, etc. They began with Social Democracy, passed through the Ibsen period, worshipped *An Enemy of the People,* finally becoming adherents of Nietzsche in theory and of Bismarck or some other social imperialist in

practice. Marxism is the antithesis of all that. It has a body of doctrines; it regards theory as the guide in practical life; and it destroys all heroism in history. In the place of the heroic factor it sets material and economic factors as the motor power of historical development. . . . The Revisionists, or Fabians, say: 'Socialism is, before all, an administrative problem; it is not a class struggle, but a clever management of public affairs! It is the Superman in local government.'

Discount the weighting of certain words with Marxist emotion and what Beer says is perfectly acceptable. Once dispute the adequacy of "material and economic factors" to make revolutions on their own, and you do have to appeal to human will and hence to "heroism." Max Beer makes the alternatives very clear and surely his position is more convincing than that of liberals who too lightly assume that we can do without the assistance alike of History and the Superman.

Beer is also right in his assertion—however sarcastic—that the Superman doctrine is implicit in the Fabian expert. He saw deeper than those who found in the latter nothing more than a dreary bureaucratic mediocrity. And he saw it long before the Webbs did. The first inkling that the Webbs had of the real needs of leadership seems to have been in the 'twenties when Beatrice called for a "dedicated Order of Socialists" resembling the Society of Jesus. At the time she was anti-soviet. A decade later, after visiting the country which Shaw was already over-enthusiastic about, she was to praise Soviet Russia for

15

having—so she alleged—made leadership a vocation.

The Webbs learnt from Shaw, and Shaw learnt from the Webbs. It is impossible to make out, as some have tried to do, that they made a merely freakish trio. They were complementary. The Webbs' weakness was an over-simplification of human nature. They regarded people as more tractable than they really are. Shaw, on the other hand, was an artist and therefore, as he said, "a specialist in human nature." The Webbs had much to learn from him about the intractability of the human animal, about the necessity of conflict and of leadership. Shaw had to learn from the Webbs the large-scale facts, the statistics, the manifold particulars of sociology. In a sense the combination of the Webbs and Shaw *is* Fabianism. This combination gave us the Fabianism of the early tracts and of the *Fabian Essays* (1889); it gave us also the Fabianism of the Minority Report and the standard history of trade-unionism. It gave us the Fabianism that "permeated the Liberals"; it gave us also the Fabianism that helped to shape and guide the Labour Party.

Between wars (1919–1939) the Fabian Society was relatively dormant; and when it woke up—how impressively! —with the outbreak of the Second World War it was in younger hands. The intermediate years, however, had a special importance in the unfolding of Fabian theory and in the development of the remarkable collaboration of Shaw and the Webbs. That the "Old Guard" did not intend to rest content with their very successful permeation of the Liberal Party, or even with the Labour Party which they had done so much to create, is already clear from a letter of Shaw's dating from before the First World War.

He wrote to his French translator that the earlier objectives of the Fabian Society were now achieved: the notion that socialist societies can reform the world by enlarging their membership had been killed; a large part of socialism had been translated into parliamentary measures so that respectable Englishmen could now be socialists as easily as Liberals or Conservatives; and, finally, the working class had been detached from the Liberal Party by the founding of the Labour Party. As for the future, the important thing, says Shaw, is to realize that the Labour Party is not a socialist party but only a radical wing of the trade unions:

> The Labour Party is good in that it represents labour but bad in that it represents poverty and ignorance, and it is anti-social in that it supports the producer against the consumer and the worker against the employer instead of supporting the workers against the idlers. The Labour Party is also bad on account of its false democracy, which substitutes the mistrust, fear, and political incapacity of the masses for genuine political talent, and which would make the people legislators instead of leaving them what they are at present, the judges of the legislators.

Fabian policy, Shaw suggests, must be to "detach the socialists from the Labour Party" and make them into a compact group of experts and leaders which will show the way to all radical parties.

This last suggestion is either merely a proposal to continue the Fabian Society or a proposal to found the kind

17

of political party which would never succeed in getting into parliament. One is not surprised therefore that after the war Sidney Webb preferred to put his energies into reorganizing the Labour Party itself as a socialist party. It was of course a hazardous task. Even today it is not clear how far the Labour Party's socialism goes. In 1924 and 1931 it scarcely seemed socialist at all.

The most pertinent criticism of the earlier Fabians was that they left too many things out of account. Shaw himself has complained that they shared too many of the prejudices of Victorian "advanced" people such as anti-clericalism and anti-militarism. Consequently they neglected to study—to give three outstanding examples—trade unionism, foreign affairs, and much of the machinery of government.

Gradually the leading Fabians managed to cover the neglected areas. Beatrice Webb was the great pioneer in the first. She and her husband became the historians of trade unions and cooperatives, thus not only filling a gap in their knowledge, but establishing a new empirical approach to sociology. What Shaw derived from their study was, as might be expected, an idea, an interpretation. Trade Unionism was, he declared, the "capitalism of the proletariat." When the workers banded together to defend the principle of selling in the highest market and giving as little as possible for their money, Proletarianism was complete. Since, moreover, the union leader's ideal was capitalism with himself getting the profits Shaw saw that the unionists were joining with the capitalists to form what the Fabians had not seen the possibility of: State Capitalism, Moralised Capitalism, a "socialism" of production, not distribution. Against this trend Shaw puts a case which is now termed "Stalinist" but which he probably derived from the American radical Edward Bellamy: one should fight, not for a "right to strike," but for the nationalization of unions (as of all other concerns) and compulsory labor for all "with death as the final penalty."

It was Shaw who first induced the Fabians to work out a more intelligent attitude to foreign affairs. When war was declared against the Boers, British liberalism, led by the young Lloyd George, was pacifist. To Shaw the pacifist position has never been convincing and, since nowadays he is accused of jingoism or muddle-headedness, it may be well to explain why. As a matter of fact Shaw himself explained why in the pamphlet "Fabianism and the Empire" and, more directly perhaps, in a letter he wrote to Hyndman at the time. Shaw's position is that once a war has begun, there being only two sides, it is usually advisable to back the lesser evil against the greater. Later, during the First World War, he went so far as to argue that you fight even for a pirate ship if you happen to be on board when it is attacked; in the letter to Hyndman he more moderately argues that the pacifism of the liberals helps the Boers to win and that this is undesirable because the Boers are less likely to do good in South Africa than the British. True, he concedes, the British Empire stands for sheer Mammonism. But it is easier for the British to pass from Mammonism to a socialist transformation than for the Boers to pass from Kruger's Old Testament fanaticism to any good thing whatsoever.

Whether Shaw's view of the Boer War was correct or not, it should be clear that his analysis was much more

19

hardheaded than that of other radicals of the day. He saw the futility of war. He also saw the futility of liberal pacifism. In the First World War he proclaimed that he found no more ethical content than in the collision of two trains, yet once the war started he thought British victory much preferable to the alternative. He was therefore equally abhorred by reactionaries and pacifists. Both groups laughed at Shaw after the war too when he consistently supported the League of Nations, which he and the Fabian Society had done not a little to start. It is characteristic that Shaw, who clearly saw that a League without power would never stop war, supported the League *faute de mieux,* and advertised its less spectacular functions. One might sum up his attitude to foreign affairs as a passionate desire to end the international anarchy linked to a sharp awareness of the power factors, political, economic, military, and psychological that stand in the way. Beside, say, H. G. Wells's proposals, Shaw's statements on international relations are tentative and few. They are also more realistic. Wells, the "scientist," generated vast, windy schemes as a boiler generates steam. Wells' thinking was nothing if not cosmic. Shaw, the artist, is more easily affected by hard facts, by brute obstacles, like nationalism, like capitalism, like the human love of dangerous illusions.

As to the third great omission in Fabian thought—the omission of a theory of government—Shaw and the Webbs have devoted a large part of their later careers to it. At the same time as they were supporting every actual and immediate step towards socialism, they were working out on paper their most systematic critique of the present system and their most sweeping proposals for reform. After the First World War the Webbs wrote (Shaw revised proof) their only full-length analysis of modern life: *The Decay of Capitalist Civilization*. They also published a plan which went far beyond the mere demand for socialism: *A Constitution for the Socialist Commonwealth of Great Britain*. This book was the starting point for all those suggestions for a new kind of government which have filled Shaw's political essays since the 'twenties. It is an attempt to sketch the institutions of a socialist society.

In her very fair-minded biography of Beatrice Webb, Mrs. Margaret Cole pooh-poohs the *Constitution* as badly written and impractical. Badly written it is. But let us hope it will not always seem impractical. Socialist literature is weak on the institutional side because socialists have too often assumed that such things will take care of themselves. The Webbs' book is important because it tries to give the socialist idea the solid content it so often lacks. It is based, like all the later books of the Fabian Trio, on the assumption that twentieth-century civilization is beyond repair, and that socialist reconstruction will have to cover every institution, economic and political. Like Shaw, the Webbs when young were thought very mild and conservative socialists; like him they are thought impractical extremists, even renegades, in their age. Yet there was no reversal of former principles. The whole development was summed up in advance in *Man and Superman*:

> All who achieve real distinction in life begin as revolutionists. The most distinguished persons become more revolutionary as they grow older,

though they are commonly supposed to become more conservative owing to their loss of faith in conventional methods of reform.

2

A Constitution for the Socialist Commonwealth of Great Britain is nowhere lengthily quoted by Shaw or even paraphrased. He endorses its main proposal—that the British government should be replaced by a new bicameral system consisting of a Political and a Social Parliament—and adds to this his own ideas. Sometimes what is peripheral for the Webbs is central for Shaw. The abolition of the Party System, cautiously hinted at by the Webbs in a footnote, is a main plank in Shaw's platform. (Perhaps he has been to school to his debating antagonist, Hilaire Belloc.) Instead of nineteenth century parliamentarism Shaw wants occupational franchise and the building of a vast hierarchical state.

The Shavian state differs from most hierarchical schemes in that power proceeds from below. It is "in touch with the people and must satisfy them." It differs from most democratic schemes in removing the higher functions of government from direct popular control. Shaw has sometimes advocated making the franchise dependent on passing tests in political science and public affairs, the tests to be harder for each level of the hierarchy; but it seems that even those who have passed no tests will be able periodically to pass judgment on the government as a whole. The public is like the purchaser who can tell whether the shoe pinches though he would not be able to make shoes himself. The doctrine that he

22

can make his own shoes Shaw calls the "mock democratic folly of pretending that the intellectual and technical work of Government can be dictated, or its ministers directly chosen, by mobs of voters." That democracy needs leadership every bit as much as any other system of government is presupposed in the following plan:

> You can conceive the new state getting a basic representative Congress to keep it in touch with its subjects. This Congress would have sufficient local knowledge to elect the local chiefs of industry throughout the country. These local chiefs can elect provincial chiefs who can elect national chiefs. These national chiefs—you may call them if you like a Cabinet—in their turn have to elect the national thinkers, for a nation needs two cabinets: an administrative Cabinet and a thinking Cabinet.

Although this plan is designed, Platonically, to make the philosopher a king and the king a philosopher, it is un-Platonic in that the base of the pyramid is a democratic franchise. It is in fact radically different from any form of aristocracy or democracy (the only two forms of government Shaw respects) that has ever existed. Only those who prefer mud-slinging to meaning could call it fascist.

Indeed it should provide the context for a more accurate account of Shaw's attitude to Mussolini and Hitler. A touchy subject, but one that should be faced: to say it should not be taken seriously is to make too large a concession to those who always laugh Shaw off. Shaw should always be taken to mean something even if he cannot al-

23

ways be taken to mean simply what he says. He can always be taken seriously; he cannot always be taken literally. People with no sense of humor find him a Mass of Contradictions. And before even the best-disposed of us can appraise Shaw's approach to fascism we must take note of the special nature of his approach to politics in general.

Shaw has never really set out to be a systematic and objective political scientist. That was the Webbs' job. Shaw's function—there is no accurate name for it—was to prod, to irritate, to enliven, to push and pull in this direction or that as the situation demanded. He was a special sort of propagandist: an artist in propaganda. He converted the trade of the Northcliffes and the Hearsts into a special craft or mission. He was not providing blueprints. Even his lengthiest political work purports only to bring out points which the political scientists have neglected, not to state an alternative political philosophy. And Shaw was entirely selfless. He didn't care if you thought him a fool provided his barbs shot home. He didn't care if you thought him a fascist if only he had undermined your own liberal complacency. The important thing was not the reputation of Shaw but the history of the world.

All Shaw's statements are "slanted." What he says is always determined by the thought: what can I do to this audience? not by the thought: what is the most objective statement about this subject? In political discussion Shaw's audience—since he became famous—has been a very large part of the British public. Consequently one can scarcely exaggerate his preoccupation with the British. Certainly his most notable limitation is his ignorance

24

of other peoples. Certainly his most noble characteristic is his passionate and lifelong attempt to reform the country in which he pretends to be an aloof foreigner. If Shaw finds something to admire in one of his quick trips abroad (Russia is the obvious example) he uses it as a stick to beat England with. If he finds something in a foreign country to dislike he is quick to add that you mustn't imagine England is any better: for British publication he changed the title of *The Future of Political Science in America* to *The Political Madhouse in America and Nearer Home*, adding a preface to rub in the last phrase. "The Inquisition," Shaws tells us elsewhere, "was a liberal institution compared to the [British] General Medical Council." The Inquisitor who condemned Joan was bad but he was "far more self-disciplined and conscientious both as priest and lawyer than any English judge ever dreams of being in a political case in which his party and class prejudices are involved." And so on. The formula has been exploited *ad nauseam*. In any hands but Shaw's it would always have seemed callow, and even in his it has become trite. It is the formula of an exasperated idealist. And it is exasperation that has driven Shaw into his most dubious declarations.

Twenty years ago Shaw entered into controversy with the eminent liberal professor, already a refugee, Gaetano Salvemini. In many ways Shaw got the worst of it. Salvemini knew Italy and Shaw did not. I doubt if he really knows any country except England. In the whole tiresome dispute he made only one good point—surely his lowest score in any controversy—but since it was his main point, for the sake of which he had provoked the whole discus-

sion, and since none of his liberal opponents has ever
tried to understand it, one may be excused for re-iterating
it here. The point was that nineteenth-century liberalism
was bankrupt, and that British socialists might wake up
to that fact, if only they could lose their inferiority complex, if only they could stop talking as men in perpetual
opposition. Shaw seems to anticipate the outsmarting of
the Labour leaders at the hands of Baldwin and Simon
in 1926 and of Baldwin and King George in 1931:

> Of course if you compare Italy with a Mazzinian
> Utopia, it is full of abuse and tyrannies. So is
> America, so is France, so is England, so is Russia.
> . . . Because I face the facts in the full knowl-
> edge that the democratic idealism of the 19th
> Century is as dead as a doornail, you say that I
> come dangerously near to the point of view of the
> British ruling class. But are you not delighted to
> find at last a Socialist who speaks and thinks as
> responsible rulers do and not as resentful slaves
> do? Of what use are Socialists who can neither
> rule nor understand what ruling means?

Of course anyone who represents Mussolini as relatively
good and British Labour as relatively bad will simply re-
mind American liberals of Charles Lindbergh and the iso-
lationists, for whom the moral in 1940 was: leave Britain
to be trampled on by the fascists. For Shaw, however, the
moral was: let Britain wake up, let Britain take thought,
and let Britain do what he has spent his life urging her to
do—adopt a socialism without Ramsay MacDonalds.

It should by now be plain that people who know nothing about Shaw except that he several times complimented Mussolini and, unlike so many liberals, never regarded Hitler as a moron must have a very eccentric picture of Shaw's politics. The Shaw the public knows and the Shaw the critics know is always the man who says outrageous things in the press, never the man who writes solid books. What Shaw actually says about fascism when not playing advocate to Mussolini's devil has been much less heeded. Here is an extract from his *Everybody's Political What's What:*

> Nowadays the Capitalist cry is: 'Nationalize what you like; municipalize all you can; turn the courts of justice into courts martial and your parliaments and corporations into boards of directors with your most popular mob orators in the chair, provided the rent, the interest, and the profits come to us as before, and the proletariat still gets nothing but its keep.'
>
> This is the great corruption of Socialism which threatens us at present. It calls itself Fascism in Italy, National Socialism (Nazi for short) in Germany, New Deal in the United States, and is clever enough to remain nameless in England; but everywhere it means the same thing: Socialist production and Unsocialist distribution. So far, out of the frying pan into the fire.

Shaw adds that Fascism is a short name for State Capitalism, that it has produced a world war, that in this war the issue was confused because Russia fought alongside "the western fascists," but that in the end the belligerents will

27

"fight for their own sides, plutocracy against democracy, Fascism against Communism." This analysis may over-simplify the issues by identifying Stalin's regime with democracy and communism. It can scarcely be taken to be favorable to fascism.

To some extent the Shavian analysis of fascism is Marx-ist—in its description of fascism as State Capitalism, for instance. Where Shaw parts company with the Marxists is in his assumption that fascism—in Italy and Germany—was supported by the masses. This assumption does not seem as unwarranted to many of us today as it did to the optimistic zealots of the 'thirties who told us that the ma-jority of Germans (they scarcely dared say of Italians) were hostile to their Leader. No less than the opinion of the zealots, Shaw's opinion was based, not on information alone, but on a presupposition about human nature. "The average citizen," the optimists said to themselves, "is a liberal." "The average citizen," says Shaw, out loud, "is a fascist."

This was no quip. Shaw has always contended that the evils of capitalism must be blamed not on the capitalists who only do what everybody would like to do but on the workers, who through ignorance, stupidity, or cowardice, let the capitalists get away with it. This acquiescence is the most fatal failure in all modern civilization. Now fascism is only a capitalism further consolidated, and fur-ther acquiesced in. The tendency of the average man to hand over responsibility to others was never more fully pandered to. It is with bitter irony that Shaw describes fascism as typically democratic, and that he says: "I do not believe in democracy."

23

Shaw is against fascism for the same reason he is against nineteenth-century liberalism: both are doctrines which relieve us of responsibility, of controlling and planning our own communal life. That is to say, they are anti-socialist doctrines. Fascism pretends to be socialist. It introduces some measure of socialist production but cannot practice socialist distribution without removing its lynchpin: capitalism. The nineteenth-century liberal prides self on the equation: liberty = free enterprise. In short, says Shaw, liberalism and fascism are rival masks of capitalism, and fascism is in some ways the better of the two. It sometimes benefited the proletariat, it gave bureaucratic status to functionaries who were formerly only casual employees, it tightened up the public services, it assailed individualism and preached putting the community first. To that extent it prepared the way for genuine socialism. Liberalism seems less apposite in the present world. It has discredited itself by preaching an abstract and negative liberty. Its characteristic modern forms are the economic doctrine of free enterprise and the political doctrine of anarchism:

> The cry of Liberty is always on the lips of the propertied classes who own the lion's share of land and capital and have nothing to fear but nationalization of these resources, because it implies that the less government activity there is the more free the people are, and because it helps to elect the thoughtless who alway support the status quo because anything unusual shocks them.

29

Liberalism can only cease to be mockery when liberty is a concrete possibility for the masses, that is, under socialism. Liberalism was born too early. It is really "a post-Communist and not a pre-Communist doctrine and therefore it has a great future before it when the world is full of Communists who will be at leisure for the greater part of their lives." For there is no liberty without leisure.

All of this is rubbing the liberal cat the wrong way. Shaw has always taken it as his role to do precisely that. "He is never so happy," Hyndman wrote over forty years ago, "as when he is running a tilt at the party with which he is, at least nominally, associated." All the most ridiculous people in his early plays, as in his late ones, are the advanced people, liberals like Roebuck Ramsden, suffragettes like Mrs. Clandon and Gloria, "disciples of Bernard Shaw" like Dubedat, whereas the capitalist and the conqueror are shown to be comparatively sane. One of Shaw's best essays is called "The Illusions of Socialism." In it he shows that socialists have carried liberal illusions to an extreme. It is not only Marxism proper but almost all forms of non-Fabian socialism that Shaw regards as "intellectually pretentious forms of proletarian Liberalism." In the course of his essay Shaw specified two major socialist illusions: the religious illusion of the day of revolution as a millennium and the dramatic illusion, "the crude Marxist melodrama of 'The Class War: or the Virtuous Worker and the Brutal Capitalist.'"

It may be that the trick of showing the enemy to be a much more sensible person than your friends is less appropriate when the enemy is Hitler than when he was Wilhelm II. (At least it is easy for us to say so, overlook-

30

ing the fact that, in America and England at least, the hatred of "the Kaiser" was much more virulent than hatred of Hitler ever was.) To stress the dangers of liberalism when civilization is theatened by illiberalism is perhaps the most suspicious item in Shaw's long political career. If we cannot quite agree with Max Beer who long ago classed Shaw with the continental intelligentsia which in such large numbers turned from Marx to Nietzsche and from Nietzsche to simple imperialism, we can see that he cast at least one look in that direction. A constant danger for the radical is that he may come to hate his rivals so much that he will join with the enemy to oppose them. In recent years we have been confronted with the spectacle of communists hating Hitler less than Churchill, and of liberals hating Hitler less than Stalin. I do not think Shaw was deeply involved in these ignominies. His championing of the rightist against the liberal is the old-fashioned devil's advocacy of a Victorian debater rather than the real diabolism that is so common today. Moreover, if Shaw's solution of the problem of power seems too Machiavellian, it is at least a resolute attempt to escape pious liberal platitude. His leftist opponents are still where they were sixty years ago—appealing either to historical necessity or to the assumed political superiority of the masses.

Actually Shaw is closer to Rousseau than to Machiavelli. Like Rousseau, Shaw seems to the casual modern reader an anarchist, a sheer rebel. Like Rousseau, Shaw seems to the more knowing reader precisely the opposite —an authoritarian. We do not really understand either Rousseau or Shaw until we see that for them liberty is a paradox, since it is achieved through its opposite, restriction. Both philosophers would agree with present-day American Republicans that a government interference means nothing if not interference with someone's liberty. Only they would add that liberty is in general achieved after this contradictory fashion.

3

Doubtless the both/and approach of a Shaw, no less than of a Rousseau, is alien to the either/or thinkers of today. Yes. Although Shaw has offered a brilliant analysis of fascism, upon the whole he is very old-fashioned. His Victorian education has limited his understanding of the twentieth century. So little has he tried to know as much about us as he knew about our grandfathers that, when he speaks of "today," we sometimes have the impression that he means 1910. He sometimes seems remote to those of us who were born into the twentieth-century *mêlée* because almost everything he knows was learnt in the nineteenth century. Yet the old-fashionedness is in most contexts less of a limitation than a merit, and we can go back to Shaw with as much pleasure and profit as to any other Victorian. He is old-fashioned but he is not obsolete. His knowledge of particular areas of contemporary fact may be faulty but his analysis of the modern world in general is valid now if it was ever valid; for the events of the twentieth century amount to tumult much more than to change, let alone progress. The classic analyses of our age are still nineteenth-century analyses.

Shaw is a Victorian socialist. Aside from the Webbs his political teachers were Henry George, Karl Marx, Stanley

32

Jevons, and Edward Bellamy. They at least are the giants. If we were to watch Shaw learning a fact here, acquiring an attitude there, picking up an idea in another place, we would have to list a score of other Victorian socialists —most important among them William Morris and Belfort Bax, Stuart-Glennie and Henry Salt. Insofar as Shavian socialism is in a broad tradition that goes back beyond the Fabians I would say it is neither in the French "Utopian" line nor the German "scientific" line nor the Russian "anarchist" line but in the British "aristocratic" line. Behind Shaw is Ruskin, and behind Ruskin is Carlyle.

Calling himself a communist, "reddest also of the red," Ruskin preached order, reverence, and authority. He believed in some such hierarchy as Shaw was to advocate (though he was not so sure it could not be hereditary). It was Ruskin who before Jevons—and by much simpler reasoning—argued that economics is not a realm of impersonal laws but a realm of human regulation, potentially a branch of human welfare. It was Ruskin who taught Shaw that there are only three ways of procuring wealth—working, begging, and stealing—and that capitalism condemns many to beg by allowing a few to steal. The corollary—that the good social order is one in which everyone works—is a cornerstone of Shavianism. The point is for Shaw not only good economics (his kind of socialism, as we have seen, finds the essential contradiction of capitalism in the coexistence of worker and idler, not worker and capitalist), it is also good philosophy. It is the philosophy of Goethe and Carlyle, summed up by Nietzsche's Zarathustra: "I labor not for my happiness, I

33

labor for my work." Ruskin has it: "Life without work is robbery. Work without art is brutality." And the whole body of Shaw's political writings might be regarded as an expansion of the best of Ruskin's dicta: "Government and cooperation are in all things the laws of life; anarchy and competition the laws of death."

What Shaw has in common with Carlyle is no less extensive than the main theme of *Sartor Resartus:* human ideals, not being eternal, must, like other kinds of clothing, be constantly discarded and replaced. Even the ideal-monger, the philosopher himself—that tailor of idealists —must be re-tailored if the dignity of man is to be assured, if the purpose of human life is to be unfolded. In the specifically social sphere Carlyle prepared the way for the Fabians in two ways. In Sidney Webb's words he was "the first man who really made a dent in the individualist shield" by subjecting his age to a point by point attack. Second, he looked forward to a collectivism which would be produced neither by historic inevitability nor by the wisdom of the populace.

The socialism of Carlyle, Ruskin, Shaw, of what I have called the British "aristocratic" line, is not scientific; it is ethical. Their belief in humanity is not faith in the common man but in the gentleman. For the gentleman is a synthesis of the democrat and the aristocrat, the follower and the leader. He is a living symbol of the fact that aristocracy is not something to be superseded but to be included in democracy, that the nobleman, if he has ceased to be a robber baron, is welcome in the new age, that we, as much as Louis XIV or George III, need men of light and leading. Moreover the gentlemanly ideal is the golden mean between two rival types—the priest and the soldier, the Pope and the Emperor or, in more recent language, the yogi and the commissar. That is why the British genius, which is for temperance, did not wait for Shaw before it formulated this ideal. Not only Carlyle and Ruskin, but such contrasted doctrinaires as Burke, Newman, and T. H. Huxley were spokesmen for it. In some unprepared remarks addressed to the National Liberal Club in 1913 Shaw said:

> What is the ideal of the gentleman? The gentleman makes a certain claim on his country to begin with. He makes a claim for a handsome and dignified existence and subsistence; and he makes that as a primary thing not to be dependent on his work in any way; not to be doled out according to the thing he has done or according to the talents that he has displayed. He says, in effect: 'I want to be a cultured human being; I want to live in the fullest sense; I require a generous subsistence for that; and I expect my country to organize itself in such a way as to secure me that.' Also the real gentleman says—and here is where the real gentleman parts company with the sham gentleman, of whom we have so many: 'In return for that I am willing to give my country the best service of which I am capable; absolutely the best. My ideal shall be also that, no matter how much I have demanded from my country, or how much my country has given me, I hope and I shall strive to give to my country

35

> in return more than it has given to me; so that
> when I die my country shall be the richer for my
> life.' . . . The real constructive scheme you
> want is the practical inculcation into everybody
> that what the country needs, and should seek
> through its social education, its social sense, and
> religious feeling, is to create gentlemen; and,
> when you create them, all other things shall be
> added unto you.

In all this Shaw was ratifying a British tradition. He was also giving it a new turn. He was giving the idea of the gentleman an economic basis. A capitalist is not a gentleman, because his ideal is to sell dear and buy cheap. A proletarian is not a gentleman, because, as the theory of value made clear, he has no value. He is a prostitute. His fate is what Shaw elsewhere calls the "only real tragedy in life: the being used by personally minded men for purposes which you recognize to be base." The capitalist economy of rent, idleness, and waste is "uneconomic" and therefore unfavorable to virtue. The capitalist idea is to get more than you give. The socialist idea, the "economic" idea, the gentlemanly idea is to give more than you get. This is the core of Shavian ethics.

The problem is how to create the civic virtue of the gentleman in the modern world. To some extent—perhaps in 5% of the population, Shaw once suggested—it already exists. If so, the credit must go to Nature which cannot be prevented from creating at least a few Fabians in every generation. For the capitalist system, far from encouraging civic virtue, encourages only the pretense of it that our politicians so eloquently flourish, and discourages the real thing by making it extremely unrewarding. It is barely possible to be a good citizen in a world where uncharitable behavior is necessary to success and even to survival. The civic virtues, Shaw concludes, are not likely to be widely practiced until capitalism is abolished. That is one reason why socialism is the necessary next step in the history of civilization.

Shaw has been criticized for his unusual definition of socialism: "equality of income and nothing else." The definition has been dismissed by many socialists as "extreme rationalism," as indicating a predilection for inhuman, mechanical, abstract order. Shaw's Marxist critics have been the severest, their main point being that, if you socialize production, exactly equal distribution is neither necessary nor desirable; distribution will be either according to the amount of work done ("socialism") or according to the needs of the worker ("communism"). Yet, if Russia is an example of "socialism" in this sense, everyone who is prepared to criticize Russia at all must wish that socialism in Shaw's sense had not been so entirely overlooked. "Society," says Shaw, "is like a machine designed to work smoothly with the oil of equality, into the bearings of which some malignant demon keeps pouring the sand of inequality." Though Shaw himself does not seem to realize it, the malignant demon has been busy in Soviet Russia. He did recognize the demon's handiwork in Germany, Italy, and America. Though he praised the fascists and the New Dealers insofar as they socialized production, he condemned them in the end because they drew the line at socialist distribution. Every kind of socialism so far tried has been at best incomplete and at worst spurious. To those who point to any of them as a model Shaw's definition of socialism is a sufficient rebuke.

If inequality is the chief barrier to civic virtue, equality is its chief prop. When no privileges are conferred by wealth or birth, the Fabian 5% can find their natural level: and they may turn out to be more than 5%. The democratic paradox of Equality—hitherto a sly deception, meaning that people are called equal but are not treated equally —begins to bear fruit when natural authority and subordination take the place of the caste and spoils systems. The democratic paradox of Liberty begins to bear fruit when equal pay guarantees to all that sufficient subsistence without which there can be no free behavior and when universal compulsory labor shortens the workman's hours, leaving him with the time in which to behave freely. The democratic paradox of Fraternity begins to bear fruit when one man's gain is not necessarily another's loss, when, though you may have "superiors" at your job, you have no "betters" in society, when human unity means, not that you confer your unwanted love upon your neighbor while pushing his face in the mud, but that you and your neighbor are at one in a common enterprise. ("You *are* your neighbor," says Shaw, observing that the murder of Marat by Charlotte Corday was really suicide: Marat killed by the spirit of Marat.)

It may seem from all this that Equality is Shaw's maid-of-all-work, one of those emotive words which enable the reformer to substitute spell-binding for sense. Yet, on the contrary, Shaw is one of the very few socialists who are candid about the limitations of socialism. "A socialist state," he says, "can be just as wicked as any other sort of state"—a remark of a very different temper from the Marxist account of the disappearance of the class struggle, the sudden cessation of dialectical conflict (unless on a purely spiritual plane), the withering of the state, and the advent of the stateless society of the free and equal. Shaw makes no promise that the state will ever wither. He knows that the socialist state will be very powerful and that all power is for evil as well as good. This is no reason for preferring irresponsibility. We must simply stop thinking of socialism as an endless good time, as unqualified freedom, an escape from the human condition. It will not change human nature overnight; there is probably a large part of human nature that it will not change at all. In some ways the capitalist's idea of socialism as a system of bureaucracy, regimentation, and tyranny is more realistic than the socialist's, always granting that by bureaucracy the capitalist means state control, by regimentation order, and by tyranny that responsibility without which there can be no real freedom.

Much of the liberal yearning of the past two hundred years has been a yearning for more freedom and more happiness than the human creature is capable of. And democracy and socialism are the causes the liberals chose for the attainment of their impossible ideals. In this sense Shaw is not a liberal. He believes in socialism because socialism will remove what have been in the past centuries the most dangerous and effective inducements to anti-social behavior and will encourage social impulses which under capitalism have existed only in spite of the system. Thus socialism offers some opportunity to men to bridge the gap which they have created between their real and their imagined world, between Pragma and Dogma. Under socialism they should be able to regulate their affairs better. They should be able to create a finer and more honorable way of life.

When Shaw is told that the poor are happy poor he need not, like other socialists, deny it. He can reply that he wants to make them, not happier, like contented pigs, but better, like the discontented Socrates. And when the idyllic picture of the withering of the state is dangled before his eyes he is not more impressed than by the "capitalist utopia" that is supposed to come from letting things slide—*laisser faire, laisser aller.* Anarchism and Capitalism are dreams of irresponsible bliss. Shaw prefers to admit that socialism will not bring as much freedom as many would like or even as much as a few people already have under capitalism. The liberal who thinks Shaw's socialism goes too far in asking equality of income is likely to think it does not go far enough in the direction of freedom and democracy. Yet we have seen that, according to Shaw, liberalism has a future. In fact the function of socialism is precisely that it allows liberalism to come into being as something other than a dream. But while the socialization of an economy is a relatively speedy affair, the progress of liberalism is necessarily slow, since it involves a radical change in the general attitude to life, a change from apathy to responsibility, which includes a change from ignorance to knowledge.

You do not have democracy until the whole population understands politics and accepts responsibility for them. In this sense no population has as yet come anywhere near to democracy. Compared with us, the first generation that attains to democracy will be a race of Supermen: and this was always the chief application which Shaw made of Nietzsche's term. The creation of Supermen is the greatest task that lies ahead of us, a longer and more arduous task than the socialist revolution. For, though the natural aristocracy of Shaw's socialist state will solve many problems, the awful problem of power before which we all tremble today can be adequately solved only by a moral improvement in the whole race. Words which Shaw wrote thirty years ago have been rendered more impressive by the invention of the atomic bomb:

> The one danger before us that nothing can avert but a general raising of human character through the deliberate cultivation and endowment of democratic virtue without consideration of property or class is the danger created by inventing weapons capable of destroying civilization faster than we produce men who can be trusted to use them wisely.

Democratic idealism with a vengeance! Shaw has no belief that any social upheaval, even socialist revolution, is enough. There is nothing for it, as he said fifty years ago (and repeated with a sinking heart in *Geneva*), but "to convince men of the immorality of abusing the majority power and then to make them moral enough to refrain from doing it on that account." There is no hope, that is to say, but that the passion for social justice which has always been at the root of British aristocratic socialism should spread to the whole population.

41

If Shaw believes in nobility, it is chiefly because *noblesse oblige*. The cardinal virtue in the Shavian scale, as perhaps we have already gathered, is responsibility. Every creed Shaw has attacked he has attacked on grounds of irresponsibility. The liberal economists shift the responsibility on to laws of supply and demand, the Marxists on to laws of history, the anarchists on to laws of nature. The Darwinists—we shall find Shaw maintaining—assign responsibility to mechanical causes, that is, to pure luck. The Christians—or many who regard themselves as such —get God to bear the burden. And when it comes to making a whipping-boy of Jesus, Shaw says:

> You will never get a high morality from people who conceive that their misdeeds are revocable and pardonable, or in a society where absolution and expiation are officially provided for us all. If there is to be no punishment there can be no forgiveness. We shall never have real moral responsibility until every one knows that his deeds are irrevocable and that his life depends on his usefulness.

This stern doctrine is something more than the "protestantism" and "puritanism" which so many have found in Shaw. It is a tough, lean naturalism without illusions. If, as Chesterton said, Shaw is the first idealist who is not also a sentimentalist, might one not add that he is the first unsentimental *naturalist?* For him life is a Promethean adventure which may entail Promethean tortures to be borne with Promethean fortitude.

Shaw's politics lead us to Shaw's philosophy. Indeed

42

everything in Shaw leads to everything else: we have had many vaster and many more scientific thinkers but few whose thinking was at the same time so manysided and so much of a piece. Shaw's views are all firmly based on a Baconian faith in human control. Like Bacon, and unlike many Baconians, Shaw includes control of the human as well as of the external world. Eschewing alike the supernaturalist myth of a God who will shield us from responsibility and the materialist myth of laws which will shield us from responsibility, man must take the burden upon his own shoulders. A perilous enterprise, rendering every problem infinitely more difficult than it is to panaceists!

Afterthought in 1957. It is proper that this chapter, like the rest of the book, should stand substantially as it was written ten years ago. But it is equally proper to note that today I could not steer between communism and anti-communism as certain passages here (see especially pages 28 and 31) indicate that I was trying, albeit unconsciously, to do.

2. VITAL ECONOMY

1

"Political Economy and Social Economy are amusing intellectual games; but Vital Economy is the Philosopher's Stone."
—JOHN TANNER, M.I.R.C.

WE HAVE SEEN THAT WHILE IT IS WELL-KNOWN THAT SHAW is a socialist it is hardly known at all what his socialism amounts to. Similarly it is well-known that Shaw has some kind of a secular religion but—except possibly for such terms as Life Force and Creative Evolution—very little of it has sunk into the general consciousness. On the one side Rationalists and Radicals denounce it as reactionary and orthodox. On the other Catholics and Conservatives denounce it as neo-pagan and heterodox. The time snobs, who include most Rationalists, Radicals, Catholics, and Conservatives, sneer at it as an already dated fad. Yet it is not as odd and arbitrary a faith as any of them think.

44

VITAL ECONOMY

Shaw's earliest background was mildly Christian—I say mildly because Shaw's father used to end an earnest recommendation of the Bible to his son by breaking into a laugh and denouncing the book as the damnedest parcel of lies ever written. The freedom of the tepidly Christian home made it easy for Shaw to proceed to the second stage of Victorian belief: belief in unbelief, faith in the liberating power of a No-God. For when religion is mainly negative, the rejection of religion seems mainly positive, and men can be enthusiastic about a vacuum. Bernard Shaw's first published utterance was a free-thinking letter to the press denouncing the Evangelists Sankey and Moody who were visiting Dublin at the time. The earliest novels, insofar as they breathe anything, breathe the agnostic atmosphere. No complete change is noticed until the fifth and last of the novels, in which socialism is preached. The conversion to socialism brought Shaw into a third and final stage.

Or was it not final? Some have felt that Shaw's faith in socialism was gradually undermined by a loss of faith in all political measures and that the religion of the Life Force arose to fill the gap. On this interpretation Shaw passed into a fourth stage—a common one in our time—political disillusionment coupled with religious faith or, at least, religious wistfulness. But if I am right about Shaw's politics, this interpretation can be correct in one respect only. Shaw never abandoned his socialism but he did come to place less faith in the usual political machinery. And, as his faith in quick progress waned, his faith in slow progress increased. As he became less and less of an optimist over the short period, he became more and more of an optimist over the long period. This sort of optimism necessarily has its roots in a kind of faith that cuts deeper than legislation, political or economic, that cuts deeper, in fact, than socialism. As Shaw's socialism grew less ingenuous, his secular religion became more important.

The religion, then, is something that co-exists with the socialism, not something that replaces it. As a matter of fact, Shaw's "irrationalism" antedates his socialism. We see it gradually emerging in the pre-socialist novels. While in the second novel Shaw was still the Rationalist with an engineer for a hero, in the third—quite deliberately—he portrays a wildly romantic artist. The view of life that is in part suggested by this portrait was later rather fully presented in three major critical essays—"The Quintessence of Ibsenism," "The Sanity of Art," and "The Perfect Wagnerite." By this time—all three treatises were written in the 'nineties—Shaw was a confirmed socialist, and the secular religion seemed to him an underpinning of his political creed. One of his unpublished manuscripts contains this avowal:

> In short we must make a religion of Socialism. We must fall back on our will to Socialism, and resort to our reason only to find out the ways and means. And this we can do only if we conceive the will as a creative energy as Lamarck did; and totally renounce and abjure Darwinism, Marxism, and all Fatalistic, penny-in-the-slot theories of evolution whatever.

But this is to anticipate.

46

VITAL ECONOMY

In one of the major critical essays three stages of belief are sketched: the old-fashioned belief in a God of wrath, the new-fashioned belief in Love, and, finally, Ibsenism, which asserts that a healthy altruism can be attained only through its apparent opposite, self-realization. Philosophically, the first stage is old-fashioned theology, the second is the Christian ethics of modern free thought, the third a philosophy of Will. Free thought has overthrown theology but, through doing so, has come to value reason too highly. In fact the whole weakness of free thought lies in its rationalism. A double weakness: it is weak in itself, and it fails to see the strength of its antagonist, religion. Once a free-thinker realizes that he has feelings and thoughts within him which science only pooh-poohs he will return to any church which claims these feelings and thoughts as its own. And, if there were no alternative, he would be right. But "Ibsenism" claims to be such an alternative.

Nineteenth-century free thought, as was being abundantly felt at the end of the century, had inherited the shallow optimistic psychology of the Enlightenment. Shaw, however, favored the psychology of the Romanticists, which was akin to that of many earlier thinkers, such as Pascal. He asserted that man is primarily a feeling, not a thinking animal. A dangerous thing to assert. Say that man is not primarily rational, and your rationalist audience will rise to its feet and denounce you as an obscurantist. They assume that you have simply inverted their idea that emotion should be dominated by reason. But neither Shaw nor the wiser of the Romanticists before him advocated the domination of reason by emotion. They said that thought and emotion should work together and not in competition.

This is anti-rationalistic but not anti-scientific thinking. Consider the control of external nature by science. The use of waterpower does not imply the elimination, the domination, of the power of the water by the even more powerful reason of man. A river is not turned back in its course; at most it is deflected or damned; the power is all its own. The control of human instinctual nature is a similar process. The feelings are our motor power. Destroy them and you destroy yourself. Try to make your reason dictator and you will be first a neurotic and soon a suicide. True, the result of dispensing with reason—if it were possible—would be equally disastrous. What the empiricist suggests is that reason play the same part in controlling human life that science plays in controlling nature.

Shaw might have taken his "irrationalism" from Pascal or Rousseau. The sources he actually cites are Ibsen—and Schopenhauer. And this is an impressive choice of sources, for it was Schopenhauer who brought home the truths of "irrationalism," if not to his own generation, at least to Nietzsche's and Shaw's. Like Nietzsche, Shaw saw that one could digest Schopenhauer's "irrationalism" and put the pessimism back on the plate. To Nietzsche and Shaw the essence of Schopenhauer was his contention that the Will is the main driving-force of human existence. To equate this Will with the Christian Soul, as Shaw does, is certainly an act of faith, but so is equating it with the Freudian Id as Thomas Mann does. Schopenhauer found the Will horrifying; Shaw finds it inspiring. In this choice

48

personal preference, necessarily, is all. Shaw prefers the optimist to the pessimist conclusion because he is alive and intends to go on living. He is interested only in a philosophy that one can accept as one's philosophy of life. Pessimism is not such a philosophy because if one really believed it one would not wish to live at all. Optimism—at face value an attitude as arbitrary as pessimism —has more validity because it is necessary to continued living. And that life should continue is a presupposition of all moral philosophy. On at least one occasion Shaw grants that pessimism has *more* to be said for it than optimism. But this only strengthens his main argument. If all the evidence is for dying and we go on living, then we are all the more compelled to accept existence "irrationally" as a wager.

In "The Sanity of Art" Shaw writes that life is "not the fulfillment of a moral law or of the deductions of reason but the satisfaction of a passion in us of which we can give no account whatsoever." The upshot of such a philosophy depends wholly upon its view of the passions. Shaw's is peculiar, at least in its wording. He destroys the antithesis of intellect and emotion by declaring that "thought is a passion." This is not mere logomachy. Shaw is saying that man is a creature of his passions but that the passions are many and various. There are refined passions like chastity and low passions like lust. There are intellectual passions like that for art and there are physical passions like that for gymnastics. The business of living consists not in the suppression of passions by something else—which in practice often means the conquest of harmless passions by ugly ones—but the training and sorting-out all passions,

49

harmless, ugly, intellectual, or physical. "It is not emotion in the raw but as evolved and fixed as intellectual conviction that will save the world." We must take comfort from the fact that human nature gives rise to altruism as well as selfishness, to conscience as well as cruelty. The hope of the race is that the passions of generosity, restraint, and goodness may prove as strong as those of egoism, aggression, and cruelty. "It is quite useless," Shaw says, "to believe that men are born free if you deny that they are born good." Conversely, if the passions were uniformly as bad as their reputation the world would be lost.

2

Those who like their philosophy sober and literal had better not read further in Shaw than the essays of the 'nineties. For in *Man and Superman* (1901–3) and *Back to Methuselah* (1921) he tries, in ways that necessarily are non-scientific, to account for what he had formerly called "a passion of which we can give no account whatever." Those who are not averse to such efforts should turn from "The Perfect Wagnerite" to the long discussion inset in *Man and Superman* and entitled "Don Juan in Hell."

It all began with a couple of Shavian jokes. When the drama critic A. B. Walkley, teasing Shaw for his sexual puritanism, suggested a play about Don Juan, Shaw's mind apparently went back to an essay he had published in 1887, "Don Giovanni Explains," in which the view is put forward that the Don was too spiritual to be satisfied by amours, that he spent his time running away from importunately amorous women, and that his reputation is based on the slanders of the slighted ladies. Such is the

VITAL ECONOMY

Don Juan of *Man and Superman,* who, though ludicrously different from the Don Juan of recent tradition, is decidedly similar to the original Don Juan of the late Middle Ages. The other joke is first found, I think, in Shaw's music criticism. It is that most people positively *like* hell, hell being the name Shaw gives to the world, not of actuality, it is true, but of popular imagination, that world of melodramatic illusions which forms the spiritual habitat of modern man.

The joking conception of Don Juan gives Shaw a spokesman for his ideas of a higher humanity. The joking conception of hell gives him a kingdom for a Shavian Devil. Two more characters are needed—a representative of womanhood to offset Don Juan and yet be complementary to him, and a representative of average mankind —the girl's father will do—to be the willing victim of the devil's arguments. Such are the vocalists in the Shavio-Mozartian quartet. They discuss the actual state of the world, as deplored equally by the devil and Juan, the devil's proposals to replace this stage of affairs with the world in which people *imagine* they are living, the world which they want to live in, and, finally, Don Juan's account of a third realm—heaven, the home of reality.

While the devil advocates everything that idealism and sentimentality can suggest to half-satisfied passions, Juan renounces all proffered pleasures in favor of arduous striving. Striving after what? Though he ridicules what men have called Progress, Juan, like Shaw, believes in a kind of progress, a much slower kind—that of the evolution of species which has already brought creation as far as man and can in the future bring it as far as—Superman.

51

The assumption is that the progressive development of species from amoeba to man is not something that merely chanced to happen. The number and complexity of extraordinary coincidences which it has involved compel us to believe in some kind of previous planning or, more likely, in some kind of striving towards future goals. Each organic change takes place to fit a need. The need for prehensile organs is felt, and fingers and toes come into being.

Now the most intricate and marvellous organ ever produced by this purposive drive—which Juan calls the Life Force—is the human brain which generates ideas, thus adding a new dimension to life itself. The average man, normally a coward, becomes a hero when you put an idea in his head. In the higher man the brain is the means to something even more remarkable. It enables him to understand life and thus to control it.

In *Back to Methuselah* the whole subject is thrashed out again from the beginning with slightly different categories and emphases. This time Shaw puts his theory in the form of a dualistic metaphysic. Life and Matter are the two basic realities. The cosmic drama begins when Life, hitherto "a whirlpool in pure force," enters into Matter and assumes the familiar shapes of the vegetable, animal, and human world. At first Life is enslaved by Matter —as all history to date sadly records. But the higher man fights against his enslavement, and when his existence is released from Matter at the time called Death, and he reverts to the pure stream of Life, he returns his original endowment with interest, thereby helping to raise the general level. "The love of economy is the root of all virtue."

Giving more than you get is the principle of Vital as of Political Economy. Thus Life spirals upwards. Eventually —this is the achievement of the Ancients or Superman— Matter will be enslaved by Life and Death thereby be abolished. Immortality will have been achieved, and Life will be pure idea. From Don Juan's "I sing the philosophic man" we have passed to the Ancient's: "The day will come when there will be no people, only thought."

Such is the theme of what Shaw has called his most significant work. The question is what we are to make of it. A few staunch Shavians have taken the theme as it stands. It has become for them the religion of the twentieth century. One philosopher attempted to provide "a formal philosophical setting for Shaw's doctrines" in a metaphysical treatise of some length—I refer to *Matter, Life, and Value* by C. E. M. Joad. Although Mr. Joad later described his effort as "not very successful," it does successfully discredit those who shrug Shaw's philosophy off as amateurish trifling. It shows that if Shaw's philosophy is re-stated in professional jargon it sounds just as plausible as any other philosophy. If I do not put an end to this chapter forthwith, it is because I think that such a re-statement and endorsement as Mr. Joad's limits rather than establishes Shaw's importance. All it proves is that Shaw might have made a good professor of philosophy. In filling out Shaw's ideas into a complete metaphysic Mr. Joad demonstrates Shaw's respectability but not, surely, his mettle. Fifteen years after writing the book, Mr. Joad complained that Shaw left his metaphysic incomplete. He did not solve the body-mind problem or the problem of free will. He did not explain *what* it is that the Ancients,

who spend their lives in contemplation, contempla\
Joad might have extended his list of lacunae indefi\
One need only read Bergson's *Creative Evolution* to \
discussions of half a dozen questions central to "irrationalism" which Shaw never copes with. (The chief of
them is the nature of Time.) Moreover, in filling out
Shaw's statements, Mr. Joad makes additions that are not
at all in the Shavian spirit. He adds to Shaw's Life and
Matter a third entity, Value. Life and Matter are always
in flux; Value, according to Mr. Joad, is not. Or, as he himself phrases it: the world of Life and Matter is the world
of becoming, the world of Value is the world of being.
Thus Mr. Joad has an answer to the question, what do the
Ancients contemplate? They contemplate objects of value
in aesthetic and ethical experience. But this pluralistic
metaphysic with three discontinuous realms is less an
elaboration than a distortion—from Mr. Joad's point of
view, a correction—of Shaw.

If *Man and Superman* and *Back to Methuselah* are
philosophical treatises they are very faulty ones. There
are contradictions as well as gaps. For example, a double
change of line on the central question of how to improve
our civilization. Three different recipes are given. In *Man
and Superman* it is eugenic breeding. In *Back to Methuselah*, as a whole, it is longevity. In *Back to Methuselah*, Part
III, it is something else again. The fairly Utopian England
of A.D. 2170 has not been attained by prolonging the lives
of men (though some "long livers" have already appeared) but by replacing British civil servants with Chinese: a recipe that might be called idealistic racism. The

remarkable thing is the nonchalance with which each of these recipes is adopted and dropped. Each, as a serious suggestion in political science, would need a great deal of defending. Eugenics? How can we deduce the nature of unborn children from that of prospective parents? Racism? Why should we believe that Shaw's tribute to the Chinese is anything but a jibe from an old Britain-baiter? Longevity? Is it really so likely to come like a thief in the night? Can we think of any of these fantastic remedies in the same way as we think of the Fabian Tracts which Shaw wrote? If not, we either have to say: Shaw is sensible in politics but his "irrationalism" is hokum; or we have to approach his Vitalist writings in a different way. If Shaw is no Bergson there are other things just as important for him to be.

Consider the politics of *Man and Superman*. Mr. Joad's analysis seems to presuppose that the protagonist John Tanner is Shaw's spokesman. Why then did Shaw give him an appearance which exactly corresponds to that of his most redoubtable political antagonist H. M. Hyndman? Why is not Tanner an heroic or at least an effective man? It is obvious that Shaw deliberately makes him —among other things—an ineffectual chatterbox. And remember that Tanner, not Shaw, is supposed to be the author of the "Revolutionist's Handbook" from which so much of our knowledge of Shavian Vitalism derives. Although so many of the ideas in the Handbook are thoroughly Shavian, they are expressed with more than the usual Shavian over-statement, in fact with the extravagance and pontificality we expect of Tanner. What then

55

is Shaw doing? Statesmen try out a dangerous idea by having one of their underlings advance it. Might not Tanner be such an underling of Shaw?

"Political Economy and Social Economy," Tanner writes, "are amusing intellectual games; but Vital Economy is the Philosopher's Stone." One could believe that this is Shaw speaking only if he had actually given up politics as hopeless instead of faithfully continuing to work for the Fabian Society. But if Tanner's outlook is not identical with Shaw's it is useful to Shaw in his attempt to integrate his politics with his religion. Take for example the demand for Supermen. We have seen how the Fabian outlook has a place for Nietzsche's higher being who is to man as man is to the ape. The Superman is perhaps the main link between Shaw's politics and his religion. Shaw had begun with socialist ethics, according to which you must change society in order to change man. The trouble was that unless you changed man he refused to change society. It was a dilemma. Shaw's way out was not to reverse his earlier decision by staking all on the prior need of inner change. He had begun by asking for change from without; he later asks for change from within, *not instead, but as well.* Shaw said, moreover, that you could not have democracy until everyone is a Superman. He did not say you could not have *socialism* till then. Until socialism is democratic and "superhuman" it will of course be attended by great evils. Shaw, as we have seen, is an unusual socialist in admitting that socialism is not a panacea. We have also seen that he operates on two time-tables: the short and the long range. On the short range he votes at each election for the lesser evil; on the

long, he deplores the fact that elections are a choice between evils and asks for a revised constitution. This dual-
ity Shaw shares with the Webbs. But his long range—
since he is a speculator—is longer than theirs. In this
longer run he sees the need for a type of manhood higher
than that of today, thus parting company with the sentimentalists who think that the common amount of wisdom
is quite enough, and with the Marxists who think that
class-interest, not stupidity, is the source of trouble.

When he finished *Man and Superman,* Shaw could
hardly have felt that he had solved his problem. He
thought of the eugenic breeding of Supermen as a desperate remedy when he found that men did not really
will democracy. Faced with the difficulty of such breeding, he (Tanner, at least) declared that men can overcome any difficulty if they will to do so. But why should
they will the breeding of Supermen—a thing that does
not appeal to them in the least—if they do not will democracy which they pay eager lip-service to? Shaw offered no solution. He simply put the whole responsibility
on John Tanner. Through him he explored the dilemma
without solving it. Tanner's solution was for Shaw a way
of forcing people to dig below their verbiage. Eugenic
breeding may not be a practical proposal. But as a suggestion thrown out by Tanner it forces people to see *why*
Superman is desperately needed. The assumption of government in Britain by Chinese sages has a similar function. So has the increase of our span of life to 300: the idea
is not that wisdom comes with age but that people who
expect to live 300 years will have to plan life more carefully than those who say "it doesn't matter, we'll soon be

57

dead." The bothersome fact that human nature seems un-
changeable will perhaps also be removed if we all have
300 years in which to change.

If they do not give a four-square treatment of all their
material, the two sprawling Vitalist plays do adequately
express the central Shavian paradox of life and thought.
We have seen how in the three major essays Shaw represented the human mind as a battle-ground of the passions,
none of which could be driven out except by a stronger
passion. It is thus quite wrong to think of Shaw as favor-
ing a "literature of ideas" in which abstract concepts do
duty for feelings. Usually Shaw is, in essay and play, opposing all and sundry ideas and championing impulse,
activity, instinct, passion, life. In one of his weekly articles
he wrote: "It is an instinct with me personally to attack
every idea which has been full grown ten years." The
paradox expressed in the Vitalist plays is that what Shaw
accepts in the place of ideas—namely, impulse, activity,
and the like—itself leads to thought, to ideas. That is
why Shaw has been alternately denounced by the critics
as the arch-rationalist and the arch-irrationalist. Again,
his position is: not Either/Or but Both/And.

3

But, I can imagine a critic protesting, the widespread
disapproval of *Man and Superman* and *Back to Methuselah* is founded less on the implausible programs which
they set forth than on the criticism they contain of Darwinism. The preface to *Back to Methuselah* is a summary
of the whole case. What Shaw says in this formal argu-

ment cannot so lightly be explained away as the fantastic incidents of his plays.

Now just as the positive metaphysic of this play, if taken simply as a metaphysic, lands one in the eternal metaphysical discussions of mind and matter, free will and determinism, so the preface lands one in those biological discussions by which, in the past two hundred years, metaphysics have been so seriously affected. After Darwin published his *Origin of Species* in 1859 there were two main schools of thought on the subject. The Darwinists believed that in the doctrine of continuity of species the great law of organic life had been discovered. The religiously orthodox believed that if man were a continuous growth from lower animals then special divine creation and with it human dignity were sacrificed. A little later, however, a number of thinkers put the whole discussion on a different basis. Of these the one who most influenced Shaw was Samuel Butler who pointed out that Darwin's special contribution was not the very acceptable doctrine of the continuity of species (which his grandfather believed in as much as he) but the doctrine of Natural Selection which Butler found by no means acceptable, because it seemed to him to make our development a matter of freakish chance or mechanical law. Darwin, he said, had "banished mind from the universe."

Thus the evolutionary controversy which had been a battle between Evolutionists and Special Creationists became a battle between Darwinists (or Mechanists) and Lamarckians (or Vitalists). Or rather it would have become such a battle if the Mechanists had ever been prepared to fight. But whether from timidity, arrogance, or sheer lack of interest, Charles Darwin gave the Mechanists a precedent for ignoring all that their opponents might have to say. The position of the Mechanists was that, even if Vitalism were correct, it was of no use in the laboratory where one had to proceed on the assumption of strict causality and mechanical law. If Vitalism were correct in claiming that in all life there was an x which was not present in dead matter, this x was of an order of reality which science could not touch. Now since our scientists are for the most part laboratory routinists with as much interest in speculation about life as a test-tube has, it is not surprising that in going ahead on premises that were necessarily mechanist they seldom gave their attention to the possible existence of entities that could not be handled in the laboratory. Insofar as they did erect their procedure into a philosophy they took a stand on both the philosophical questions of *Back to Methuselah:* mind and matter, free will and determinism. Being champions of the mysterious x, the Vitalists postulated the existence of mind, which is cause as well as effect, and affirmed free will. The publication of Darwin's book proved nothing one way or another. No philosophic problem was created, let alone solved, by it. Age-old controversies were re-opened and reanimated. We often hear, of course, from one group of people, that "Darwinism has been proved false by the discoveries of Mr. Y" and, from another group, that "Darwinism has been proved true by the discoveries of Mr. Z." But the body-mind problem, the problem of free will and necessity—these are simply not susceptible of final solution. One may, with the extreme school of positivists, declare the whole discussion meaningless. Or one may take sides.

Being a poet, Shaw could never declare anything meaningless. He took sides. And the Vitalist side was the only one he could possibly be on. He became the willing champion of Buffon, Lamarck, and Butler against Darwin, Huxley, and Weismann. Shaw's is so purely an espousal of free will against determinism, of mind against materialism, above all of the *x*—the soul—against mechanism, that there is scarcely any need to follow him into specifically biological arguments. It is not even true that Shaw "denied" Natural Selection. He said:

> Natural Selection must have played an immense part in adapting life to our planet; but it is Creative Evolution that adapts the planet to our continual aspiration to greater knowledge and greater power.

This is not the statement of one school of scientists arguing with another. It is the statement of a religionist arguing against scientism.

Scientism is the attitude of the man who, on Huxley's advice, believes something only when the evidence for it is overwhelming. To Butler and Shaw this attitude seemed profoundly impractical. For it means suspending belief in practically everything. The area as yet covered by exact science is very small. If, as the scientists sometimes recommend, we wait till exact science has covered a field before making up our minds about it we shall still be suspending judgment on our deathbeds. And meanwhile our less scientific fellow-men will not have been so squeamish. The decisions which we declined to make will have been made "unscientifically" by others. As moral agents we have simply been immobilized.

The scientist assumes that decisions not scientifically based are all *equally* unreliable. It is at this point that Butler and Shaw protest. They point to the processes that are performed by nature—human and non-human—without full understanding. "The unconscious self is the real genius," says John Tanner, adding: "Except during the nine months before he draws his first breath, no man manages his affairs as well as a tree does." In other words, if waiting till scientific method has been applied to all areas of life were the only remedy of our ills, the job should be given up as hopeless. Luckily, Butler and Shaw assert, many things that are not scientifically controlled function perfectly well. Butler saw this as a physiological and psychological matter. Shaw has more often stated it in theological terms. Outside help is needed for salvation; works will never be sufficient; grace is needed. Or as the Irishman puts it in *The Black Girl:*

> There's somethin in us that's dhrivin at Him,
> and somethin out of us that's dhrivin at Him.

Again it is Both/And. The inner and the outer, works and grace, will and nature, conscious and unconscious—all are necessary to salvation.

The preface to *Back to Methuselah*, then, should not be read mainly as an essay on organic evolution. It is a confession of faith and a denunciation of unbelief. The scientists long ago had convinced Shaw that supernatural Christianity is done for; but what they gave him in its place was no adequate substitute. As in economics, the great error in biology, he concludes, is to imagine that all life is regulated by impersonal forces. Both Marx and Darwin started from Malthus's picture of the automatic survival of the fittest in the remorseless struggle for existence. Real economy begins when we make welfare the goal and control the method. Real biology begins when life is viewed poetically rather than mechanically, religiously rather than scientifically. What the cash nexus is in economics, the struggle for existence is in biology. If life is not more than this, it must be made so.

Accordingly, Lorenz Oken, who found in nature the workings of the Holy Ghost, is worth more to Shaw than all the Darwins. And this, not the defence of ordinary Vitalism, is the main point of the famous preface. Shaw dissociates himself even from the Vitalists:

> The Old Vitalists, in postulating a Vital Force,
> were setting up a comparatively mechanical con-
> ception as against the divine idea of the life
> breathed into the clay nostrils of Adam, whereby
> he became a living soul.

This divine idea is of course the *New* Vitalism. (Shaw does not give us any idea who the New Vitalists are, apart from himself.) And we have here not a school of biological thought but a religion; not a "new religion," either, but a very old one. "There is no question of a new religion," says Shaw, "but rather of redistilling the eternal spirit of religion." He wants to replace the purely analytic attitude to nature, and the purely heuristic one, with the spirit of wonder and reverence as it is found in religion

63

BERNARD SHAW

and poetry, as it is found in Blake's poem "Auguries of
Innocence" and Goethe's rhapsody "Die Natur."

4

As a theologian Shaw is very unpretentious. What he
again and again says about God is that He exists but that
He is very different from the Jehovah of the Jewish-
Christian tradition who is, first, a bully tyrannizing over
humanity and, later, a sentimental busybody slobbering
over humanity and never giving it a rest from His impor-
tunate affection. In his story *The Adventures of the Black
Girl in Her Search for God* Shaw specifies several other
phases of Deity; but the conclusion as to all of them is
that they are too crude or too flattering. Shaw's God is less
personal and less perfect. He is much too busy to be interested in counting hairs or watching the fall of spar-
rows. Above all, He is not yet finished. He is an evolving
God, learning, as we learn, by trial and error. A headline
reporting a Shavian speech once read: *God Makes Mis-
takes—Bernard Shaw*. Such was Shaw's account of the
problem of evil.

This theology is obviously even more rudimentary and
insufficient than the Shavian metaphysics and science. It
is even more in need of interpretation—as Tolstoy seems
to have felt when Shaw exchanged letters with him concerning *Man and Superman*. Tolstoy wrote: "You seem
yourself to recognize a God who has got definite aims com-
prehensible to you" and chided Shaw for flippancy. He
was wrong on both counts. Shaw was not flippant, and
neither was his God quite what Tolstoy implied. Soon
after *Methuselah* came out, Shaw was asked the ultimate

religious question: "do you believe that there must be 'somebody behind the something'?" He replied: "No. I believe there is something behind the somebody. All bodies are products of the Life Force (*whatever that might be*)." [1] In other words the Life Force is another of those ultimates of which "we can give no account whatever." The world is not, as in Christian theology, neatly circumscribed by a creator. It is shrouded in mystery. Then what is God? Shaw advises:

> When you are asked, "Where is God? Who is God?" stand up and say, "I am God, and here is God," not as yet completed, but still advancing towards completion, just insomuch as I am working for the purpose of the universe, working for the good of society, and the whole world, instead of merely looking after my personal ends.

If a theology is, by definition, literally true in the eyes of its adherents, this is not a theology. It is a theological allegory. It is metaphor in which theology is the vehicle of a non-theological meaning. Compare it with Blanco Posnet's "shewing-up":

> . . . there's a rotten game and there's a great game. I played the rotten game but the great game was played on me; and now I'm for the great game every time. Amen.

Or with a statement more literal than either, from the "Epistle Dedicatory" to *Man and Superman*:

[1] My italics [E.B.].

65

This is the true joy in life, the being used for a purpose recognized by yourself as a mighty one; the being thoroughly worn out before you are thrown on the scrap heap; the being a force of Nature instead of a feverish selfish little clod of ailments and grievances complaining that the world will not devote itself to making you happy. And also the only real tragedy in life is the being used by personally minded men for purposes which you recognize to be base.

Shaw is not talking about God in the Christian sense but about human ethics. He is saying that, like happiness, goodness is achieved as a by-product of working for an object higher than one's own goodness and happiness.

For Shaw, then, "God" is a symbol of the ideal. Man has pictured God in various guises—from Jehovah to the Life Force. Even John Dewey and A. N. Whitehead have not been able to do without Him. In what sense has He objective existence? This is not the kind of question Shaw has given his attention to. One might assume that he agreed with his friend Beatrice Webb, who wrote:

How each of us determines our scale of values no one knows. For my own part, I find it best to live "as if" the soul of man were in communion with a superhuman force which makes for righteousness.

On the other hand, theologians might give the name Pantheism to the Shavian belief in the oneness and sacredness of Nature without whose cooperation man's virtue would be vain. But supposing Nature is not so sincerely benevolent as she seems? Supposing God does not "make for righteousness"? In his correspondence with Tolstoy Shaw faced even this possibility. He asked: "Suppose the world were only one of God's jokes, would you work any the less to make it a good joke instead of a bad one?" Tolstoy was pained. But Shaw's thought was ten layers deeper than cynicism. In this query he was back again at the very beginning of his positive thought, back at the beginning of things where the choice between the negative and the affirmative attitudes to life has to be made by sheer subjective preference. It was a gamble, but Shaw, like Carlyle and Nietzsche with their everlasting yeas, had accepted it. He followed his master, Samuel Butler, who also worded his choice theologically: "I *bet* that my Redeemer liveth."

Shaw's theology is no theology but a symbolism. It is chiefly a use of religious language. Not only does Shaw use the central term God quite unblushingly. His works are full of the words and phrases of the Bible, the church services, and the hymnal, from Major Barbara's "My God, why hast Thou forsaken me?" which scandalized London, to Saint Joan's "How long, O Lord, how long?" which made London think him a Christian. His first play has the pseudo-Biblical title, *Widowers' Houses*.[2] Several of his last plays suggest the theme of Doomsday, and one of them acts it out. Another play retells the story of Genesis and sets up as a contribution to a new Vitalist Bible. An-

[2] *Matthew XXIII, 14:* "Woe unto you, scribes and Pharisees, hypocrites! for ye devour widows' houses, and for a pretence make long prayer: therefore ye shall receive the greater damnation."

other is the life of a saint. Two prefaces contain Shavian portraits of Jesus; Paul and Pilate, the fanatic founder of "Crosstianity" and the suave *real-politiker*, are in turn presented as anti-Christs. And Shaw has perhaps put more clergymen on the stage than any other playwright of any period. From all this we are entitled to deduce not only that Shaw was bred on the Bible, retained an absorbing interest in Christianity, and was in politics very much of a theocrat, but also that he was trying to make the religious language which he was brought up on go to work for the religion which he grew up to.

Like many of Shaw's devices the use of religious language in strained meanings has grown tiresome with endless repetition. Sometimes it sounds far-fetched as when he says:

> The true Fall of Man occurred when he lost his intellectual innocence by trying to pluck the apple of knowledge from the upas tree of the teaching profession.

Sometimes it has to be ponderously explained:

> Even when I speak of Confirmation I do not mean the Church ceremony but the assumption of responsibility for one's opinions which it formalizes.

If the device is not always a flippancy, what is Shaw trying to do with it? Many would say that he is trying to lend an aura of sanctity, tradition, and authority to his own secular, modern, and home-made creed. Obviously there is something in this. Yet obviously if the device remained so ponderous Shaw's religious language could never have had more force than the Biblical quotations and echoes in newspaper editorials, political speeches, and Broadway plays. Why are the Biblical *cris de coeur* of Barbara and Joan so effective? Not surely because very much of their original context is carried over by association. The connection between the Bible and Shaw's play is an irony. The emotion which the lines convey must be Shaw's own; and much of it is generated by the Shavian context. It is not a matter of an old emotion and a new creed. The emotion is ever new to any artist who can re-create it; the homelessness of Shaw's girl heroines is as old as humanity. The Biblical language of Shaw at its best is as fully assimilated to his own medium and as responsive to his touch as the Homeric language and the classical imagery of some of our poets. It is by such means that he tries to "re-create the spirit of eternal religion."

Most often Shaw does not stoop to explain what he is doing with his Christian language. That is why only the fairly astute have found him heterodox. Sometimes, however, a joke gives the show away, as in the peroration to his beautiful essay—the whole of which shows the depth of Shaw's early interest in religion—"On Going to Church":

I am a resolute Protestant; I believe in the Holy Catholic Church; in the Holy Trinity of Father, Son (or Mother, Daughter) and Spirit; in the Communion of Saints, the Life to Come, the Immaculate Conception, and the everyday reality of Godhead and the Kingdom of Heaven. Also I

69

believe that salvation depends on redemption
from belief in miracles; and I regard Saint Athanasius as an irreligious fool. . . .

A Christian believer who had never heard of Shaw would
probably dismiss this as a meaningless and not very funny
joke. Yet Shaw's meaning is substantial: that he is a sort
of Protestant in his belief in protest and individual conscience; yet a Catholic too in that he wants a universal
faith; a believer also in the sanctity of birth, fatherhood,
motherhood, sonship, daughterhood, and in the kinship of
the great men of the spirit, in the divinity of all life, in the
potential earthly ubiquity of heaven. Such a set of beliefs constitutes a Shavian theology. The churches and the
orthodox theologians are irreligious.

5

In the last chapter we saw how Shaw did not try to
beat the political thinkers on their own ground, did not
try to lay down a complete scheme of political philosophy,
political reform, or descriptive sociology, but touched on
all these subjects supplying a fact or an idea that had been
overlooked, pointing to a subterfuge or a self-deception,
laying bare hidden assumptions, and the like. Shaw's relation to professional thinkers in philosophy, biology, and
religion resembles his relation to the professionals of political thought. It is—one might almost say—a tangential
relation. Just as a foreign traveller may write a more serv-
iceable book about a country than most of its inhabitants
could, so Shaw has paid an extraordinarily fruitful visit
to many countries of the mind. Thus we find one who had

but a moderate competence in musical technique becoming one of the supreme music critics. Even Shaw's incursions into science have been praised by the few scientists strong enough to take his strictures in good part. The eminent crystallographer J. D. Bernal commends Shaw's "natural, almost effortless grasp of the commonsense scepticism which is the life-blood of scientific advance" and adds: "Explicitly Shaw may stand out against current science: implicitly he understands it." Mr. Bernal says that the preface to *Back to Methuselah* "should form part of every biological student's education" because it analyses the social context of Darwinism, a side of the subject that biological students would otherwise learn nothing of. In other words, Shaw's preface is supplementary and corrective. Had H. G. Wells understood this he would not have condemned Shaw for "dancing round" and "philandering with" the facts. He might have acknowledged that Shaw's supplements and correctives were at least as valuable as his own summaries of orthodox Darwinism.

It is not an affair of subject matter only. Shaw has a peculiar polemical *method,* the simplest thing about which is, as we know, that he "slants" his utterances, thinking of effect, not of objectivity. The best-known characteristic of the method is pure exaggeration. According to Shaw unless you say a thing irritatingly you might as well not say it at all. "It is always necessary to overstate a case startlingly to make people sit up and listen to it, and to frighten them into acting on it. I myself do this habitually and deliberately." Everyone is familiar with quips about Shaw himself or Shakespeare or the General Medical Council or the human race that are simple exaggerations of a truth.

71

One of the characteristic results of the Shavian procedure—and one to which Shaw is himself supremely indifferent—is the amount of logical contradiction which it involves.

For instance, Shaw uses the same word in almost opposite senses. Take such words as *gentleman, science,* and *democracy.* In a speech quoted above (p. 35) *gentleman* is the name given to Shaw's ideal type; in *Man and Superman* and its appendices it is the name given to the rich parasite ("I am a gentleman: I live by robbing the poor.") Shaw writes: "All problems are finally *scientific* problems" in the preface to a play ridiculing the claims of medical *science.* In all expositions of his artistic approach he claims to write a "natural history" that is "genuinely *scientific*" yet on other occasions he will say: "*Science* is always wrong and religion is always right" and "Impostor for impostor I prefer the mystic to the *scientist.*" His own political allegiance has always been to what he regards as "genuine *democratic* socialism" yet he is not in the least averse to saying "I do not believe in *democracy.*" Are these polemics really so deceiving? Is it not obvious that in each case Shaw postulates a genuine article—gentleman, science, democracy—and in each case the spurious product which has stolen the market? "I do not believe in democracy." This from Bernard Shaw! The things he pretends not to believe in for the sake of irritating his public are of course precisely the things he believes in most ardently. But they have been degraded till the words mean the opposite of what they originally meant. The contradiction here is not in Shaw but in society at large.

72

Well, it might be retorted, if Shaw's exaggerations have a function yet at best they are only half-truths. Precisely. The art of epigram and apothegm is the art of salutary half-truth; and a very fine art it is. Shaw utters half-truths, first, because, as has been noted, half-truths jolt people into paying attention, second, because he would never presume to think he could utter The Whole Truth, and, third, because there is usually a side of the truth which deserves special notice, having been obscured by our stupidity, sentimentality, and fear. The half of the truth which Shaw ignores is always the "easy" half, the half which needs no repeating because it is shouted from the housetops, because it is a half-truth that is firmly established to the point of being a menace.

For example: "Compared with Weismann the Kaiser was as innocent as a lamb." What is the Shavian strategy here? The starting point is the opinion of the British public that the Kaiser was the main, if not the sole, cause of the First World War. In effect Shaw ironically indulges this view with the reflection: "You think the Kaiser very guilty: in that case, Weismann is even more guilty. Of course to make the cloistered well-meaning scientist the cause of war is extravagant polemics; but so was making the cloistered well-meaning Kaiser the cause of war. Or were you using the Kaiser's name as a symbol? In that case I shall use Weismann's as a symbol. In place of the Monarch who launched the ship with oratorical champagne I shall indict the Scientist who put the steam in the engine, who supplied the Idea."

The tendency to use names as symbols may be found throughout Shaw's writings. One recalls his apology for

73

using dramatists' names in this way in his theatre criticism:

> In justice to many well-known persons who are
> handled rather recklessly in the following pages,
> I beg my readers not to mistake my journalistic
> utterances for final estimates of their worth and
> achievements as dramatic artists and authors.
> . . . I must therefore warn the reader that what
> he is about to study is not a series of judgments
> aiming at impartiality, but a siege laid to the the-
> atre of the XIXth Century by an author who had
> to cut his own way into it at the point of the pen,
> and throw some of its defenders into the moat.

One might say that Shaw has never chosen an enemy
except when his name could be used as a symbol of a
general vice. (This is the obverse of the proposition that
Shaw's attacks are never personal.) In his early days the
symbol was Marx or his English disciple Hyndman; later
it was more often Darwin and his German disciple Weismann. Or Shaw might take the field against the fashionable coiner of a new formula—Max Nordau in the 'nineties, Pavlov in the 'twenties. The names he championed
were also used abstractly, like the names Nietzsche championed. *The Quintessence of Ibsenism* and *The Perfect
Wagnerite* parallel rather interestingly *Schopenhauer als
Erzieher* and *Richard Wagner in Bayreuth* in that they
are *unzeitgemässe Betrachtungen* by a young man who is
presenting his own philosophy in the guise of Ibsen's,
Wagner's, or Schopenhauer's, these names being rallying

points, oriflammes, for the *avant-garde*. All "slanting" is the doctoring of writing with a particular audience in view. Nietzsche and Shaw have in mind the modern intelligentsia that is their public. Nietzsche would never have wanted a larger audience; and Shaw has never been under the "proletarian" writer's illusion that he is, or might be, read by the masses.

Of course, by his jokes, his blarney, his tone, his irony, Shaw expresses an attitude to every section of the intelligentsia whose interests he touches on. There is, for example, a running joke in his works against the aesthete, for Shaw believes the intellect should be stronger than the fancy and the sense of life stronger than the sense of beauty. If there are readers who have determined his strategy more than any others they are the most powerful groups in the whole intelligentsia: the liberals and the scientists.

The liberals are used to the phenomenon of "slanted" writing. They denounce its use in the reactionary press and freely practise it in their own. (Not, of course, *all* liberals *all* the time. Throughout this passage I criticize broad tendencies in modern liberalism but, I hope, from a fundamentally liberal point of view.) In journalism, reactionary and liberal alike, the function of "slanting" is to permit reader and writer to ooze virtue without paying for it. It is true that liberal writers disguise their conformity by attacking the genteel classes, but then they have their own cohorts to appeal to. Of late years writing that is "slanted" by radical conformism has been more of a plague (within the intelligentsia) than reactionary distortion. It has resulted in the moral corruption of a great part of the intelligentsia, a corruption labelled "Stalinism" by anti-Stalin leftists, but really just as common among near-Stalinists, ex-Stalinists, and non-Stalinists. The corruption consists (among other things) in being able to see in history only a battle between the Right People and the Wrong People and in fitting one's judgments of all other matters to this Procrustean bed. Thus the main point in discussion of a writer is whether he is Ours or not: the battle has raged over all the masters from Shakespeare to Dostoevsky. One of the chief demerits of the method is that you are never interested in your own real opinion. You do not say what you think nor even, precisely, what you think you ought to think, but what you think other people ought to think. Thus you warn your public against Franz Kafka, because he did not believe in the common man, though you would be affronted if anyone suggested *you* had suffered any harm from your Kafka readings.

I describe the liberal malady in contemporary terms. But one must be clear about the fact that Shaw, though friendly to Stalin, has been anti-"Stalinist" for two generations. His essay "The Illusions of Socialism" is the best analysis of "Stalinist" thinking ever written. Nor is it an isolated work. Here is what Shaw told his *Saturday Review* readers:

> Men do every day, with a frightful fatalism, abjectly accept for themselves as well as others all the consequences of theories as to what they ought to feel and ought to believe, although they not only do not so feel or believe, but often feel

and believe the very reverse, and find themselves
forced to act on their real feeling and belief in
supreme moments which they are willing with
a tragically ridiculous self-abnegation to expiate
afterwards even with their lives.

Anyone who knows the history of liberals and Marxists in
the twentieth century, anyone who knows the history of
a liberal or Marxist magazine is bound to acknowledge the
prescience of these lines.

Shaw knows the political animal. He wrote: "Bourgeois
morality is largely a system of making cheap virtue a cloak
for disastrous vices," and he insisted that Bohemia is a
bourgeois institution, and that radical groups consisted of
people who were not good enough for bourgeois society
as well as of those who were too good for it. He saw that
the vice of the radical is self-righteousness and that the
chief manifestation of this vice is lip-service. We all "com-
pound for sins we are inclined to / By damning those we
have no mind to," and the liberal salvationist has in our
time outdone most previous practitioners of this art. Shaw
once described socialism as "a movement in which every
man is a hero and every woman a heroine *ex officio*." Have
we not met people whose heroism consists in having read
Malraux instead of Proust?

Now Shaw acquired his peculiar tone and attitude in a
personal fight against all this sixty years ago. He preferred
the role of Devil's Advocate to that of hero *ex officio*. He
blasphemed against every god of the lip-servers' idolatry,
especially against Demos the king of their gods. This is a
very unpopular game to play, and doubtless Shaw's work

shows some wear and tear. But he never gave up the game, never played safe, never allowed himself to be put on the defensive. In Bernard Shaw there are no evasions, no apologies, no relaxations. Shaw has said many things which as they stand are not true. Yet he is much less deceiving than many writers with Truth on their sleeve and Facts in their filing cabinet. For he knows that the distinction is not between Truth and Untruth but between partial truth with one motive and partial truth with another. Shaw's motives are "above suspicion." (The phrase is common; the reality, rare.) Though endowed with the most extraordinary flow of words our time has heard, Shaw has assiduously abjured claptrap. And this is why few liberals understand him.

Shaw's speech is "slanted" the wrong way. He does not include his audience in an embrace. He does not court the approving smirk of any group. Not content with "bewildering the bourgeois," he bewilders the liberal too. Unused to the spectacle of man so utterly independent— a free lance who is really free—the sectaries have been forced to pigeonhole him. Must not an opponent of the liberals be a fascist? Certainly Shaw objected to participation in the liberal game of Jack the Giant Killer (a favorite version of the Right People versus the Wrong). What if Jack happens to be a fool and the Giant beneficent in comparison? The liberals, tied to moral generalizations, fixed categories, and melodramatic attitudes are on Jack's side irrespective of circumstances. Shaw had only to refer to Mussolini and Hitler without the ritual exorcisms and Edmund Wilson was deploring the loss of youthful enthusiasms and declaring that Shaw was not a "practising socialist." Practising socialist indeed—as if socialism were a personal morality! Shaw had not changed: he had written his first play to explain that socialism was not something an individual could "practise."

There was an irony also about the liberal charge that Shaw had capitulated to sheer power, that he was a sort of comical Pétain, an Irish Hauptmann. What the liberals naturally did not see was that Shaw was not in the position of a Pétain or even a Hauptmann, that he was an unpersecuted intellectual talking to—liberals. In these circumstances the easiest of all things, the thoroughly conformist thing, was to praise Jack and condemn the Giant. After all a radical intellectual belongs to the circles that read and write *The New Statesman, The Nation, The New Republic.* What courage was needed to oppose Hitler in *them?* When the liberals solved the moral problem with cocktail parties for Spanish Relief, the old teetotaller did not attend.

If the liberals are victims of a spurious moralism, the scientists are victims of sheer amorality. Or perhaps one should say that the victims of science are the victims of sheer amorality, for obviously there are scientists with as much moral stamina as anyone else. The *victims* of science form a larger class. They are the people to whom all scientific advance is in itself good. One hears the spokesman of this scientism in the newsreel which cheers some hideous new invention. One notes it in the common assumption that scientific research *must* go on even though it cost billions of dollars, even though it threaten civilization. Bernard Shaw used to incur ridicule when he inferred that if you began by baking a dog for the furtherance of

79

science you would end by baking your mother for the furtherance of science. Yet atrocities very like this were perpetrated in the German concentration camps. Again Shaw's remark was extravagant; but again its extravagance was as nothing compared with the extravagance of what actually happened.

Shaw was one of the first to distinguish between people who understand science and people who are befuddled by it, between the few who comprehend scientific methods and findings and the vast public to whom science is an array of spectacular results and fascinating symbols, to whom, in fact, science is something about as scientific as voodoo. It is with this latter group—the public at large—that Shaw is concerned. Their attitude to science constitutes a new and gross superstition. The scientist has become a priest who like other priests insists that the public accept his doctrines on authority. Your individual judgment (that the sun goes round the earth, for instance) is shown to be misleading. Nothing that seems to be so is so. Science creates for us a mental world of bewildering incomprehensibles. Instead of tangible commonsense evidence it staggers the imagination with statistics and deadens the brain with abstract formulae. In such an age the mind of the citizen is a hodge-podge of beliefs which the citizen could not in any way substantiate and images which differ from those of the primitive myth chiefly in being far less coherent and beautiful. The new priest, moreover, is inferior to the old in two important respects. First, he has no help to offer either in morality or in that expansion and development of consciousness which is the fruit of "religious experience." Second, his authority undermines itself by too frequent changes of doctrine: the cloak of infallibility sits ill on priests who change their minds.

Commonsense, individual judgment, responsibility for one's actions, belief in purposeful activity—the new superstition threatened all these Shavian allegiances. And Shaw deployed all his ordnance against it. His simplest weapon was the joke. He laughed off the proposition that the sun is 93 million miles away with a "Nonsense: look at it!" He computed that the moon was but some 37 miles off. He denounced as "blazing nonsense" a mathematics based on such assumptions as that a curve is a collection of straight lines. To the logician he said: "I have always the right to treat your logical principles as a *reductio ad absurdum.*"

It will not escape notice that all these quips have the same drift as Shaw's critique of Darwinism. They are a Romantic's plea for the evidence of the senses. As Blake and Keats rejected the Newtonianism that told them color was in their eyes and not in the rainbow, so Shaw rejects the Scientism that tells us our relation to the sun is a matter of statistics, not of sight, the mathematics that prefers the abstraction of accumulated straight lines to the concrete reality of the curve, the logic whose laws are so gray a caricature of the green tree of life. Shaw's pose as the man who believes that the sun goes round the earth dramatizes his attachment to first-hand sensory judgment. It also performs the almost exactly contrary function of demonstrating that the non-scientist's notion of a science is unscientific and will remain so unless science is presented to us in a new way.

In school I was set to perform certain algebraic operations, but left in such a complete ignorance of their nature that I guessed for myself that a + b was shorthand for Eggs and Bacon. Consequently I rejected equations as utter nonsense for the next twenty or thirty years . . . until one day J. L. Joynes, amazed at my ignorance, told me that a and b meant neither bacon and eggs nor brandy and Bibles. But, being the son of a famous Eton master and educated accordingly, he failed to explain what they did mean; and not until I had in the course of my literary work to take the matter into serious consideration did I find out for myself.

This passage shows that Shaw has no objection to science itself. But he knows that what passes for the scientific mind of a scientific age is the superstitious mind of a barbarous age blown up with the conceit of an entirely imaginary enlightenment.

The whole development seemed to Shaw summed up in the rise of what was virtually a new institution: the medical profession. Although medicine and surgery are old enough practices, and Molière himself has warned us against their practitioners, it was only in the nineteenth century, especially the later nineteenth century, that the medical profession became the thing we know today: a group of men receiving high social and moral status as initiates into the highest and deepest mysteries of Democracy's partner in godhead, Science. Shaw's life runs parallel with this extraordinary development. He noted that, as traditional religion declined, the confidence of men in doctors increased. If every scientist was a priest of a new religion, the doctor was still a witch-doctor, establishing his prestige by an array of hocus-pocus—from the illegible Latin of his placebos to the monastic discipline, the masked and white-coated ceremonials, of his hospitals. In the modernity of their apparatus the doctors are exactly as scientific as Californian evangelists who adorn their churches with microphones and chromium-plating instead of incense and stained glass.

There was a time when one would have had to argue about the exact rightness and wrongness of every statement Shaw made about medicine, when indeed one would have had to defend Shaw against the charge of sheer wrongheadedness. Today, I think, there is no need either to endorse every Shavian verdict or to be shamefaced about the general tenor of his indictment. J. D. Bernal acknowledges that the preface to *The Doctor's Dilemma* has the same sort of importance for doctors as the preface to *Back to Methuselah* has for biologists: it is the outstanding account of the sociology—the social pathology—of their field. Mr. Bernal makes the most interesting concessions even on those points where Shaw was always thought most perverse: vaccination and vivisection. As to the first, he praises Shaw for exposing the "absurdities" of "the period of the early enthusiasm and excesses of the germ theory, where scientists as much as doctors took Pasteur's work as divine revelation and thought that all disease was due to germs." The whole Shavian argument against vaccination Bernal finds to be sound enough criticism of inoculatory practices at the time when *The Doc-*

tor's Dilemma was written. Although he does not share Shaw's uncompromising opposition to vivisection he admits that

(i) "It is certainly also true that the greater proportion of animal experiments—as the greater proportion of all experiments—prove nothing."

(ii) "If we had to learn science all over again from the start we could undoubtedly do it in a far more humane way."

and

(iii) "If all men and all scientists were ideally wise and honorable they might have discovered what they have discovered without recourse to any animal experiments."

From the third admission Mr. Bernal expects us to conclude that since no one is ideally wise and honorable we should reverse what would otherwise be our opinion. But why the adverb *ideally?* Wisdom and honor are terms that have no meaning at all for men who regard scientific advance as in itself good. They are luxuries that the pursuer of knowledge at all costs cannot afford. Contrariwise, when Shaw attacks the disastrous amorality of science he is speaking as an adherent of wisdom and honor. Amorality is for Shaw the ultimate horror because it is the ultimate form of irresponsibility. Immorality is spasmodic and very human. Scientific amorality is systematic and fiendish. To the impulsive sadism of nature it adds a cruelty that is the more ruthless for being sheer indifference. And the "pursuit of knowledge" is not an adequate excuse:

> The cruel (loving to read the descriptions of his experiments), the selfish (hoping for cures), the sportsman (anxious to be kept in countenance) and the cowardly (seeking an excuse for tolerating an evil they dare not attack) will accept his [the scientist's] excuse: the humane will not. The final conflict is not then between the excuses in their logical disguise of scientific arguments, but between the cruel will and the humane will.

6

Shaw's teasing of the liberals and the scientists is not badinage. It is his arraignment of the scribes and pharisees. It is, further, an integral part of a comprehensive analysis of civilization. "The final conflict is . . . between the cruel will and the humane will." This is one of a dozen Shavian formulations of the problem of living. To thumb through the Prefaces is to come across one diagnosis after another of the diseases of modern life. In the course of an autobiographical preface we come upon this:

> Property is theft; respectability founded on poverty is blasphemy; marriage founded on property is prostitution; it is easier for a camel to go through the eye of a needle than for a rich man to enter the kingdom of heaven.

In a preface instructing reviewers in Shaw's intellectual heritage we are told, by the way:

BERNARD SHAW

Our laws make law impossible; our liberties destroy all freedom; our property is organized robbery; our morality is an impudent hypocrisy; our wisdom is administered by inexperienced or mal-experienced dupes, our power wielded by cowards or weaklings, and our honor false in all its points.

In *Man and Superman* itself, far more impressive than the romance of the Life Force are the satirical tirades against our world:

Its sympathies are all with misery, with poverty, with starvation of the body and of the heart. I call on it to sympathize with joy, with love, with happiness, with beauty. . . . Give me warmth of heart, true sincerity, the bond of sympathy with love and joy. . . .

This is the devil speaking. His diagnosis is correct, but the remedy he prescribes—idealism—is as bad as the disease. Hell is not better than earth, as Don Juan explains:

Here you call your appearance beauty, your emotions love, your sentiments heroism, your aspirations virtue, just as you did on earth; but here there are no hard facts to contradict you, no ironic contrast of your needs with your pretensions, no human comedy, nothing but a perpetual romance, a universal melodrama.

In *John Bull's Other Island*, Father Keegan's heresy is that he regards this world as hell:

86

This world, sir, is very clearly a place of torment and penance, a place where the fool flourishes and the good and wise are hated and persecuted, a place where men and women torture one another in the name of love; where children are scourged and enslaved in the name of parental duty and education; where the weak in body are poisoned and mutilated in the name of healing, and the weak in character are put to the horrible torture of imprisonment, not for hours but for years, in the name of justice. It is a place where the hardest toil is a refuge from the horror and tedium of pleasure, and where charity and good works are done only for hire to ransom the souls of the spoiler and the sybarite. . . .

In such an essay as "The Impossibilities of Anarchism" Shaw's diagnosis is even more specific. In a parenthesis that lasts for several pages Shaw concedes that the anarchist analysis of bourgeois life is correct:

I fully admit and vehemently urge that the State is at present simply a huge machine for robbing and slave-driving the poor by brute force. You may, if you are a stupid or comfortably off person, think that the policeman at the corner is the guardian of law and order—that the gaol, with those instruments of torture, the tread-mill, plank bed, solitary cell, cat o' nine tails, and gallows, is a place to make people cease to do evil and learn to do well. But the primary function of the policeman, and that for which his other func-

tions are only blinds, is to see that you do not lie
down to sleep in this country without paying an
idler for the privilege; that you do not taste bread
until you have paid the idler's toll in the price of
it; that you do not resist the starving blackleg
who is dragging you down to his level for the
idler's profit by offering to do your work for a
starvation wage. Attempt any of these things and
you will be haled off and tortured in the name of
law and order, honesty, social equilibrium, safety
of property and person, public duty, Christianity,
morality, and what not, as a vagrant, a thief and
a rioter. Your soldier, ostensibly a heroic and pa-
triotic defender of his country, is really an unfor-
tunate man driven by destitution to offer himself
as food for powder for the sake of regular rations,
shelter and clothing. . . . And *his* primary function is to come to the rescue of the policeman
when the latter is overpowered. Members of Parliament, whose sole qualifications for election
were £1000 loose cash, an independent income,
and a vulgar strain of ambition; parsons quoting
scripture for the purposes of the squire; lawyers
selling their services to the highest bidder at the
bar, and maintaining the supremacy of the money
class on the bench; juries of employers masquer-
ading as the peers of proletarians in the dock;
University professors elaborating the process
known as the education of a gentleman; artists
striving to tickle the fancy or flatter the vanity
of the aristocrat or plutocrat; workmen doing

their work as badly and slowly as they dare so as to make the most of their job; employers starving and overworking their hands and adulterating their goods as much as *they* dare: these are the actual living material of those imposing abstractions known as the State, the Church, the Law, the Constitution, Education, the Fine Arts, and Industry. Every institution, as Bakounin saw, religious, political, financial, judicial, and so on, is corrupted by the fact that the men in it either belong to the propertied class themselves or must sell themselves to it in order to live. . . . The ordinary man is insensible to the fraud just as he is insensible to the taste of water, which, being constantly in contact with his mucous membrane, seems to have no taste at all. . . . The insensibility, however, is not quite complete; for there is a period in life which is called the age of disillusion, which means the age at which a man discovers that his honest and generous impulses are incompatible with success in business; that the institutions he has reverenced are shams; and that he must join the conspiracy or go the wall. . . .

In such passages as this, surely, the Shavian vision is at its sharpest. Shaw exposes modern society as one "huge conspiracy and hypocrisy." He calls for something better. And he sees his chance in the conscience of youth at the stage of "disillusion."

Having noted in earlier sections of this chapter so many

things that Shaw seems to be doing and is not doing we are now in a position to see what he *is* doing. "I am by profession," he says, "what is called an original thinker, my business being to question and test all the established creeds and codes to see how far they are still valid and how far worn out or superseded, and even to draft new creeds and codes." Shaw's use of the word *original* is rather special. When he called Caesar "genuinely original" he added that Caesar could "estimate the value of truth, money, or success in any particular instance quite independently of convention and moral generalization." It is by a happy symbolism that Shaw portrays himself as a Caesar, a practical, public man, for his peculiarity as a thinker is the constant practical and public relevance of all his ideas. Though Shaw's polemics are only obliquely related to the propositions of scientists, theologians, and philosophers, he stands four-square to the concerns of the public. He is a practical moralist—practical in that he always asks "Is it feasible?" and moral in that he always asks "Is it right?" He handles ideas only insofar as they are matters of right and wrong, only insofar—one might almost say—as they are matters of life and death.

When we ask what Shaw has been doing if he has not been contributing to philosophy, theology, or science, the answer is that he has been making a moral analysis of contemporary civilization. Such an analysis requires incursions into metaphysics, religions, biology, but Shaw has always subordinated these to his central purpose. The analysis, moreover, is not that of a spectator but of a passionate reformer and participant. That is why it is not conducted in an "objective" manner. Shaw, so to say, is not writing military history or laying down the principles of military science. He is conducting a campaign. His analysis of a situation is revealed, therefore, in the strategy which he uses to change it, the strategy of the "original thinker" or, to use Shaw's other term, the "artist philosopher." Insofar as this strategy is not a product of Shaw's peculiar temper and genius it is that of the meliorist thinker in all ages, especially is it in the tradition of the eighteenth-century *philosophes*. Do we not call Voltaire and Rousseau *philosophes* precisely because they changed the meaning of the word *philosopher* until it had much the same content as Shaw's "original thinker" and "artist philosopher," namely, a man of letters, immersed in the thought of his time, who gives his best energies to defending what he believes to be the simple human foundations against the rotten superstructure of modern civilization? The *philosophe* is fired with what Tolstoy called *Weltverbesserungswahn*—which Shaw translated "worldbettermentcraze." But, like all true revolutionaries, the *philosophe* is at bottom a conservative whose desire to pull down is backed by positive faith in what will be left when the destruction is over. Though he has brought the heavenly city down to earth, he remains, in a Shavio-Pickwickian sense, a believer in "Father, Son (or Mother, Daughter) and Spirit." Though he has remained a proponent of Political Economy, "the science by which civilization stands or falls," he has seen that Political Economy is but part of Vital Economy. Far from trying, after the fashion of unconservative or lunatic revolutionaries, to impose upon society ideas not native to it, Bernard Shaw took a stand *for* society *against* "modern

91

ideas," including liberalism and science. "I am prepared," he wrote, "to back human society against any idea, positive or negative, that can be brought into the field against it." And this remark is the perfect cue for a discussion of Shaw's most highly studied presentation of the conflict between society and ideas, feelings and notions: his theatre.

3. THE THEATRE

1

My plays are sui generis.

—BERNARD SHAW

IF THE WIDESPREAD PREJUDICE AGAINST SHAVIAN DRAMA
were more articulate it might take the form of a syllogism:
Problem Plays are an inferior genre; Shaw's plays are
Problem Plays; therefore Shaw's plays are inferior.

What is a Problem Play? Although it is a modern term
there is no more agreement about it than about tragedy
and comedy. To the unlettered the term probably suggests propaganda and little else. To academic critics it
has almost become a term to cover modern drama in general. The modern age, we are told, has abandoned the
classic norms of tragedy and comedy to put in their place
the Problem Play which is wholly devoted to ephemeral
social questions like votes for women and prison conditions. Some writers assume that the Problem Play has a

thesis, a solution to its problem. Others find the justification of the word Problem in the fact that the play ends on a question-mark.

It would be possible to ignore the term altogether had not Bernard Shaw brandished it himself. In the manifesto-like preface to *Mrs. Warren's Profession* he wrote: "Only in the Problem Play is there any real drama." Although this is the kind of remark which anti-Shavians pounce on, its context yields an unexpected meaning. Shaw is dividing drama into two categories, the frivolous and the serious, his name for the latter being Problem Play.

In 1895 when a London periodical announced a symposium on the Problem Play Shaw's statement was far from unorthodox. He wrote:

> The material of the dramatist is always some conflict of human feeling with circumstances; so that, since institutions are circumstances, every social question furnishes material for drama. But every drama does not involve a social question, because human feeling may be in conflict with circumstances which are not institutions, which raise no question at all, which are part of human destiny.

And further:

> To this day your great dramatic poet is never a socialist, nor an individualist, nor a positivist, nor a materialist, nor any other sort of 'ist,' though he comprehends all the 'isms,' and is generally

quoted and claimed by all the sections as an adherent. Social questions are too sectional, too topical, too temporal to move a man to the mighty effort which is needed to produce great poetry. Prison reform may nerve Charles Reade to produce an effective and businesslike prose melodrama; but it could never produce *Hamlet*, *Faust*, or *Peer Gynt*.

The whole article might have been written by a professor of literature—except for one heterodoxy:

A Doll's House will be as flat as ditchwater when *A Midsummer Night's Dream* will still be as fresh as paint; but it will have done more work in the world; and that is enough for the highest genius.

In other words, literary greatness is not the only criterion; there is also social utility.

Now while Shaw appreciates the importance of the great poet who "comprehends all the 'isms,'" he has made it his job to champion the other, utilitarian kind of talent. The great poet, if he has been dead long enough, needs no championing, for he is never attacked. Nor would literary greatness itself ever be attacked; it suffers more often from reverence than from challenge. Provoked by this fact, the Quixotic Shaw assails a Shakespeare and praises a Brieux. More to the point, he assails Shakespeare and praises Shaw. In the preface to one of his novels he tells us first that it isn't a very good novel and then draws himself up to inform us that anyway it is of the first order

95

while Shakespeare is of the second. However, Shaw is only discussing orders of *morality*. It was not he after all, but a more generally respected writer, who asserted his preference for *Uncle Tom's Cabin* over *Othello*.

Is the attitude of the self-confessed Problem Playwright a simple moralism like Tolstoy's? Certainly *What Is Art?* could not be more highly spoken of than it was in Shaw's review of it. Yet Shaw boggles at Tolstoy's chief criterion—popularity. His own severity towards the arts is more akin to Plato's: the existence of aesthetic criteria is not denied, but the arts are seen also as a sensual lure.

> I am as fond of fine music and handsome buildings as Milton was, or Cromwell, or Bunyan; but if I found that they were becoming the instruments of a systematic idolatry of sensuousness, I would hold it good statesmanship to blow every cathedral in the world to pieces with dynamite, organ and all, without the least heed to the screams of the art critics and cultured voluptuaries.

It is dangerous, however, to go thus far with Shaw and no farther. For the puritanism which warns of the dangers of sensuousness is but the negative side of a philosophy which makes a great deal—perhaps too much—of the arts. Shaw warns against dangers which were very real for himself. Growing up in the stuffy milieu of Protestant Dublin he had from an early age found in the arts that route to richer emotional experience which many find in religion:

> What power did I find in Ireland religious enough
> to redeem me from this abomination of desola-
> tion? Quite simply, the power of art.

Or again:

> If religion is that which binds men to one an-
> other, and irreligion that which sunders, then
> must I testify that I found the religion of my
> country in its musical genius and its irreligion in
> its churches and drawing-rooms.

Shaw the art critic declared that the art-gallery was the
church of modern times; Shaw the theatre critic declared
the theatre a cathedral. Professor Edward J. Dent observes that Shaw the music critic took up and elaborated
an idea of Handel's and Beethoven's: that music has of
itself (that is, without being specifically ecclesiastical)
religious force. Shaw described the Ninth Symphony as
"religious music, and its performance a celebration rather
than an entertainment. I am highly susceptible," he goes
on, "to the force of all truly religious music, no matter to
what Church it belongs; but the music of my own Church
—for which I may be allowed, like other people, to have
partiality—is to be found in *Die Zauberflöte* and the
Ninth Symphony."

The fact that Shaw makes so much of music is enough
to show that his didactic theory of art is not merely a demand for a message. Absolute music has no message; but
according to Shaw, it has nevertheless an ethical, nay, a
religious function. It stirs, it inspires, it enlarges our consciousness. It is the breath of the Life Force. Shaw is

97

again at one with Nietzsche in finding in art the supreme tonic—in art itself, in color, sound, and form, not in a message. Charles Reade and the Ibsen of *A Doll's House* are useful; Mozart and Rembrandt and Shakespeare are great.

For Shaw "music" and "message" are not only two separate arts. They are also two sides of the one art of literature, the great poets being musicians, the useful poets being evangelists. In his *Dramatic Opinions* and elsewhere Shaw insists that Shakespeare is great chiefly as a musician. He has no message; is not philosophical; is no master of psychological realism; therefore we must not look to content abstracted from form if we wish to find the source of his greatness. Shaw knows his Shakespeare backwards and had as his purpose in assailing him the laudable motive of discouraging the bardolatry of Victorian critics and actors. ("The bardolatry I shook up was simple ignorance: the bardolaters never read him.") Moreover Shaw defended actors who understood Shakespeare—like Forbes-Robertson—against actors who exploited him—like Henry Irving. He complained against the constant cutting of Shakespeare's scripts. He championed his underrated plays such as *All's Well* and *Troilus*. His limitation is that he does not trouble to understand the drama of earlier periods *on its own terms*. He is merely disgusted by Webster and Congreve. Although his constant seeking-out of bad psychology in Shakespeare will probably appeal to the dominant school of Shakespeare critics today, as showing that Shaw saw through the humbug of Victorian psychological criticism, his complaining of the lack of philosophy and higher motive in (for example) the history plays shows only that Shaw is judging Shakespeare by the standards of Ibsen. When he declares: "Shakespeare survives by what he has in common with Ibsen, not by what he has in common with Webster and the rest" Shaw is confessing that he *likes* only what Shakespeare has in common with Ibsen and is not interested in what he has in common with Webster.

There is no need to lecture Shaw about this. His aim as a dramatic critic was freely confessed:

> I postulated as desirable a certain kind of play in which I was destined ten years later to make my mark as a playwright . . . and I brought everybody, authors, actors, managers, to the one test: were they coming my way or staying in the old grooves?

This kind of prejudice is often present in a critic's mind; the rare thing is that he should admit it. But the admission does not cancel the offense. Shaw is not a literary critic at all. Asked to contribute to a Keats Memorial Volume he protests: "I find myself with nothing to say except that you cannot write about Keats" and proceeds to find a passage in "Isabella" in which "the immense indictment of the profiteers and exploiters with which Marx has shaken capitalistic civilization to its foundation even to its overthrow in Russia is epitomized"! When Dixon Scott wrote what remains the best of all descriptions of Shavian style, Shaw commented: "It was very much as if I had told him the house was on fire, and he had said, 'How admirably monosyllabic!'" Again this sounds like Tolstoy or the Marxist critics of the nineteen-thirties. But again we have to remember that Shaw has not denied the existence of aesthetic criteria; he has only said that they are not always paramount.

For Shaw, as he boasts, is a journalist. He is grinding, not the sword of justice, but the axe of amelioration. His remarks about Shakespeare do not all look well in the context of Shakespeare criticism where the scholars see them; but they look very well indeed in the context of Victorian opinion and Lyceum productions where his weekly readers saw them. Shaw is not a scholar. His judgment of works of art is not prepared by the exercise of historical imagination upon masses of fact. It is the spontaneous judgment of a highly sensitive, highly intelligent individual living plump in his own time. "I deal with all periods," he once wrote, "but I never study any period but the present, which I have not yet mastered and never shall." In some ways Shaw is our Dr. Johnson, inviting trouble by complete candor and complete lack of shame. Any critic who reported his own immediate responses to works of art as consistently as these two would as often as they make a fool of himself. But after all their bard-baiting, their praise of Shakespeare has a truer ring than that of the scholars and the actor-managers.[1]

If Shaw is not, like Johnson, a great literary critic, it is because he is pre-occupied (unconsciously, as he might say) with his creative work. He has nothing to say *about* it precisely because he is busy *doing* it. When he does talk about it he often gives evidence of good natural taste but

[1] Johnson went further than Shaw in one respect: "Love is only one of many passions, and, as it has no great influence upon the sum of life, it has little operation in the dramas of a poet who caught his ideas from the living world."

100

seldom knows what to say. The old dichotomy of form and content only makes matters worse for him. Because his feeling for form and technique is natural and undifferentiated, he talks always about content and advises his biographer to do the same when discussing the Shavian life-work. If we want to know, then, just what actually happened to the Problem Play in Shaw's hands we must disregard the legend that he has explained everything in his prefaces and look at the plays for ourselves.

2

The two plays which first made Shaw known as a playwright are, technically considered, crude inversions of accepted patterns. Shaw took up a couple of plays by less skilled and more conventional hands—William Archer's *Rhinegold* and Janet Achurch's *Mrs. Daintry's Daughter* [2] —and by "inverting" the characters arrived at *Widowers' Houses* and *Mrs. Warren's Profession.* After half a century these plays look no more like masterpieces than they did in the 'nineties. But it is not true that they are utterly dated and dead. Since Hollywood has perpetuated the themes, characters, situations, and attitudes which Shaw inverted, his very earliest plays still have point. The subject is the ethics of individualism. Shaw confronts his audience with people apparently very similar to those they expect to find in all popular fiction and theatre. In *Widowers' Houses* he shows a young man suddenly discovering that the dowry of his bride-to-be is wealth which her father procured by extreme exploitation of the poor, and making the expected gesture of disdaining to accept the

[2] The full truth is more complex, as *Rhinegold* was "vaguely suggested" by an Augier play, *Mrs. Daintry* less vaguely by a "French novel"—perhaps Maupassant's *Yvette.*

money. With this act, which belongs to the world of fiction and individualism, the Shavianizing of Archer's play begins. The first inversion is that of the heroine's response. She does *not* undertake to give up all for love and marry her husband penniless. The ultimate inversion is that the young man, finding that his own unearned income is derived from the same source as his prospective father-in-law's, reverses his disdainful gesture, makes love again to the lady, and thus provides Shaw, not with the unhappy ending of the continental naturalists, but with the happy ending of ordinary English melodrama Shavianized.

After the event the innovations of *Widowers' Houses* are not amazing. Shaw himself pooh-poohs the play. In relation to the Victorian theatre, however, it was a prodigious feat; it remains the most revolutionary act in modern English drama. But, if expediency is any criterion, Shaw had brought much too much reality into the unreal theatre. The critics leapt at his throat with their characteristic mixture of outraged innocence and fiendish glee. Caught off guard, Shaw confessed to being an artist.

> You will please judge it [*Widowers' Houses*] not as a pamphlet in dialogue but as in intention a work of art as much as any comedy of Molière's is a work of art, and as pretending to be a better made play for actual use and long wear on the boards than anything that has as yet been turned out by the patent constructive machinery.

However, he quickly recovered the pretence that this play (performed exactly twice at a club theatre) would help to change England:

And I claim that its value in both respects is enhanced by the fact that it deals with a burning social question, and is deliberately intended to induce people to vote on the Progressive side at the next County Council election in London.

The campaign was continued in *Mrs. Warren's Profession* which has much the same story: a young person discovers that the wealth which has paid for her upbringing was earned by immoral means. Though Mrs. Warren's profession is not the levying of rackrent, the moral is not very different. In both plays Shaw is saying that the system, not the individual, is responsible—which to him means, not that no one is guilty, but that everyone is guilty. It is impossible for a man to escape responsibility with a disdainful gesture. Harry Trench's guilt is, if anything, greater than Sartorius's because Sartorius has at least had to face the task of getting in the rents himself. Mrs. Warren's guilt is less than that of the capitalist bully Sir George Crofts who reaps the benefits without doing the work. Mrs. Warren is the counterpart of Sartorius and she is drawn in more flattering colors. Though today one hears *Mrs. Warren's Profession* spoken of patronizingly, it is hard to see how Shaw could more boldly have affronted Victorian values. Within the scheme of bourgeois morality and bourgeois fiction a prostitute must be either strong and villainous or weak and virtuous. Shaw's procuress is neither the one nor the other. She was therefore unintelligible to Victorian readers; and I have found her unintelligible to young Americans in the nineteen-forties. If Shaw is not attacking her, they think, must he not be defending her? Or is the point not to take sides? Is to know all to forgive all? Shaw himself tried to explain when he told his public that he was attacking them, not his characters. Society was guilty. And socialism was the remedy.

This latter statement was not made in either play. Only one Shavian work of art does make it: his last novel, *The Unsocial Socialist*. Already in the first plays socialism is an unstated corollary. How is it that Shaw the celebrated socialist, Shaw the declared propagandist, does not write socialist plays, does not even write plays about strikes, revolts, workers? The fact is that while Shaw is a socialist in his treatises, and perhaps chiefly a socialist, he realizes —as we have seen—that neither socialism, nor capitalism, nor feudalism, nor any other such ism can be the basis of an art, even so social an art as comedy. Unlike the Socialist Realists of a later day Shaw refused to present the struggles of socialists and capitalists as crusades of right against wrong. The human comedy consisted too obviously of such facts as that socialists are not angels nor capitalists devils. And Shaw's interest as an artist has always been in the human situation as he found it and not simply as he desired it (except in some later sections of *Back to Methuselah* where he is at his worst as a playwright). As an observer of the human situation Shaw saw a conflict that cut across all the doctrinal divisions and that cut under them. He once tried to explain to the doctrinaire Hyndman what it was:

> You are an economic revolutionary on a medie-
> val basis of pure chivalry—Bayard educated by
> Marx. I am a moral revolutionary, interested, not

in the class war, but in the struggle between human vitality and the artificial system of morality, and distinguishing, not between capitalist and proletarian, but between moralist and natural historian.

It seems that on his conversion to socialism (1882–3) Shaw expected to be a socialist writer in the ordinary sense. He immediately wrote *The Unsocial Socialist*. In 1885 he began *Widowers' Houses*. Yet *Mrs. Warren's Profession* is the last frontal attack he made on capitalism in his plays. From then on they are primarily about the "struggle between human vitality and the artificial system of morality." Not that this subject was suddenly invented. It is implicit even in the novels and in the two plays which had as their primary intention the defense of collectivism against individualism. The energetic, sometimes daimonic women, are the first Shavian incarnation of "vitality," later known as the Life Force. It was *Cashel Byron's Profession* that provoked R. L. Stevenson's much-quoted ejaculation: "I say, Archer, my God, what women!" The heroine of *Widowers' Houses* gave as much offense as the critique of capitalism by haling her maid across the stage by the hair. *Mrs. Warren's Profession* has been criticized on the grounds that the main problem is obscured by the emergence of a strong emotional nexus that ties Vivie to her mother. The vitality that in Shaw's earlier works was more or less kept under comes bubbling here to the surface.

Two scenes in the play are first-rate. One is the scene which opens as a denunciation of Mrs. Warren by Vivie

and works round by way of a taut fighting dialogue to
Vivie's fascinated: "My dear mother: you are a wonder-
ful woman: you are stronger than all England." The other
is the final scene, no less disconcerting to Victorians, in
which the mother-daughter conflict is presented with a
poignant irony only equalled in modern drama by certain
scenes in Ibsen and Strindberg. In the earlier scene it was
Mrs. Warren who said: "If there's a thing I hate in a
woman it's want of character." And now Vivie finds herself her mother's daughter—but precisely for that reason
bound to break with her mother. "My work is not your
work and my way not your way." Whereupon the mother
turns upon Vivie with a depth of passion such as had not
been heard in British drama for two centuries. "I kept
myself lonely for you. You've no right to turn on me now
and refuse to do your duty as a daughter. . . . I was a
good mother and because I made my daughter a good
woman she turns me out as if I was a leper."

The arguments, of course, are those of the respectable
Victorian parent, a point Vivie does not miss: "If I had
been you, mother, I might have done as you did; but I
should not have lived one life and believed in another.
You are a conventional woman at heart. That is why I am
bidding you goodbye. . . ." In *Widowers' Houses* the
young man and the young woman both accept the situation and the ending is "happy." In *Mrs. Warren's Profession* it is the "unhappy" ending that Shaw travesties: the
boy does not get the girl; mother and child are parted;
yet Vivie is happy. She refuses to accept the situation—
not out of an individualistic heroine's smug disdain, not
out of socialist conviction, but out of spontaneous vital

protest, out of the feeling of having her own life to live. The events and discoveries of the play are her education, for which her career at Newnham was not even a preparation, and for the first of many times in Shavian drama the core and culmination of the play is a personal crisis, a disillusionment, almost a conversion. A soul is born.

The struggle between human vitality and artificial system which is the basis of Shavian comedy finds its chief manifestation in the struggle of the inner light of genuine conscience and healthy impulse against conventional ethics. The conventional ethics of modern life Shaw finds to be identical with those of stage melodrama.

> Nothing is more significant than the statement that "all the world's a stage." The whole world *is* ruled by theatrical illusion. Between the Caesars, the emperors, the Christian heroes, the Grand Old Men, the kings, prophets, saints, heroes, and judges, of the newspapers and popular imagination, and the actual Juliuses, Napoleons, Gordons, Gladstones, and so on, there is the same difference as between Hamlet and Sir Henry Irving. The case is not one of fanciful similitude, but of identity. The great critics are those who penetrate and understand the illusion: the great men are those who, as dramatists planning the development of nations, or as actors carrying out the drama, are behind the scenes of the world. . . .

Here we begin to see why the stage, and particularly the late-Victorian stage, was apt to Shaw's purposes. He ridiculed the unreality of Victorian melodrama by letting in a flood of "natural history." But he found that the unreality was also real: the illusions of melodrama were precisely those which men fall victim to in "real" life. Hence the inversion of melodrama—a device found in Shaw from beginning to end—was not an arbitrary trick but an integral part of an interpretation of life.

We have seen it in use in two of his earliest plays; but there the basic conflict is between collectivism and individualism; only later is the conflict between vitality and system pervasive. The pattern of a new, definitely Shavian comedy is more clearly observable in the *Three Plays for Puritans* which cap the first decade of Shaw's work in the theatre: *The Devil's Disciple, Caesar and Cleopatra,* and *Captain Brassbound's Conversion.* In each of the *Three Plays for Puritans* we see a protagonist who stands for vitality and natural history in the midst of a group who stand for system and melodrama. In each a second character—or antagonist—is educated, helped to grow up, if not actually "converted," by the protagonist. In fact this process of education is in each case the "inner" action of the play; the "outer" action consists of the noise and swagger of melodrama.

The first of the three plays—*The Devil's Disciple*—is also the crudest (though not the least popular, because the average audience enjoys in it the thing satirized—melodrama—a good deal more than the satire). Just because it is crude the play affords a clear instance of Shavian inversion. Every incident in the play—from the announcement of the legacy to the last-minute rescue at the scaffold—is a standard item of Victorian melodrama; so is every character from the dashing hero to the little orphan chee-ild Essie. When Shaw himself calls the play "threadbare melodrama" he means presumably that it is melodrama insufficiently Shavianized, insufficiently transformed into a satire upon melodrama. The dialogue of the first two acts might almost have been written by anybody—a thing one could not say of a single page of mature Shaw. The most fully Shavian passages of the play—those in which Burgoyne speaks—are inserted without the establishment of any very significant relationship between Burgoyne and the main story.

Shaw started, so he tells us, from a central situation: that of a young man's allowing himself to be led off to the gallows in someone else's place. This sacrificial act, derived perhaps from *A Tale of Two Cities*, is then interpreted unmelodramatically. Its noble motivation is removed: Dick is not giving up his life because he thinks more of the other man than of himself. More important, the *ig*noble motive is also removed. Dick is not in love with the man's wife and is not acting to impress her with his heroism. He acts out of spontaneous feeling and entirely without motive. We have noted that Shaw is sceptical about ideas because he believes in something that underlies them—feeling, vitality, conscience, natural virtue, for "it is quite useless to declare that all men are born free if you deny that they are born good." Good deeds are not performed for motives, but for their own sake. Though not all men who do only what they want to do are good men, no man who does what he does not want to do is a good man. Dick Dudgeon *wants* to sacrifice himself. His mother, whose whole life is self-sacrifice, is a

109

bad woman because she thinks that virtue lies in self-denial, in the fact that she makes herself miserable.

The play abounds in outer action of the kind Shaw is often criticized for not having: physical, violent action, event, pursuit, crisis, escape. Yet, to be sure, lovers of soap opera and westerns would want to delete a good deal of his dialogue, since it is taken up to a large extent with the inner, psychological action. Now, although Shaw takes his outer actions from here, there, and everywhere, and achieves variety by sheer acquisitiveness, his inner actions follow one from another, are, in fact, a continuous working-out of one or two problems that have worried Shaw throughout his life. The inner action of *The Devil's Disciple*, for instance, is taken over from an earlier play, *Candida*. In both plays we see an apparently idyllic Christian home broken into by an eccentric outsider. In both plays the result of the encounter is that one of the three people is utterly disillusioned (Morell, Judith), one is "educated" in the sense of being enabled to see that his true nature is not what he thought it was (Marchbanks, Anderson), and one operates as a catalyst (Candida, Dick Dudgeon), effecting change without being changed, this last character being eponymous. The duplication does not extend to psychology. In the earlier play the wife is the catalyst, in the later play the outsider. The protagonists are Candida and Dick Dudgeon, the antagonists Eugene Marchbanks and Judith, and the two parsons are, so to say, victims of the clash. There is no common moral, except that each man should act according to the law of his own nature. Judith learns that she is really a wife, and not an Isolde, Eugene learns that he can stand alone and is not a Tristan. As for the two parsons, Shaw uses both his favorite processes: one is disillusioned, the other converted.

In Captain Brassbound the two processes are for the first time successfully combined: he is both disillusioned and converted. The problem of melodrama and ethics is now examined in relation to the crucial ethical matter of punishment. The British judge Hallam and the outlaw Brassbound are alike victims of the ethics of retribution. For the judge the crude code of the jungle is disguised and sanctified by the Law, for Brassbound by the romance of revenge. Minor characters are integrated with the major ones to shed light on the central theme. The major characters indeed *are* the minor characters more closely examined and at a higher level of consciousness. Like the missionary Rankin, whose conversion of savages to Christianity is the conversion of Christianity to savagery, Hallam represents the fraud of civilization. Like the slumboy Drinkwater, whose imagination is fed by pulp fiction, Brassbound, whose imagination feeds on photographs and reports of his unhappy mother, represents the fraud of the primitive and the romantic, of the non-civilized. Unlike the other men, however, Brassbound is not irreclaimable. His soul has not yet been strangled by the "artificial system of morality." Confronted with the natural goodness of Lady Cicely, he quails. And when the foolish mask of the Avenger is torn from him he finds the secret of mastery.

The whole framework of *The Devil's Disciple* and *Captain Brassbound's Conversion* is that of Victorian melodrama. *Caesar and Cleopatra* is a less obvious case. The kind of melodrama which it parodies is today largely forgotten, though some of our historical movies and costume plays are near enough to it. Nineteenth-century playwrights from Sheridan Knowles and Bulwer-Lytton to Sardou and Tennyson had provided the stage with lavish historical dramas which imposed a solemn edifice of pageantry and poetry upon a foundation of melodrama. One should remember that the author of the *The Man of Destiny* was also the critic of Sardou's *Madame Sans-Gêne* in which a very different Napoleon appears. Reviewing the Lyceum production Shaw said that Sardou's Napoleon felt nothing, saw nothing, and did nothing "that might not as appropriately have been felt, seen, and done by his valet. . . . He is nothing but the jealous husband of a thousand fashionable dramas, talking Buonapartiana." The dictator of the Lyceum Theatre, Henry Irving, refused to do really modern drama because he was preoccupied with such plays as *Madame Sans-Gêne* and with their unwitting progenitor, Shakespeare. Shaw's history plays are part of his campaign against the twin foes of modern drama: Sardoodledom and Bardolatry.

What first struck people about the history plays was that Shaw was debunking heroes. He seemed to be a pioneer of "fictional biography" in which we are comforted with the idea that the so-called great man is an ordinary chap like ourselves. But, as usual, Shaw was not playing a simple trick of this sort. He was stating a double paradox. He *did* bring the hero off his pedestal, but only to demonstrate that the flesh-and-blood man was much more of a hero than the statue and the legend. Shaw's point is that the statuesque heroes of Sardoodledom are not great men at all. They are inflated idiots. The really great man, Shaw implies, might well have a very common-place appearance and manner because his superiority rests to a large extent on his unusual closeness to prosaic fact. Shaw's Egyptians and Austrians have all the melodramatic hero's dignity and unreality; Caesar and Napoleon defeat them precisely by being less "heroic."

Thus the Shavian history plays are inverted melodramas every bit as much as the other *Plays for Puritans*. *Caesar and Cleopatra* is a melodrama in which the supposed prime agent of melodramatic incident—the hero—refuses to perform either of the two types of melodramatic action: he refuses to avenge himself and he refuses to make love. The play is a neat five-act structure in which Caesar is the Shavian protagonist, Cleopatra the Shavian antagonist. Caesar is the teacher, Cleopatra the pupil. So far there is nothing to surprise the reader of *Candida, The Devil's Disciple*, and *Captain Brassbound's Conversion*. But although Cleopatra, like Marchbanks, Anderson, and Brassbound, grows up as much as she is capable of doing—she begins as a mere child and under Caesar's influence becomes a woman—her capacities are limited. She is of a lower nature, and her growth, to use the metaphor of the play itself, is from a kitten to a cat. The proficiency she develops is precisely in the areas which Caesar keeps out of: revenge and erotic passion.

Shaw himself has eloquently explained that the *Three Plays* are *for Puritans* because the moral criteria are anti-melodramatic and therefore anti-erotic. (Is it not an essential doctrine of melodrama that love is omnipotent and omniscient?) Yet the critics are wrong in imagining that Shaw shies off from the erotic theme; William Archer was nearer the mark in accusing Shaw of being obsessed with sex. In each of the three plays—as in *Candida*—there is an approach to a stock kind of "love interest." Lady Cicely almost falls for Brassbound; Judith does fall for Dick Dudgeon; and a liaison between Caesar and Cleopatra is rumored in Alexandria. In all three plays, however, Eros is thwarted. Lady Cicely is saved by a bell; Judith's passion is unrequited and she gets over it; Cleopatra realizes that Caesar is above love. Nevertheless this last is the only play in which the consummation of romantic love is suggested. Mark Antony, who never sets foot on the stage, hovers on the edges of the play; the future spells the assassination of Caesar and the romance of Antony.

When he leaves Rufio in command and Cleopatra queen in Egypt, Caesar knows that there is nothing left but for himself to be killed and for the cycle of murder and revenge to be resumed:

> To the end of history murder shall breed murder,
> always in the name of right and honor and peace,
> until the gods are tired of blood and create a race
> that can understand.

This realization is the climax of the inner action of the play. In the earlier scenes we have learnt to know Caesar as the alienated hero—part brute, part woman, part god. We have seen him as the leader who makes decisions on grounds of pure expediency. In his indifference to the burning of the library we see the indifference of the history-maker to the historian, of the doer to the sayer—another aspect of "puritanism." The first three Acts consist of three incidents which progressively reveal Caesar and educate Cleopatra. In the last two Acts Cleopatra is grown up, and the conflict between protagonist and antagonist blazes forth. Cleopatra has the people's favorite killed because he is plotting against her. She plausibly claims that he was Caesar's enemy too:

> If one man in Alexandria can be found to say that I did wrong, I swear to have myself crucified on the door of the palace by my own slaves.

To which Caesar replies:

> If one man in all the world can be found, now or forever, to *know* that you did wrong, that man will have either to conquer the world as I have or be crucified by it.

Against the world-view of melodrama only two kinds of men can stand out, the man who is too strong to be attacked and the man who is too humble to mind, the conqueror and the saint, Caesar and Christ. The character of Caesar, conqueror and commissar, is the largest thing attempted in Shavian drama up to this point. It was followed by what is virtually a fourth Play for Puritans— *Man and Superman*—in which the antitype of the man of action is not the erotic woman but the man of ideas. But here we move out of Shaw's dramatic nonage.

3

Reviewing Shaw's first decade in the theatre, one can see that, taking up the materials of the theatre as he found them, and enriching them with thoughts and attitudes he had learnt from life and literature, Shaw

115

created a new type of comedy. Compare any of his plays with the kind of play he is parodying or otherwise modifying and his own contribution to the drama will be evident. Were we to have entered a theatre in 1900 the things that would have struck us in a Shaw play, assuming that we were sympathetic enough to notice them, would have been—in order of their saliency—the endlessly witty and eloquent talk, the wideness of reference in the dialogue, the incredible liveliness of the characters, the swift tempo, the sudden and unexpected reverses (especially anticlimaxes), in a phrase, the unusual energy coupled with the unusual intellect. And the gist of the early reviews is that, though it wasn't drama, it was something as serious as it was entertaining, as brilliant as it was funny. The more intelligent reviewers began by gravely observing that it wasn't drama and ended by saying precisely the opposite. Shaw is not a dramatist, says one, but a preacher and satirist—"incidentally, no doubt, he often gives us very good drama indeed." "The chief characteristics of Mr. Bernard Shaw's plays," says another, "are not precisely dramatic," yet he goes on to say of the new drama, "the special mode of its manifestation does belong to the stage." "As a conscientious critic," says a third, "I have pointed out that Mr. Shaw's abundance of ideas spoils his plays. I may add as a man," he somewhat disarmingly goes on, "that to me it is their great attraction."

It all boils down to the fact that Shaw's plays were good in an unfamiliar way. What was new about them? Though this question has been partly answered already it may be of interest to recall Shaw's own answer. He located the newness of Ibsen (and for "Ibsen," throughout *The Quin-*

116

tessence of Ibsenism, we should read "Shaw") in two things: his naturalism and his use of discussion. The naturalism is arrived at primarily by the replacement of romance and melodrama by "natural history." This entails a vast extension of subject matter. Invariably naturalism has meant an extension of subject matter, so to say, downwards—towards the inclusion of low life and animal passions. Shaw made this extension in his Unpleasant Plays. A more characteristically Shavian extension of subject matter was the extension *upwards* in the Pleasant Plays and the *Three Plays for Puritans,* an extension towards the inclusion of the higher passions—the passion for beauty, for goodness, for control. Sardoodledom had removed from the theatre most of the serious interests of civilized men. Nobody did more than Shaw to bring them all back. And nobody brought them back more entertainingly.

As for the use of discussion, Shaw observes that the conventional nineteenth-century play consisted of an exposition, a complication, and a denouement, but that Ibsen, in *A Doll's House,* replaced the denouement by a discussion, and thus made the essential technical innovation in modern drama. Luckily Shaw goes on to qualify this over-simplification with the observation that the new element of discussion may sometimes be found at the beginning (one thinks of *The Apple Cart*) or in the middle (one thinks of *Man and Superman*) or it may interpenetrate the whole action—one thinks of a dozen Shaw plays. As so often, Shaw's critical comment is too simple to cover his practice. A Shavian play is not to be equated with a non-Shavian play plus discussion. The truth is far more complicated. Shaw is perfectly capable of writing a *drama* which is as personal and emotional as one of Ibsen's. He has also written much disquisitory dialogue. Personal plays—such as *Candida*—and discussion plays—such as *Getting Married*—are, in fact, the twin poles of Shavian drama. Without denying the existence of either, one should see that the bulk of Shaw's plays are on middle ground between the poles.

Another distinction is called for. There are broadly two different kinds of discussion in Shavian drama. The one has become a byword because, until Shaw proved the contrary, everyone denied that it could be dramatic. I refer to the discussion of problems for their inherent interest. "Don Juan in Hell," "The Doctrine of the Brothers Barnabas," *In Good King Charles's Golden Days* are instances. In these nothing is more important than the discussion itself. The other type of discussion is more usual on the stage—discussion as an emanation of conflict between persons. Shaw is expert at writing verbal duels in which the acerbity and the interest derive not from the questions discussed but from situation and character. The discussions in *Major Barbara* and *John Bull's Other Island* are of this type. Of course our two types are again twin poles, and most of Shavian dialogue is between the extremes. It is therefore not enough to say, on the one hand, that Shaw makes the ideas themselves dramatic, for this implies that he eschews drama of character and situation. It is not enough to say, on the other hand, that Shaw after all wrote *Candida*, for this implies that Shaw is at his best only when he is closest to conventional patterns, only when the discussions never venture far from the human crisis that is being enacted. One must take particular cases to see how Shaw is drawn now to one magnetic pole, now to another, and how at his best he feels and expresses tension from the pull of both. To analyse particular plays will also afford an opportunity of illustrating other points that so far have remained mere generalizations.

Pygmalion is a characteristic instance of a personal play. And it is characteristic that many people think of it as very disquisitory. At least it at first seems to conform to Shaw's formula: exposition, complication, discussion. But let us take a closer look.

Pygmalion is the story, in five Acts, of Henry Higgins' attempt to make a duchess out of a flower girl. Act I is really a sort of prologue in which the two main characters encounter each other. The action proper starts in Act II when Higgins decides to make the experiment. In Act III the experiment reaches its first stage when Eliza appears in upper-class company behaving like an imperfectly functioning mechanical doll. Readers of Bergson will understand why this scene gets more laughs than all the others put together, so that to the groundlings the rest of the play seems a prolonged anti-climax. Has not Shaw blundered? What ought to be the climax seems to have been left out: it is between Acts III and IV that Eliza is finally passed off as a duchess at an ambassador's party. Would not Sarcey have called this the *scène à faire?* When the curtain goes up on Act IV all is over; Eliza has triumphed. Higgins is satisfied, bored, and wondering what to do next. The comedy is over. But there are two more acts!

"The play is now virtually over but the characters will

119

discuss it at length for two Acts more." Such is the curtain line of Act I in a later Shaw play. It is one of those Shavian jokes which appear to be against Shaw but are really against the vulgar opinion of Shaw. The two Acts that follow (in *Too True To Be Good*) are *not* a discussion of what happens in Act I. Nor are the last two acts of *Pygmalion* as purely disquisitory as they at first seem.

Certainly, the big event occurs between the Acts, and the last two Acts *are* a "discussion" of the consequences. But the discussion is of the second of the types defined above: it is not so much that the consequences are discussed as that the consequences are worked out and determined by a conflict that is expressed in verbal swordplay. There is no pretence of objectivity. Each character speaks for himself, and speaks, not as a contributor to a debate, but as one whose life is at stake. Eliza is talking to free herself. Higgins is talking to keep his domination over her. The conclusion of conversations of this kind is not the statement of a principle (as in Plato's symposia or even Shaw's *Getting Married*) but the making of a decision. Ibsen's Nora slams the door, his Ellida decides to stay at home. What happens to Eliza? What *can* happen, now that the flower girl is a duchess, the statue a flesh-and-blood Galatea?

In the original romance, so lyrically revived by Shaw's friend William Morris, Pygmalion marries Galatea. Might not something of the kind be possible for Shaw, since Pygmalion is a life-giver, a symbol of vitality, since in Eliza the crime of poverty has been overcome, the sin of ignorance cancelled? Or might not Higgins and Eliza be the "artist man" and "mother woman" discussed in *Man and Superman?* They might—if Shaw actually went to work so allegorically, so abstractly, so idealistically. Actually *Pygmalion: a Romance* stands related to Romance precisely as *The Devil's Disciple* stands to Melodrama or *Candida* to Domestic Drama. It is a serious parody, a translation into the language of "natural history." The primary inversion is that of Pygmalion's character. The Pygmalion of Romance turns a statue into a human being. The Pygmalion of "natural history" tries to turn a human being into a statue, tries to make of Eliza Doolittle a mechanical doll in the role of a duchess. Or rather he tries to make from one kind of doll—a flower girl who cannot afford the luxury of being human—another kind of doll—a duchess to whom manners are an adequate substitute for morals.

There is a character named Pygmalion in *Back to Methuselah.* He is a sort of Frankenstein or Pavlov. He thinks that you can put together a man by assembling mechanical parts. Henry Higgins also thinks he has made a person—or at least an amenable slave—when he has "assembled" a duchess. But the monster turns against Frankenstein. Forces have been brought into play of which the man-maker knows nothing. And Shaw's Pygmalion has helped into being a creature even more mysterious than a monster: a human being.

If the first stage of Higgins' experiment was reached when Eliza made her *faux pas* before Mrs. Higgins' friends, and the second when she appeared in triumph at the ball, Shaw, who does not believe in endings, sees her through two more stages in the final acts of his play, leaving her still very much in flux at the end. The third

121

stage is rebellion. Eliza's feelings are wounded because, after the reception, Higgins does not treat her kindly, but talks of her as a guinea pig. Eliza has acquired finer feelings.

> While some have felt that the play should end with the reception, others have felt that it could end with the suggestion that Eliza has begun to rebel. It seems, indeed, that the creator of the role of Eliza thought this. In her memoirs Mrs. Patrick Campbell wrote:

> The last act of the play did not travel across the footlights with as clear dramatic sequence as the preceding acts—owing entirely to the fault of the author.

The sympathetic analyst of the play will more probably agree with Shaw himself who, Mrs. Campbell says, "declared I might be able to play a tune with one finger, but a full orchestral score was Greek to me." The fifth act of *Pygmalion* is far from superfluous. It is the climax. The arousing of Eliza's resentment in the fourth Act was the birth of a soul. But to be born is not enough. One must also grow up. Growing up is the fourth and last stage of Eliza's evolution. This consummation is reached in the final "discussion" with Higgins—a piece of dialogue that is superb comedy not only because of its wit and content but also because it proceeds from a dramatic situation, perhaps the most dramatic of all dramatic situations: two completely articulate characters engaged in a battle of words on which both their fates depend. It is a Strindbergian battle of wills. But not of sex. Higgins will never marry. He wants to remain in the relation of God the

122

Creator as far as Eliza is concerned. For her part Eliza will marry. But she won't marry Higgins.

The play ends with Higgins' knowingly declaring that Eliza is about to do his shopping for him despite her protestations to the contrary: a statement which actors and critics often take to mean that the pair are a Benedick and Beatrice who will marry in the end. One need not quote Shaw's own sequel to prove the contrary. The whole point of the great culminating scene is that Eliza has now become not only a person but an independent person. The climax is sharp:

LIZA: If I can't have kindness, I'll have independence.

HIGGINS: Independence? That's middle class blasphemy. We are all dependent on one another, every soul of us on earth.

LIZA: (*rising determinedly*) I'll let you see whether I'm dependent on you. If you can preach, I can teach. I'll go and be a teacher.

HIGGINS: What'll you teach, in heaven's name?

LIZA: What you taught me. I'll teach phonetics.

HIGGINS: Ha! ha! ha!

LIZA: I'll offer myself as an assistant to Professor Nepean.

HIGGINS: (*rising in a fury*) What! That impostor! That humbug! That toadying ignoramus! Teach him *my* methods! *my* discoveries! You take one step in

123

> his direction and I'll wring your neck.
> (*He lays hands on her.*) Do you hear?
>
> LIZA: (*defiantly non-resistant*) Wring away.
> What do I care? I knew you'd strike
> me some day. (*He lets her go, stamp-
> ing with rage. . . .*)

With this cry of victory (it rings in my ears in the intona-
tion of Miss Gertrude Lawrence who succeeded where
Mrs. Patrick Campbell seems to have failed) Eliza wins
her freedom. Higgins had said: "I can do without anybody. I have my own soul." And now Eliza can say:
"Now . . . I'm not afraid of you and can do without
you." After this it does not matter whether Eliza does
the shopping or not. The situation is clear. Eliza's fate is
settled as far as Higgins is concerned. The story of the
experiment is over. Otherwise her fate is as unsettled as
yours or mine. This is a true naturalistic ending—not an
arbitrary break, but a conclusion which is also a beginning.

Pygmalion is a singularly elegant structure. If again we
call Act I the prologue, the play falls into two parts of
two Acts apiece. Both parts are Pygmalion myths. In the
first a duchess is made out of a flower girl. In the second
a woman is made out of a duchess. Since these two parts
are the main, inner action the omission of the climax of
the outer action—the ambassador's reception—will seem
particularly discreet, economical, and dramatic. The
movie version of *Pygmalion* was not the richer for its inclusion. To include a climax that is no climax only blurs

124

the outline of the play. *Pygmalion* is essentially theatrical in construction. It is built in chunks, two by two. The fluidity of the screen is quite inappropriate to it. On the screen, as in the novel, a development of character naturally occurs gradually and smoothly. Natasha in *War and Peace* passes imperceptibly from girlhood to womanhood; Eliza in *Pygmalion* proceeds in dramatically marked stages—one, two, three, four, Act by Act. Perhaps we never realized before the Shaw movies how utterly "of the theatre" the Shaw plays are.

As we might have learned to expect, *Pygmalion* follows the pattern of earlier Shavian works, not duplicating them but following up another aspect of a similar problem. We have seen how the eponymous character is often the representative of vitality and that he remains constant like a catalyst while producing change in others, especially in the antagonist whom he is educating, disillusioning, or converting. *Pygmalion* diverges from the type in that the life-giver, for all his credentials, and his title of Pygmalion, is suspect. He is not really a life-giver at all. To be sure, Eliza is even more palpably his pupil than Judith was Dick's or Brassbound Lady Cicely's. But the "education of Eliza" in Acts I to III is a caricature of the true process. In the end Eliza turns the tables on Higgins, for she, finally, is the vital one, and he is the prisoner of "system," particularly of his profession.

Ironically parallel with the story of Eliza is the story of her father. Alfred Doolittle is also suddenly lifted out of slumdom by the caprice of Pygmalion-Higgins. He too has to break bread with dukes and duchesses. Unlike his daughter, however, he is not reborn. He is too far gone for that. He is the same rich as he was poor, the same or worse; for riches carry awful responsibilities, and Doolittle commits the cardinal sin on the Shavian scale—he is irresponsible. In the career of the undeserving poor suddenly become undeserving rich Shaw writes his *social* comedy, his Unpleasant Play, while in the career of his deserving daughter he writes his *human* comedy, his Pleasant Play. Those who think that *Pygmalion* is about class society are thinking of Doolittle's comedy rather than Eliza's. The two are carefully related by parallelism and contrast. One might work out an interpretation of the play by comparing their relation to the chief "artificial system" depicted in it—middle-class morality.

In short, the merit of *Pygmalion* cannot be explained by Shaw's own account of the nature of modern drama, much less by popular or academic opinion concerning Problem Plays, Discussion Drama, Drama of Ideas, and the like. It is a good play by perfectly orthodox standards and needs no theory to defend it. It is Shavian, not in being made up of political or philosophic discussions, but in being based on the standard conflict of vitality and system, in working out this conflict through an inversion of romance, in bringing matters to a head in a battle of wills and words, in having an inner psychological action in counterpoint to the outer romantic action, in existing on two contrasted levels of mentality, both of which are related to the main theme, in delighting and surprising us with a constant flow of verbal music and more than verbal wit.

126

4

If *Pygmalion* is a fair example of a personal play, which plays of Shaw are best called disquisitory? Shaw himself first applied the term to *Getting Married* which, with *Misalliance*, remains the most celebrated and straightforward example of the genre, though the method is found earlier in "Don Juan in Hell" and later in a series of plays ending, for the present, with *In Good King Charles's Golden Days*.

Although many people think of all Shaw's plays as discussion plays, Shaw was already a veteran playwright when he first wrote a full-length play consisting of a series of conversations unbroken by act or scene divisions. *Getting Married* is not a variant of farce, melodrama, or any other established kind of dramatic structure. It is something new—a new dramaturgy and not, as its critics thought, a mere pamphlet in dialogue form. It is closer even to orthodox dramaturgy than to pamphleteering.

Though the mode of presentation is endless talk, the plot-pattern is orthodox if unobtrusive. The whole discussion is built around a situation; and in the course of the play the outcome is decided. A young couple is about to be married. A last-minute obstacle arises, as on the stage such obstacles often do. All that is unusual is the nature of the obstacle: a pamphlet on marriage by Belfort Bax. The difficulties accumulate, but suddenly there occurs a pleasant reversal: the couple have slipped out and been married in spite of all. There are also sub-plots. A divorced couple are re-united. The man who was to have been the second husband of the divorcée goes off to form a Platonic-Shavian *ménage à trois* with a happily married couple.

The conversational mode should not blind us to the fact that there is plot enough here for any comedy. What distinguishes Shaw's play is, first, the mode itself which tends to hide the plot and, second, the oblique relation of plot to theme. A plot may be used straightforwardly as in ordinary story-telling and play-writing. It may be used ironically as in Shavian inversions of melodrama. But if Shaw's melodramas may be said to turn the plot upside down, his disquisitory plays, so to say, leave it alone, isolate it, treat it with contumely. Given the plot of *The Devil's Disciple* you might guess what would happen to it in Shaw's hands. Given the plot of *Getting Married* you would remain completely in the dark. For if in the personal plays the dialogue is tied to the main situations and events, in the disquisitory plays the dialogue gets the upper hand. Yet the plot is not reduced to complete impotence. There is still interaction between theme and plot, between the ideas and their narrative vehicle. The new factor is that the ideas are now becoming more dramatic than the events. In *The Devil's Disciple* we have a violent plot with the more silent and interesting inner action in the background. In *Getting Married* the plot is in the background, for the inner action has become more adequately vocal. The point has been reached at which Shaw can bring it into the foreground.

The basic situation, the inner and outer action are not the only genuinely dramatic ingredients of *Getting Married*. The characters also are very theatrical. Like so many

of Shaw's creations, they are close relatives of the manni-
kins of popular Victorian theatre. Consider for a moment
the rather colorless juvenile leads, the comic greengrocer,
the funny army officer, the benign bishop, the old maid,
the solid matron, the religious fanatic. These people hail,
not from the stratosphere of abstract thought, but from
the boards. It is a characteristic of all the disquisitory
plays that the characters are more than usually stagey, if
not farcical, as if Shaw, far from trying to academicize
the drama, were afraid of his own didacticism, and were
determined to spice it with every trick of the trade. In this
respect Shaw is a less intellectual and more conventional
dramatist than Molière, as James Bridie once showed
by parallel passages from *The Doctor's Dilemma* and
L'Amour Médecin.

Discussion of social problems on the one hand, brilliant acting and abundant comic business on the other—
this, however, is not the complete Shavian recipe. The
real art of the disquisitory plays lies in the unique solution found there to the problem of the Problem Play. The
solution lies in Shaw's handling of the ideas which, as I
have said, are now in the foreground. Shaw's handling
of ideas is "of the theatre" most obviously because he so
well knows how to confront spokesmen of different outlooks. To this task Shaw brings his unequalled gift of
sympathizing with both sides. He once said that he has
no soul because, Proteus-like, he can see the world only
through the creatures he creates, each of whom differs
from the other. This is not a matter of fairmindedness
merely. It is a matter of a particular mentality, a particular way of observing life. Shaw's way is the dramatist's

129

way. For him ideas perform like characters. In aid of this special gift he re-introduces the pre-naturalistic convention that stage characters may be endowed with an artificial amount of self-consciousness. And the device is of use not only technically in permitting greater explicitness but also dramatically in permitting greater eloquence, in producing that feeling that we are getting somewhere which is of the essence of Shavian dialogue. Listen to Hotchkiss in *Getting Married*:

> I am a snob. Why not? The whole strength of England lies in the fact that the enormous majority of the English people are snobs. They insult poverty. They despise vulgarity. They love nobility. They admire exclusiveness. They will not obey a man risen from the ranks. They never trust one of their own class. I agree with them. I share their instincts. In my undergraduate days I was a Republican—a Socialist. I tried hard to feel towards a common man as I do towards a duke. I couldn't. Neither can you. Well, why should we be ashamed of this aspiration towards what is above us? Why don't I say that an honest man's the noblest work of God? Because I don't think so. If he's not a gentleman, I don't care whether he's honest or not: I shouldn't let his son marry my daughter. . . .

This is very simple prose. At least it *sounds* very simple, which is the important thing in the theatre. Yet its athleticism and vitality are of a quality unique in literature. Splendid in itself, this mode of utterance is especially splendid for comedy. One recognizes its purity and its nobility if one walks from the matinee of a slick Broadway play to an evening performance of Shaw or if one sees a Shaw movie immediately after an average Hollywood product. There are very few dramatic poets whose voice alone carries more authority.

Shaw raised his drama above the level of other men's Problem Plays not only by understanding the problems better, not only by knowing the technique of drama better and arranging more skilfully his contrasts and confrontations, his polemics and conflicts, not only, even, by being able to give such a prodigious stage vitality to difficult questions in philosophy and life, but above all by being able to provide an artistic mould for all those things, a mould which we might call—music. W. H. Auden says:

> All his life Shaw has been devoted to music (he was probably the best music critic who ever lived) and, as he tells us, it was from Mozart's *Don Giovanni* that he learned "how to write seriously without being dull"; and this devotion is, perhaps, the clue to his work. For all his theatre about propaganda, his writing has an effect nearer to that of music than the work of any of the so-called pure writers.

One need not follow Mr. Auden in using this argument as an excuse for not taking Shaw's "propaganda" seriously. The melody and rhythm of Shaw's dialogue reinforce rather than cancel its meaning. But Mr. Auden's words do help us to realize how, in being more of a "musician" than the poetic dramatists themselves, Shaw

131

is at the opposite pole of art from the problem playwrights who were his colleagues, friends, and disciples.

In mature Shavian drama the music is ubiquitous. Its special importance in the disquisitory plays lies in the fact that there it is not only pervasive but paramount. The disquisitory plays are Shavian sonatas. The most successful of them is *Heartbreak House;* and, the Shavian music being what it is, this play is also the most chock-full of Shavian ideas. (After this play the "drama of ideas" can never be regarded as the antithesis of poetic drama.) It is subtitled "a fantasia in the Russian manner on English themes," which means that Shaw had been reading Tolstoy, seeing some Chekhov plays, and had been given a germinal idea for a play particularly by *The Light Shines in Darkness* and *The Cherry Orchard.* One must issue a warning, though, to our lynx-eyed students of literary sources. Shaw's citing of precedents is often whimsical, not to say extravagant. He justifies his dramatic prefaces by the precedent of Dryden whose prefaces were actually of a quite different sort. He asks us to believe that *The Millionairess* is Jonsonian. As to sources proper, Shaw often gets an idea from an earlier work which has no necessary relation to it. He sees a performance of *Everyman* and thinks: why not Everywoman? The result is the character of Ann Whitefield in *Man and Superman!* And he tries to put us at ease with *Getting Married* and *Misalliance* by invoking the classical unities!

How far from these jokes and whimsies is the Chekhovism of *Heartbreak House?* The play is genuinely Chekhovian in that its people are cultured talkers, members of a decadent rich class, who never do anything; the scene is a country house; the method consists of stringing together rather weary conversations in a musical, nonlogical manner. One might list half a dozen more Chekhovisms, but the conclusion must be that these are only the externals of Chekhov's art and thought and that if Shaw had made a play out of these elements alone it would not be a very good play.

The Chekhovism is superficial. The play is deeply Shavian. Just as in writing *The Shewing-Up of Blanco Posnet* Shaw may have thought he was inspired by Tolstoy's *Power of Darkness*, whereas he really was rewriting his own *Devil's Disciple,* so in *Heartbreak House* he may have believed himself an English Chekhov (or he may have been teasing us), whereas he is really following up his own *Getting Married* and *Misalliance.* The three plays form a trilogy of which the latest is the crown and culmination.

The links between the three are both of form and content. All three plays are about the cultured classes. All three are full of erotic adventures of a similar type. All three are in the form of strings of conversations in drawing rooms. All three embody Shaw's unchanging attitude to upper-class life. More interesting than the mere duplications (which are numerous) are the steadily growing intensity of mood and the steadily broadening range of theme.

Getting Married is bright and brittle: it is full of the kind of near-brashness that alienates many from Shaw. The moral of the play is that marriage is an insoluble problem, its insolubility consisting in the fact that while marriage is a single institution, the natural relations between the sexes are of many different patterns. What makes Shaw's comedy comic, quizzical, and wise is that it admits that there is no alternative to marriage. It is bad; but to reject it is worse. It is a procrustean bed; but the alternative is no bed at all. The second irony (and by now we are used to double ironies) is that problems of marriage and sex cannot be solved by any consideration of marriage and sex but only by much wider considerations. Deeper than the need for a bedfellow is the need for "Christian fellowship." The climax of the play, which characteristically is a musical climax and not a climax in the plot, is the Mayoress's speech, spoken in a trance, of which the theme is that love is one thing and the demands of erotic convention are another:

> When you loved me I gave you the whole sun and stars to play with. I gave you eternity in a single moment, strength of the mountains in one clasp of your arms, and the volume of all the seas in one impulse of your souls. A moment only; but was it not enough? Were you not paid then for all the rest of your struggle on earth? Must I mend your clothes and sweep your floors as well? Was it not enough? I paid the price without bargaining: I bore the children without flinching: was that a reason for heaping fresh burdens on me? I carried the child in my arms: must I carry the father too? . . . We spent eternity together; and you ask me for a little lifetime more. We possessed all the universe together; and you ask me to give you my scanty wages as well. . . .

> I gave you your own soul: you ask me for my
> body as a plaything. Was it not enough?

The setting of *Misalliance* is even more obviously a
Heartbreak House:

> HYPATIA: It never stops: talk, talk, talk, talk.
> That's my life. All the day I listen to
> papa talking; at dinner I listen to
> papa talking. . . .
>
> LORD SUMMERHAYS: Were we very dull?
>
> HYPATIA: Not at all: you were very clever.
> That's what's so hard to bear, because
> it makes it so difficult to avoid listen-
> ing. You see, I'm young: and I do so
> want something to happen. My
> mother tells me that when I'm her
> age, I shall be only too glad that noth-
> ing's happened; but I'm not her age;
> so what good is that to me? There's
> my father in the garden, meditating
> on his destiny. All very well for him;
> he's had a destiny to meditate on; but
> I haven't had any destiny yet. . . .

The atmosphere of *Misalliance* is more intense than that
of *Getting Married*. The accusing finger is pointed at all
three classes of the community (Matthew Arnold's bar-
barians, philistines, and populace) by Lina Szczepa-
nowska, the goddess from the twentieth-century machine:
she crashes into the garden of this Heartbreak House in
her airplane. If *Getting Married* demonstrates the diver-

sity and mysteriousness of sexual relationships, *Misalliance* demonstrates the diversity and mysteriousness of family relationships.

Neither play is entirely unrelated in its structure to the personal plays. Both, for instance, end with the union of a vital character, a descendant of the Shavian protagonist of the *Plays for Puritans,* and an intellectual but wrongheaded character, a descendant of the Shavian antagonist who needs to be "educated." The difference between the disquisitory and personal plays in this respect is that in the former the protagonist and antagonist have dwindled. They are only members of a group. For this too is one of the main characteristics of the disquisitory plays: they have no protagonist. Even if the plot centers on two or three characters, the play as a whole does not. The personal plays tend often to be concertos for two soloists and orchestra; the disquisitory plays are symphonies.

Heartbreak House is the finest example of the genre. In its plot the protagonist and antagonist survive. Just as Mrs. George undertakes the "education" of Hotchkiss at the end of *Getting Married,* and Lina that of Bentley Summerhays at the end of *Misalliance,* so at the end of *Heartbreak House* a male embodiment of the Life Force —Captain Shotover—is "educating" the young and disillusioned Ellie Dunn. In fact this personal drama is embedded in the disquisitory play. And Ellie's education is pushed further than that of Shaw's earlier antagonists. By the middle of Act I she has been disillusioned about romantic love, like Judith Anderson. Unlike Judith, and more like Major Barbara, she passes from romance to pay her respects to money. "Turning your back on Undershaft and Bodger," Barbara said, "is turning your back on life." But "life" thus understood also collapses beneath Ellie Dunn's feet. Under her tutor, old Captain Shotover, she thinks at first that she has reached a kind of peace on the other side of despair, that she is now "one of those who are so sufficient to themselves that they are only happy when they are stripped of everything, even of hope."

We never learn what happens to the disillusioned antagonists of such plays as *Candida* in which Morell is at the end crushed and speechless. In *Heartbreak House*, however, we are not allowed to remain in doubt. Ellie's peace of mind is not lasting, for she finds that

> there seems to be nothing real in the world except my father and Shakespeare. Marcus's tigers are false; Mr. Mangan's millions are false; there is nothing really strong and true about Hesione but her beautiful black hair; and Lady Utterword's is too pretty to be real. The one thing that was left to me was the Captain's seventh degree of concentration; and that turns out to be—

"Rum," says the Captain, while Hesione confesses that her hair is dyed. The play ends with an air raid that is fatal to two members of the group. Hesione expresses the wish that the bombers will come again and Ellie, "radiant at the prospect," cries "Oh, I hope so!" She has been thrice disillusioned—once in each Act, by Hector, by Mangan, by Shotover—and is, in a sense, back at the beginning again, in love with romance. Only the romance which *now* brings color into her life is that of a kind of warfare that threatens civilization.

137

The story of Ellie Dunn, neatly arranged in three Acts, could easily have made a personal play. But if in *Heartbreak House* her story is the center of the action it is a center not very much more important than anything on the periphery. In the *theme* of the play it is the group that matters. In the *form* of the play it is the group that is presented in an endless shifting of the camera (so to speak) from one couple or trio to another. Although the method is Chekhovian, Shaw's characters are not. Chekhov's people are felt, so to say, from the inside; they are creatures of feeling, never very far from the pathetic. Shaw's are closer to traditional puppets of comedy. They are more crudely representative of classes of men, more deliberately allegorical, than Chekhov's. Later, in *The Simpleton of the Unexpected Isles,* Shaw would frankly state that four of his people simply represent Love, Pride, Heroism, and Empire. And it has been pointed out that the Shotover daughters and their men represent the same four forces: Hesione is Love, Ariadne is Empire, Randall Utterword is Pride, and Hector is Heroism. One might add that all the other characters "stand for things"— Mangan for business and realism, Shotover for aged intellect—and that, in general, one of Shaw's worst tendencies is to create characters who have no function except to illustrate a point. The burglar episode, for instance, makes a point that is repeated in Shaw's great pamphlet *Imprisonment.*

Luckily for *Heartbreak House,* this reductive account of the people does not do them justice. The things his characters stand for, the points they illustrate, are only a part of their being. Beyond this they have a double vitality: they have the life of the great comedic types, that special theatrical life which, "artificial" though it is, all too few stage people have had since the rise of naturalism; and, second, they have a yet subtler form of life, a form which only first-rate playwrights have been able to create, a life which consists in an illusion, an aura, a flavor of lifelikeness. When a character has this sort of life you feel that his existence stretches back beyond what is visible and audible on the stage, that his reality, as you apprehend it from your seat in the stalls, is more than merely theatrical.

In most of his early plays Shaw had given the sense of this second kind of life chiefly by letting a strong aroma of actuality mingle with the musty smell of the theatre. His Dick Dudgeons and Caesars and Lady Cicelies were whiffs of actuality. Now although the sense of the real is induced in *Heartbreak House* partly by the same method, a more extraordinary means is also employed, extraordinary, that is, for Shaw (though not for Chekhov whom he has his eye on): a haunting, haunted atmosphere. In speaking to his biographer about the genesis of his plays, Shaw said that *Heartbreak House* "began with an atmosphere." It seems to have been written by pure inspiration with a minimum of conscious planning. Not that this, as some have assumed, makes the play unique among Shaw's works. All along Shaw has belonged to the school of inspired writers from whom works of art erupt rather than to the school of conscious makers. All along he has been able to create an atmosphere in the theatre. Even the special atmosphere of *Heartbreak House* was not created *ad hoc*. There is a trace of it already in *Getting*

139

Married: Mrs. George's trance might almost be regarded as a try-out for the later play. In *Misalliance* the clash between Lina and the inmates of this other Heartbreak House generates the same kind of electricity as the later play is charged with. It is only in the latter, however, that the darkness, the mystery, and the poignancy are pervasive, so that the title has to shift from the suggestion of a problem play—*Getting Married, Misalliance*—to the suggestion of a state of society and a state of mind.

Heartbreak House might be called The Nightmare of a Fabian. All Shaw's themes are in it. You might learn from it his teachings on love, religion, education, politics. But you are unlikely to do so, not only because the treatment is so brief and allusive but because the play is not an argument in their favor. It is a demonstration that they are all being disregarded or defeated. It is a picture of failure. The world belongs to the Mangans, the Utterwords, and the Hushabyes. In the world where these men wield the power stands the lonely figure of old Captain Shotover, the man of mind. What he is seeking is what Shaw has always been seeking, like Plato before him: a way of uniting wisdom and power. The Fabians had tried by "permeation" to make the men of power wise. But the men of power preferred a world war to the world's wisdom. Shotover has given them up as hopeless. He is trying to attain power *by means of* mind. When he attains the "seventh degree of concentration" he will be able to explode dynamite by mere thinking. "A mind ray that will explode the ammunition in the belt of my adversary before he can point his gun at me" will implement thought with power. Shaw is borrowing the "Vril" of Bulwer-

Lytton. But unlike the scientific romancers he does not have his "hero" *find* the ray he seeks. Shaw has seldom used his drama of ideas for the depicting of easy ideal solutions for hard real problems. In *Heartbreak House* the protagonist and antagonist have shrunk to "a crazy old sea captain and a young singer who adores him." There is aspiration in the play. Ellie wants "life with a blessing"—Shaw's primary ideal in capsule form. And just as Mrs. George could say "I've been myself" and Lina: "I am unbought," so Shotover can say "I had my life": he tells Ellie:

> I was ten times happier on the bridge in the ty-
> phoon, or frozen into Arctic ice for months in
> darkness, than you or they have ever been. You
> are looking for a rich husband. At your age I
> looked for hardship, danger, horror, and death,
> that I might feel the life in me more intensely.

Nevertheless, the captain is now old and crazy. The aspirations of men are being crushed by the great twin-sources of power (and ironically enough they are the twin-sources of comedy): love and money. For "the knowledge that these people are there to render all our aspirations barren prevents us having the aspirations." The first Act ends with a request for "deeper darkness," the last with the threat that if we do not learn navigation the ship will founder. It is the threat of the atom bomb.

The end of *Heartbreak House* is the beginning of the later Shavian drama. In a sense all the plays after this are disquisitory plays (except *Saint Joan*, and even *Saint Joan*

141

has a large disquisitory element). They branch out in two directions. First, the disquisition is developed into the fantasy, as in *Misalliance* it had already begun to do. All the fantastic disquisitions are about what we now call the problem of the atomic age. *The Simpleton of the Unexpected Isles* ends with the doomsday promised in *Heartbreak House* (though the structure of the later play is too flimsy to support the idea). *Geneva* ends, one might almost say, with the reported bursting of the bomb: a messenger announces the end of the world. *The Apple Cart* and *On the Rocks* take up the problem of British government. They are the only satisfying new departures in later Shavian drama. The cabinet meetings in both are something that Shaw *had* to give us someday—a rounded picture of the political madhouse which directs our destinies. Technically the cabinet scenes are constructed on the pattern of the discussions in *Getting Married*. ("The Doctrine of the Brothers Barnabas" is also preparatory: it contains Shaw's first portraits of twentieth century statesmen.) *The Simpleton* reduces the complex figures of *Heartbreak House* to allegorical symbols and *Too True To Be Good* is also more of a reduction than an extension of the earlier play. It *is* an extension, though, in that it catches the mood of a later generation. Heartbreak House was the habitat of cultured pre-war Europe; Aubrey, the Sweetie, and the Patient are the new post-war generation (first represented by Savvy, the flapper of "The Doctrine of the Brothers Barnabas"). But Shavian characterization is a topic that takes us beyond the frontiers of the disquisitory play. It deserves attention on its own account.

142

5

Because distinctions between modern and earlier drama have usually been made by partisans of the one or the other, we are far from knowing what the differences really are. But few would dispute that modern drama has in general been more resolutely psychological. Ibsen and Chekhov are perhaps the greatest of all psychological playwrights. Shaw is not so thoroughly psychological as they, not so concerned with the recesses of the spirit, not so interested in building up complete spiritual biographies. But if, as we are told nowadays, Shakespeare took situations and adapted his characters to them in a rather makeshift manner, Shaw, though not denying the need of dramatic situation, and admitting that many of his own plays have grown out of the central situation, is much more particular about plausibility of behavior. Tolstoy expressed the modern attitude when he said: "You can invent anything you like but you cannot invent psychology," and Shaw echoes him with: "Absurdity is the one thing that does not matter on the stage, provided it is not psychological absurdity." He told his biographer: "My procedure is to imagine characters and let them rip."

What kind of characters? As we have seen, Shaw's people are stage types, Victorian or simply perennial, modified by his conception of real life. We have also seen that when his people are inadequate it is not in being too literal, too flatly naturalistic, too "real," but in being too stagey, in not having been dipped in real life at all. What

143

is there about little Essie that does not belong to ham melodrama of any period? Shaw's servants, matrons, and vacuous young men—with certain exceptions—are barely removed from the ordinary article of the commercial stage. "My characters," Shaw once said, "are the familiar harlequin and columbine, clown and pantaloon." Sometimes they are lifted out of other writers. Shaw himself has permitted us to see in Mrs. Dudgeon and Bohun the Mrs. Clennam and Jaggers of Dickens. Mendoza is a Conan Doyle character, and his brigand-colleagues are variants of the Pirates of Penzance. But to talk of a "variant" in Shaw is to imply the introduction of a non-conventional, non-literary element. The pirates of Gilbert were themselves a parody of romance. (And not un-Shavian: "I don't think much of our profession," says the the Pirate King, "but, contrasted with respectability, it is comparatively honest.") Shaw parodies the parody by infusing into it a much stronger dose of "reality." The sulky Social Democrat is Harry Quelch, once a well-known non-Fabian radical. Not that a thing is real in art simply because it has a non-literary origin; it is not Shaw's mimicking of Quelch that gives force to his scene but the fact that he converts the conventional rivalry of bold bad men into the real rivalry of political doctrinaires.

Since the Victorian audience understood well enough, or at least took for granted, its own stage types, Shaw's energies, insofar as he ventured into criticism, were concentrated on explaining and defending his infusion of a "real" element. The explanation and the defence pervade his weekly pieces for *The Saturday Review*. Once he came to the rescue of *Arms and the Man* in an admirable essay

144

entitled "A Dramatic Realist to His Critics," where he explains how the infusing of "reality" affects dramatic characters:

> It does not concern me that, according to certain ethical systems, all human beings fall into classes labelled liar, coward, thief, and so on. . . . As a realist dramatist . . . it is my business to get outside these systems. For instance, in the play of mine which is most in evidence in London just now, the heroine has been classified by critics as a minx, a liar, and a *poseuse.* I have nothing to do with that: the only moral question for me is, does she do good or harm? If you admit that she does good, that she generously saves another man's life and wisely extricates herself from a false position with another man, then you may classify her as you please—brave, generous, and affectionate; or artful, dangerous, faithless—it is all one to me: you can no more prejudice me for or against her by such artificial categorizing than you could have made Molière dislike Monsieur Jourdain by a lecture on the vanity and pretentiousness of that amiable *bourgeois gentilhomme.*

It is clear from these lines that Shaw was challenging the basic conventions of character on the Victorian stage. And anyone who challenges the current conventions of the stage is asking for a different attitude from his audience and different methods from his actors. If he practises what he preaches his work must in the very nature of

145

things—habit being what it is—be declared "not drama." It was this deviation from the conventions that linked Shaw's cause with Ibsen's. In *The Quintessence*, Shaw demanded an Ibsen theatre, for the actors who could break with the Victorian tradition to act Ibsen could also act Shaw. Both required a new naturalism, a new sense of "reality." In other respects Shavian drama is, in Shaw's own words, "utterly unlike Ibsen in its stage methods and its Socialist view of human misery."

The upshot is that Shaw repudiates the villain and hero system, not in sheer contrariness, nor yet out of a love for that drab naturalism which replaces black and white with an even gray. Shaw wanted to bring in "reality," and reality for him was neither black, white, nor gray but all the colors of the rainbow. Furthermore, his morality does not replace vice and virtue with a mediocrity in which vice and virtue are found in equal proportions in every man. His repudiation of the hero and the villain has quite a different point. Consider the stage villain. He is a man whose moral standards are the exact opposite of ours, and

> This is a totally different phenomenon from the survivals of the ape and tiger in a normal man. The average man is covetous, lazy, selfish; but he is not malevolent, nor capable of saying to himself, "Evil: be thou my good." He only does wrong as a means to an end, which he always represents to himself as a right end. The case is exactly reversed with a villain; and it is my melancholy duty to add that we sometimes find it hard to avoid a cynical suspicion that the bal-

146

ance of social advantage is on the side of gifted
villainy, since we see the able villain, Mephis-
topheles-like, doing a huge amount of good in
order to win the power to do a little darling evil,
out of which he is as likely as not to be cheated in
the end; whilst your normal respectable man will
countenance, connive at, and grovel his way
through all sorts of meanness, baseness, servility,
and cruel indifference to suffering in order to
enjoy a miserable two-pennorth of social position, piety, comfort, and domestic affection, of
which he, too, is often ironically defrauded by
Fate.

Mazzini Dunn is such a "normal respectable man," whose
dealings with Mangan have involved him in something
other than gentlemanly behavior:

MAZZINI: What am I?
SHOTOVER: A thief, a pirate, and a murderer.
MAZZINI: I assure you you are mistaken.
SHOTOVER: An adventurous life; but what does
           it end in? Respectability. A ladylike
           daughter. The language and appear-
           ance of a city missionary. . . .

Shaw replaces the hero-and-villain psychology with a
tragi-comedy of the real. The method he adopts is not to
ignore the tradition of heroes and villains but to show that
it is itself real—as a superstition. A great part of the tragi-
comedy of the real arises from the interaction of such
superstition with natural fact.

We have seen how the new kind of life which Shaw's people possess required and received new dramaturgic patterns. When we dispense with heroes we have people who do wrong, but since we have also dispensed with villains they do wrong only for ends they regard as right. This means that every person is right from his own point of view—a situation which, as Hegel and Hebbel knew, is highly dramatic. The pattern suits naturally with the full and "artificial" articulateness of Shavian characters and explains their procedure. Hotchkiss tells us outright that he is a snob. His counterpart in real life would not do so, not because he is less honest or less talkative, but because he would not be conscious of snobbery as a means to an end. Many critics seem to have regarded the Shavian pattern as a mere joke until they heard discussions of Nationalism and Protestantism on the lips of medieval dignitaries in *Saint Joan*. And then, still failing to realize how far this sort of thing was part and parcel of Shavian drama, they indignantly protested against anachronism.

One might analyse further the tragi-comedy of the real, noting how Shaw shows that one man is a number of different people, that a "rogue" has his points of honor, that a "good" man has his points of dishonor, and how all these things are not only hometruths but material for comedy. A less technical and perhaps more fruitful approach is through the characters themselves. What types of character has Shaw, with his new method, been able to create?

The word *types* may be used without shame. All comedy, as Bergson rightly insists, deals in types. Nor is the word an exact antithesis to "individuals." "Begin with an individual," says Scott Fitzgerald, "and before you know

148

it you find that you have created a type." Shaw certainly
began with individuals. John Tanner was Hyndman,
Adolphus Cusins was Gilbert Murray, Dubedat was Karl
Marx's son-in-law, dozens of Shavian characters are portraits of his friends. And when he succeeded in giving
them life, he had created types, perhaps the greatest gallery of human types since Dickens and Balzac, and a gallery, like theirs, unified by the unmistakable individuality
of their author's thought and feeling.

How shall one speak of this lively crowd of creatures?
One must make distinctions, and the most elementary distinction is that between main and minor characters, a
dichotomy not as devoid of substance as it sounds. In
Greek tragedy it is a distinction between principal and
chorus, participant and onlooker, and in much modern
drama, including Shaw's, it retains something of this
original meaning. Main characters in Shaw are either
straightforward embodiments of that vitality which is the
great positive force in his world or they are battlegrounds
for the struggle between vitality and its opposite, "artificial system." The minor characters, on the other hand,
are pure victims of system, existing in complete contrast
to the vital heroes. Thus the simplest Shavian pattern is
to show a solitary representative of "evolutionary appe-
tite" among machine-made minds. We have seen something of this pattern in the *Three Plays for Puritans*. King
Magnus among the politicians is a later example showing
the conflict between vitality and system as a contrast between a mature person and professional men. This is one
of the oldest comic contrasts. From the first, comedy has
defended the human against that corruption of the human

149

which takes place when a man comes to identify himself with his social function—of being a doctor, a soldier, a statesman, or even a son, a husband, a father. The Shavianizing of this perennially comic perception entails its absorption into vitalism and socialism. One of the ways in which Shaw absorbs it into his vitalism is by reversing the allocation of roles: the mass of his characters are the corrupted professionals of comic tradition, but opposing them is the man of vitality. He absorbs it into his socialism by combining it with a collectivist ethics which had never before, perhaps, found its way to the stage.

You will probably find no Shaw play in which the contrast of amateur and professional, of person and petrifaction, is not present. If Shaw is not only showing us a Dick Dudgeon, a Caesar, a Lady Cicely, a Joan, a Magnus, in contrast with professional men taken *en masse,* he is showing us the parson Morell in contrast with the curate Lexy, Bluntschli in contrast with Sergius, the Man of Destiny in contrast with the Lieutenant, Father Keegan in contrast with Father Dempsey, General Burgoyne in contrast with Major Swindon, Undershaft in contrast with his son Stephen, Private Meek in contrast with Colonel Tallboys. In arranging these pairs Shaw combines the old antithesis of amateur and professional with a yet older one which, we are told, is the oldest confrontation in all comedy. This is the confrontation in the earliest Greek comedy of the Ironist and the Impostor, the Ironist in Shaw being always the soft-spoken vital man in harmony with himself, the Impostor being the professional man who has ideologies and habits instead of ideas and impulses. Many of the greatest scenes in Shaw are duels between these two.

If the main distinction between Shaw's characters, true to his whole theory of drama, is that between the vital people and the mechanized people, there are a couple of other antitheses which cut across this one, though they have chiefly to do with the vital characters. These are the antithesis of male and female and the antithesis of the actual and the ideal.

6

According to Meredith, comedy can only exist where women have a high status, since it depends upon a battle between the sexes in which victory, if attained at all, is decidedly pyrrhic. We have seen that Shaw's first notable innovation in art was his creation of "unwomanly" heroines. (He once said that good women are all manly, "good men being equally all womanly men.") In his fight against the "romantic" love of popular fiction and drama Shaw showed that women are at once lower and higher than the fragile heroines of Dickens. They are lower because they lose their tempers like Blanche of *Widowers' Houses*. They are lower because their love is physical. Here is the first love scene in Shavian drama:

> They stand face to face . . . she provocative, taunting, half-defying, half-inviting him to advance, in a flush of undisguised animal excitement. It suddenly flashes on him that all this ferocity is erotic: that she is making love to him.

151

His eye lights up: a cunning expression comes
into the corner of his mouth. . . .

Shavian heroines are also *higher* than Dickensian heroines. Higher, like Lady Cicely and Lina and Mrs. George,
in their superiority to erotics, in their naturalness and in
their grandeur, in the nobility of their purpose and the
effectiveness of their behavior. Higher like Barbara and
Jennifer and Lavinia and above all Joan in their soaring
aspirations, their passion for realizing the ideal.

The relation between the sexes, throughout Shaw's
works, has two levels. There is the famous Higher Relationship, which has given Shaw his reputation for sexless-
ness. The point of the *Three Plays for Puritans* was to
show, in each play, a man and a woman with something
larger than a romance on their hands. Read the plays
closely, though, and you will see that this is no brushing-
aside of sex by one who pretends to do without it. In each
play—as we have noted—there is the shadow of a sex relationship between hero and heroine. Cupid, so to say,
hovers over all six of them; his shadow is one of the
subtlest and most interesting Shavian characters. In other
plays there are many relationships which look "dangerous" but are not. In *Getting Married* and *The Apple Cart*
Shaw replaces the eternal triangle with a Platonic triangle. In *Candida* and *The Devil's Disciple* adultery is
held at arm's length with some difficulty. It is a wonder
that Shaw has escaped the charge of prurience.

For the most part the biological comedy is taken to be
relatively low, the near-prurient spiritual comedy high.
The one great exception is *Man and Superman,* in which

152

the relation between the two levels is sought. It is a biological comedy with spiritual overtones, a spiritual comedy with a biological ground bass.

You would gather from the Epistle Dedicatory that *Man and Superman* has a world-shattering theme. A line of thought somewhat as follows—it is almost an anthropological myth—is expounded. Woman is the prime mover in the evolutionary process. While woman is creating and forming the race, man, needed only for a moment in the biological process, is left free to develop secondary interests, intellectual and social. Fearing to lose him, woman lures him back to domesticity by all possible means, among other things by a feigned interest in his intellectual and social pursuits.

This contest between the sexes we might call the lower biological comedy. Shaw indicates that a higher comedy —he calls it a tragedy—is enacted when the man is a genius and will not be led back to the woman. Unlike the ordinary straying male, a genius is not a truant from life. He escapes from the home only to fulfill as high a function of the Life Force as woman herself. For if woman preserves and creates life, genius is the means by which man becomes conscious of living. If he flees woman, his mother, he is the favorite child of his father, the Life Force. Without the woman there is no life, without him there is no value. When the artist man flees the mother woman, and the mother woman pursues the artist man, an irresistible force meets an immovable object.

Whether Shaw ever intended to present this "tragic" impasse in *Man and Superman* is not clear. He has certainly not done so. Tanner, as we have seen, cannot be regarded as an unequivocally great man. His appearance is a caricature of Hyndman. His behavior is often that of a brilliant gasbag. A stage-direction describes Ann Whitefield as a "vital genius," but then we have to be careful to base our judgment of the play on the dialogue itself and not on Shaw's busy comments. Whatever his initial intention, Shaw has given us the lower biological comedy in which we have, not an impasse, not two irresistible forces, but the snapping-up of a clever young man by a shrewd young woman.

The Epistle Dedicatory contains some very big talk. It also sums up the play as "a trumpery story of modern London life, a life in which, as you know, the ordinary man's main business is to get means to keep up the position and habits of a gentleman and the ordinary woman's business is to get married." Turn to the play itself, resolutely ignore all its glittering adornments, and you will discover—among other things—a Victorian farce in four neatly arranged acts. The dialogue is of course interpenetrated with discussion. Not only is there abundant witticism on every possible topic. In each Act one main object of satire is added to the main story through the agency of extra characters—Ramsden the Liberal, Straker the New Man, Mendoza and his band of Radicals, Hector Malone, Sr., the Irish-American. Finally, Shaw uses the counterpoint of main plot and sub-plot. Ann begins by getting an inheritance and then spends her time landing a man. Violet begins by landing a man and then spends her time making sure she gets an inheritance too. Thus the two perennial comic themes—love and money—are treated with the perennial levity of farce.

And so *Man and Superman,* regarded by Shavians as a bible rivalling the "metabiological pentateuch" *Back to Methuselah,* regarded by anti-Shavians as a pompous bore, is—aside from the discussion in hell—a farce of the order of *You Never Can Tell.* In fact it looks back to the latter as much as it looks forward to the former. *You Never Can Tell* and *Man and Superman* sharpen Gilbertian satire to a finer edge than Gilbert himself ever gave it. I have in mind not only Mendoza's political pirates of Penzance but the fooling with family relationships that runs through both plays. With the exception of the opening of Becque's *La Parisienne* the story of Violet's marriage in Act I of *Man and Superman* is probably the cleverest piece of histrionic deception in all modern comedy. To think of Bohun and his father William, of Mendoza and Louisa Straker (not to mention Guinness and Bill Dunn or the ancestry of Juggins) is to realize once again that Shaw had not been a Victorian theatre-goer for nothing.

We have seen how he raised his pseudo-melodramas above melodrama. How does he raise his pseudo-farce above farce? The most obviously unusual feature of the play viewed as a Victorian farce is—as one would expect —a Shavian inversion. The woman courts the man. But one learns also to expect that the primary simple inversion in a Shavian play is only the beginning of the irony. By giving an active sexual role to a woman Shaw not only shocks the Victorians. He implements his own anthropological myth. More important, he broadens the whole basis of relations between the sexes as shown on the stage. "The natural attraction of the sexes" he presents as a physical, biological fact. Which is low and shocking. But the

155

second irony is that this "lowness" is interpreted—and incontrovertibly—as "higher" than the conventional view, for what Ann Whitefield wants is not sexual pleasure but motherhood. *Man and Superman,* as I have said, is a fourth Play for Puritans.

Now in each *Play for Puritans* we found a protagonist standing for the Life Force and an antagonist who had against his will to be "educated" by the protagonist. According to the pattern, Tanner would be the protagonist, a role he seems to be well fitted for by his creed, his knowledge, his eloquence, and his pedagogical passion. He poses as the veritable high priest of the Life Force. But in *Man and Superman,* as in *Pygmalion* later, protagonist and antagonist are reversed. Though Tanner *preaches* the Life Force, Ann *is* the Life Force. In the end he goes to school to her. If the play has the standard Shaw theme of vitality versus system, its upshot is that the apostle of vitality is himself the slave of system, for like other doctrines vitalism can lose its vitality. Tanner is system, Ann spontaneous life.

If *Man and Superman* is far from containing the tragedy mentioned in the Epistle, it also rises far above the farce that is its basis. Nor is the tragic theme altogether ignored. It is not the Epistle but the play that contains the sentence: "Of all human struggles there is none so treacherous and remorseless as the struggle between the artist man and the mother woman." But though the "mother woman" who inspired the sentence is Ann Whitefield, the "artist man" here referred to is the poet Octavius, who in reality is not much of an artist and even less of a man. The speaker—the impartial observer!—is Tanner, who is not an artist but a political theorist. What is Shaw doing with his tragic idea? Is he not looking at it slantwise, shyly declining to use it? It might be said that Tanner is more of an artist in the Shavian sense than Octavius, as Caesar is more of an artist than Apollodorus. But is he? Is he?— not as an idea in a preface but as an actuality in the play? The destiny that Ann and Tanner work out is precisely that of the lower biological comedy. Tanner's intellectual pretensions shrink to nothing before Ann's reality. Tanner is brought to heel precisely as Shaw says the genius is not.

Octavius is not a genius either. Those who think all Shaw's artists the same have compared him with Marchbanks. But Marchbanks probably *was* a genius, though, at the beginning, an immature one. Marchbanks would have seen through Tanner, and would have placed himself as an immovable object in the way of Ann, had she exerted upon him her irresistible force. There is a play in this, but Shaw did not write it. His artists—for that matter it is true of most of his people, "typical" as they are—never exactly duplicate each other. Octavius is isolated like Marchbanks, but for him isolation is frankly a *pis aller*. The triangle Dick-Judith-Anderson was different from the triangle Marchbanks-Candida-Morell, and the triangle Octavius-Ann-Tanner is different again. In all of them Shaw touches some very delicate springs. His central situation is crude but here on the margin is something subtle and mysterious. Those who are disappointed that Shaw did not attempt a Strindbergian tragedy of love can find some compensation in his equally curious triangular tragi-comedies.

157

7

If Shaw's plays are in the first place the meeting-ground of vitality and artificial system and in the second of male and female they are in the third place an arena for the problem of human ideals and their relation to practice. His characters may be ranged on a scale of mind, ideas, aspirations, beliefs and on a scale of action, practicality, effectiveness. At one extreme there are men of mind who make as little contact with the world of action as possible. Such are most of Shaw's artists. At the other extreme are men of action who lack all speculative interests and ideal impulses. Such are Shaw's professional men: soldiers, politicians, doctors. At a little distance from the one extreme are the men of mind who are interested in this world even if they can do nothing about it. Such, in their different ways, are Tanner, Cusins, Keegan, Shotover, and Magnus. At a little distance from the other extreme are certain practical men with a deep intellectual interest in the meaning of action. Such are the businessmen Undershaft and Tarleton, the soldiers Napoleon and Caesar.

The conversations which all these men, of mind or of action, have with each other have, perhaps, more nervous energy, a more galvanic rhythm, than any other disquisitory passages in all Shaw. For they are all pushing, probing towards the solution of the problem of morals in action. They are all part of the search for the philosopher-king. Keegan talks with the politician Broadbent, Shotover with the businessman Mangan, Magnus with his cabinet. Most strikingly, perhaps, Undershaft talks with Professor Cusins. They are agreed that there is no hope until the millionaires are professors of Greek and the professors of Greek are millionaires.

Although the problem enters into all Shaw's plays there is one special repository for it: the history play. We have seen that *Caesar and Cleopatra* is a melodrama and one of the *Three Plays for Puritans*. It is also the second of three history plays—*The Man of Destiny*, and *Saint Joan* are the other two—in which Shaw worked at his problem by connecting it with great historical figures. One must however be very clear about the fact that Shaw never tried to do the job of the professional historian. As his way is, he informs everybody that his plays are utterly historical and defends their most whimsical anachronisms in notes that are not uniformly funny. However, there were scholars who fell for it and earnestly corrected Shaw's facts in solemn articles. A whole book was written to "refute" *Saint Joan*.

Shaw's claim was that he knew history intuitively! He writes his plays, reads the history books afterwards, and finds—so he says—that he was right all along, for "given Caesar and a certain set of circumstances I know what would happen." Those who think this a naive confession are themselves naive. Many of them would prefer to Shavian history plays those fictional biographies which, though they are based on research, every fact guaranteed, are humanly absurd—*kitsch* in Metro-Goldwyn-Mayer settings designed by historical researchers. Shaw's method is the opposite. He retains his right to be absurd in everything but psychology. And he recognizes a limitation in all historical writing which our historians would be wise to grant: that our understanding of an historical

159

character is a highly subjective affair. What Shaw confesses as a personal shortcoming is a general human one:

> As a dramatist I have no clue to any historical or other personage save that part of him which is also myself, and which may be nine tenths of him or ninety-nine hundredths, as the case may be (if, indeed, I do not transcend the creature), but which, anyhow, is all that can ever come within my knowledge of his soul.

Shaw differs from a sound historian not in being more subjective but in not being a historian at all. In his "history plays" Shaw was not interested in the peculiar character of each period—Napoleonic, ancient, or medieval—but in indicating what has not changed. Seeing and hearing people much like ourselves (or better) the audience learns that no progress has been made during historical time. As theme, these settings are part of the game Shaw plays with his audience; as technique, they are a parody of the Lyceum and other period pieces. Just as in *You Never Can Tell* he boasts of giving the gallery all it wants by way of good wine and carnival dresses, so he might boast of the good time he gives his audiences with his historical costumes. Apollodorus's flight to the pharos he calls a "prodigious harlequin leap."

Another purpose Shaw has in choosing historical characters for his plays about power is that such characters have a mysterious authority. Napoleon, Caesar, and Joan actually existed. The audience therefore feels them to be real and tangible. And it is a fact that Chesterton would have enjoyed that when an historical personage is famous we call him "legendary." Shaw chooses only "legendary" names from history's pages. And his plays have much more reference to the legend than to the fact. (Who knows "the fact" anyway? Shaw would ask.) Just as the whole show is something of a parody of the *kitsch* costume play, the character of the hero is always a variant —never a debunking—of the popular legend: the granite-faced Caesar, Napoleon as he appears in David's portraits, Joan as interpreted by Schiller or Mark Twain.

The Man of Destiny is the crudest of the three plays. Napoleon is little more than a parody of *l'Empereur,* though a parody that should make the audience smile on the wrong side of its face, since the hero's heroism is not really impugned. Shaw has made it clear that he means the piece as a theatrical exercise for virtuosi; and Gordon Craig says that the stage-business is a transcript of some of Henry Irving's favorite stage behavior. If Napoleon is more than a puppet it is because Shaw tries to infuse into him something of himself, as one would gather at least from the stage direction:

> He has prodigious powers of work, and a clear realistic knowledge of human nature in public affairs. . . . He is imaginative without illusions, and creative without religion, loyalty, patriotism or any of the common ideals. Not that he is incapable of these ideals: on the contrary, he has swallowed them all in his boyhood, and now, having a keen dramatic faculty, is extremely clever at playing upon them by the arts of the actor and stage manager. Withal, he is no spoiled child.

161

Poverty, ill-luck, the shifts of impecunious shabby-gentility, repeated failure as a would-be author, humiliation as a rebuffed time-server . . . these trials have ground his conceit out of him, and forced him to be self-sufficient and to understand that to such men as he is the world will give nothing that he cannot take from it by force.

When Shaw insists on making his hero so like himself, the character has more reality in the stage direction than in the play. Another way of using one's own personality is to make of it the measuring-rod for what is *not* oneself: one can measure *difference* with it as well as likeness. In Caesar, though there is a lot of Shaw too, there is happily something also of the not-Shaw. Napoleon seems to have taken up action only because he failed as a writer: an interpretation later re-embodied in the Napoleon of *Back to Methuselah*. Napoleon, that is, is a Shaw *manqué;* Caesar, so the author seems to admit, is a Shaw *plus*. The play is (if you insist) a delusion of grandeur. This time one may quote one of his notes without flattering Shaw since the conception here outlined is also conveyed by the play itself:

I have been careful to attribute nothing but originality to him. Originality gives a man an air of frankness, generosity, and magnanimity by enabling him to estimate the value of truth, money, or success in any particular instance quite independently of convention and moral generalization. . . . He knows that the real moment of success is not the moment apparent to the crowd. Hence, in order to produce an impression of complete disinterestedness and magnanimity, he has only to act with entire selfishness; and this is perhaps the only sense in which a man can be said to be *naturally* great. It is in this sense that I have represented Caesar as great. Having virtue, he has no need of goodness. He is neither forgiving, frank, nor generous, because a man who is too great to resent has nothing to forgive; a man who says things that other people are afraid to say need be no more frank than Bismarck was; and there is no generosity in giving things you do not want to people of whom you intend to make use. This distinction between virtue and goodness is not understood in England: hence the poverty of our drama in heroes. Our stage attempts at them are mere goody-goodies. . . .

As these lines suggest, *Caesar and Cleopatra*, subtitled *A History Lesson*, and doubtless teaching a lesson to such historians as are ready to learn, is really a lesson in political psychology. As such, it is much more than a "defense of dictatorship" because it shows Caesar's genius to be paradoxical, even equivocal, rather than good. The central paradox of Caesar is that, while his clemency raises him above the hatchet-men, he is all the time dependent on the "honest" hatchet-man Rufio and sometimes on the "dishonest" hatchet-man Lucius Septimius. Shaw is not so doctrinaire as to hope to remove the paradox and resolve the contradiction. He only shows how the paradox works out. Rufio, the "practical" man, is less practical than Caesar in military and political strategy; Caesar, the dreamer, knows how. In this paradox there is no real contradiction. But it is a double-paradox, and in its second half lies the snag. At the end, when Caesar's fate is to be determined, it is Rufio who is practical in foreseeing Caesar's death in Rome. At this point we see that Caesar really *is* a dreamer who will sail blithely to his death rather than play for safety. His oration to the sphinx was not hokum. It prepared us for the double paradox.

Paradox, not synthesis. Caesar is not a Superman. He is not a philosopher-king, first, because he is not altogether a philosopher, and, second, because as king he fails at last, and his empire bursts asunder. If the higher man must either conquer the world or be crucified by it, *Caesar and Cleopatra* does not make it clear that the conquest is preferable to the crucifixion.

The plays that follow show—or inadequately conceal—increasing uneasiness over the gulf between theory and practice, talking and doing, right and might. In each, Shaw places representatives of several—usually three—positions side by side. In *Man and Superman*, John Tanner is the unpractical talker; Roebuck Ramsden is the "practical" liberal—as unpractical as Tanner really—whose views were advanced thirty years ago. The practical one of the three is Ann Whitefield who has no ideas either old-fashioned or up-to-date. Ann's creativeness could scarcely be Shaw's last word. Even in this play Shaw finds a higher status for the man of thought, if only in another world.

What has become of the Caesarian hero who not only

has his apartness and mystery but what Shaw calls "the only imagination worth having: the power of imagining things as they are," not to mention his gift for *acting* on his insights? In *John Bull's Other Island* the Shavio-Caesarian mind is, so to say, split into its two component parts: the alienation is given to Father Keegan, the practical ruthlessness to Larry Doyle. The chief result of this unhappy fission is that Keegan and Doyle have each to play second fiddle to Roebuck Ramsden, now reincarnate as Broadbent. It is not surprising that Shaw's critics, who at first assume that Shaw is a straightforward radical propagandist and later call him "confused" because he declines to be straightforwardly radical, find the pattern bewildering. One of them reports the magnificent final scene of *John Bull* in this manner:

> A queer three-sided contest now takes place between Keegan, who knows what is right but does nothing, Doyle, who knows what is right but does what is wrong, and Broadbent, who does what is wrong but is quite convinced that he is doing right. (Herbert Skimpole)

This is an accurate summary, as far as it goes, of a scene whose "queerness" consists in the fact that the man who wears the straitjacket of artificial system is no longer a child in the hands of a "vital" hero. Broadbent is ridiculous, it is true, but the last laugh is on the others, including the vital ones—Keegan and Doyle—whom he outdoes in all practical matters. In *Caesar and Cleopatra* the idea of Caesarism is slightly ambiguous because of the partial dependence of Caesar on Rufio and Lucius

165

Septimius. In *John Bull,* which portrays a country where realism and idealism have been fatally split, we find the unoriginal and machine-made type all too effective. It is Shaw's first political play and—significantly—one of the saddest things he ever wrote.

Generalizing from *Three Plays for Puritans,* some critics have assumed that *all* Shaw's plays show a vital hero surrounded by the victims of artificial system. Yet we have seen that this pattern is subtly inverted in *Man and Superman* and *Pygmalion* where—such is Shaw's version of the female and male principles—the heroine is the vital one and the hero only a vitalist. It is inverted also in *John Bull* where the central character is Broadbent who is a devout idealist and by that token the archetype of Shavian villainy. In *Major Barbara,* the central trio— Undershaft, Barbara, Cusins—differs as much from Broadbent, Keegan, and Doyle as from Ramsden, Ann, and Tanner. This time the successful man is a modern Caesar, at home with himself, imaginative in the Shavian sense, very much the vital hero. The idealistic heroine, though at the outset far gone in illusions, is jolted back to reality at the famous emotional climax of the play. The young professor of Greek who is to be Undershaft's successor will unite —we are asked to hope—realism and idealism, practicality and wisdom, in an almost superhuman union.

Such at any rate seems to be the intention of the play. It is not quite realized. Barbara's final conversion has much less force than her previous disillusionment. Undershaft remains far more impressive than Cusins. Seemingly Shaw started out to demonstrate that poverty is a crime and therefore that there is more good sense in the career of an Undershaft than in that of a Snobby Price. His play was to have been called *Andrew Undershaft's Profession,* presumably in ironic parallelism with *Mrs. Warren's Profession,* which showed exactly the opposite side of the truth. Probably the idea of making Cusins the synthesis of Barbara's idealism and her father's realism came to Shaw later, perhaps *too* late. His devil's advocacy remains all too effective. Like so many other writers, he makes his monster so impressive that no good man can match him. He so brilliantly proves that "money is the most important thing in the world" that he cannot quite enforce the fundamental Shavian principle that selling yourself is the ultimate horror, that "money was not born in the light." Superficial observers have said that, though Shaw's early businessmen—Crofts, Burgess, Lickcheese—are rogues, his later ones—Undershaft, Tarleton—betray Shaw's growing conservatism. For Shaw, however, Undershaft and Tarleton are realities which he was trying to understand and do justice to. The businessman in a much later play—*Heartbreak House*—is also a rogue; in that play and in many to follow the original Shavian position is re-affirmed.

Not that *Major Barbara* was for Shaw a pure eccentricity. Its heroine for example is evidence of a new approach. In his earlier period Shaw had surprised his audience with two kinds of women: capable, unromantic women like Vivie, Candida, Lady Cicely, and acquisitive, passionate women like Mrs. Warren and Blanche Sartorius. After the latter type has culminated in Ann Whitefield, it apparently ceases to be important for Shaw, reappearing only in such termagants as Hypatia and the

167

Millionairess; the "mother woman" dies out. Even the self-possessed capable type is less frequent. Shaw's newer New Women are often simply abundant, independent daughters of the Life Force like Lina, Mrs. George, Margaret Knox and Eliza (after her emancipation). A few of them are something subtler. Starting with Nora in *John Bull,* several of Shaw's heroines constitute a new Shavian type: the girlish type, innocent in a fresh un-Victorian way, refined by civilization yet on fire with God. Barbara, Lavinia, and Jennifer Dubedat are most obviously of this stamp.

If the early possessive heroines culminated in Ann Whitefield, the late girl heroines culminate in Joan. *Saint Joan* is an attempt at several kinds of synthesis, one of Shaw's periodic attempts to gather together in one work all that had been on his mind through several preceding works, to unite and transcend them. Joan unites the down-to-earth practicality of the Lady Cicely's, the vitality of the Lina's, and carries as far as Shaw can take it the spirituality of the girl heroines. When Mrs. Shaw suggested Joan as a subject to her husband, and when he read the records of Joan's trial as made available by Jules Quicherat, Shaw must have realized that here was an opportunity to study and recreate a person who united in herself so much that he had divided between his practical and his idealistic characters. It almost seems that if Joan had never existed Shaw would have had to invent her.

What does the career of this living synthesis demonstrate? Whether Joan can be thought to have "succeeded" depends wholly upon the criterion of success. In war she outdoes the most gifted professional soldiers: she was a success. Yet, after her victories, she is outdone by the same professionals: she was a failure. The effect of her victories was lasting: she was a success. She was outwitted and burnt: she was a failure. Yet after her death the practical men decided that they had made a mistake: she was a success. Would they then like to have her back again? No, that would be inconvenient: she is a failure.

So far the play might be a romantic defense of Joan. But Shaw is after bigger game. *Saint Joan* is his most ambitious drama and—if, as we should, we count *Man and Superman* as two plays, *Back to Methuselah* as five—his longest. It is also the only play in which Shaw essays what in his discussion of *Man and Superman* he called a tragic conflict—that is, an *irreconcilable* conflict. It was never true that Shaw's plays "almost invariably ended cheerfully enough with a precise indication of the solution," as Edmund Wilson once alleged. We have seen how *Caesar and Cleopatra* and *Major Barbara* end on unsolved dilemmas. But in these plays the problems are patched up, if not solved; and in neither case is irreconcilability at the center of the action. In *Saint Joan* it is. The irresistible force of her genius meets the immovable object of social order. Shaw is not writing an "individualist" defense of Joan; or a "collectivist" defense of social order. He depicts the clash.

In this he deviates from the practice of his predecessors in drama and biography, and shocks the historians and would-be historians of two extreme wings, Catholic and Rationalist. The Catholic canonization of Joan in 1921 was, so to speak, the occasion of Shaw's play, and the

169

Epilogue in which he deals with that event is an integral part of his tragi-comedy. Now this second Catholic rehabilitation of Joan—like the first which occurred a generation after her death—involved the complete repudiation of the men who had sentenced her. Since Shaw was in a manner rehabilitating these men, and since he regarded Joan as a genius in a natural way, rather than a saint and martyr in a supernatural way, the Catholic opposition was quite inevitable. Oddly enough the Rationalists agreed with the Catholics as to the villainy of Joan's judges; to doubt it would have been to doubt the whole basis of their anti-clericalism. And so it was possible for the Anglo-Catholic T. S. Eliot and the Rationalist J. M. Robertson to join hands over what they believed to be the corpse of Shaw.

For those who understand the drift of Shaw's history plays the controversies over the facts in *Saint Joan* are irrelevant. Aside from Quicherat, it seems that all Shaw read about Joan were the plays and biographies that had helped to create her Legend—or rather her Legends, for Joan is every sort of villain or heroine to every sort of sect. Shaw cannot see her—cannot see anybody, least of all a genius—as either villain or heroine. Nor can he allow her judges to be assigned the opposite role—villains if she is a heroine, heroes if she is a villain. To Shaw the versions of Joan provided by Shakespeare, Schiller, Mark Twain and the rest are all melodramatic variations on an impossible theme. They see the characters of all concerned as morally one-sided and the conclusion of Joan's story as a simple phenomenon: simply pathetic, simply

170

glorious, simply atrocious, simply a good thing, or simply a bad. These legends cannot satisfy Shaw, who began his investigation of human nature by rejecting villains and heroes. He must show Joan as a credible human being and, unlike most of our "humanizing" biographers, he must make her *greatness* credible. As for the vast forces which crushed her, since they are of human creation, he must make them credible too. If Joan's judges were really cheap politicians then her story had best be left alone as a cheap story. If there is drama in it, it lies in the collision of two forces, both profoundly human, both eminently defensible, both, perhaps, necessary.

Shaw's play is about the individual and the collective or—if we think of it in terms of time—the simultaneous need for stability and change. Shaw cannot with the anarchists and their myriad unconscious sympathizers resent authority; he finds it requisite for order and permanence. He cannot with the authoritarians reject nonconformity; he finds it requisite for all human development. He must therefore show Joan, the nonconformist, as good; and he must show the Inquisitors as reasonable. The Inquisitor must be convinced and convincing; yet Joan must be no Agnes Bernauer. Shaw feels no "Teutonic" glee in the sacrifice of an individual to the goddess of history and no anarchistic joy in the defiance of church and state. His purpose and his achievement were to maintain an exact balance between Joan and her judges. We have seen how often Shaw has made opposing views dramatic. In *Saint Joan* the happy fact about his impartiality is that he seems to be, not on *neither* side (like, say, Galsworthy in *Strife*)

171

but on *both* sides. Those who have found Shaw's both/and a brash eclecticism should here be given pause. The both/and of *Saint Joan* is not an easy "best of both worlds." It is a combination with awful consequences. And Shaw's noble characterization carries the play beyond the political historical theme to an ultimate question: will this world ever be a home for higher men?

I am not suggesting that the play is satisfying in all respects. Many of the details are quite unimpressive: Joan's dialect is silly, her occasional prose poetry forced, many of the jokes (such as the one against the Shavian Englishman) decidedly musty. Dividing the play, as Shaw has hinted, into a Romance (Scenes I, II, III), a Tragedy (Scenes IV, V, VI), and a Comedy (the Epilogue), the Romance seems much inferior to the other two parts. Yet one has only to compare *Saint Joan* with the *Plays for Puritans* to see that Shaw's art and thought had deepened since 1900. In 1900 Shaw would have represented Joan as pure Vitality fighting against pure System. Perhaps he would have inverted the melodrama in some way, but he would not have avoided it. And, I think, he would have had to cut short his story before the death of Joan, leaving you with the threads in your hands to tie up as you please —as at the end of *Caesar*. In the first two decades of the twentieth century Shaw's faith in Vitality doubtless took some hard knocks; *Saint Joan* might easily have been pessimistic. But though he had long scorned the simple Progress of the older liberals, Shaw declined the easy path of the disillusioned radical into pessimism or otherworldliness. His sense of catastrophe and failure is balanced by his genius for admiration and love.

8

It should by this time be clear how little the phrase Problem Play contributes to the understanding of Shavian drama. Perhaps we are now in a position to say in general terms what the affiliations of Shavian comedy really are.

As a man Shaw was the friend and colleague of such Problem Playwrights and naturalists as Galsworthy and Granville-Barker who, along with a hundred other lesser men, tried to substitute a flat, gray reality for the artifice of Scribe's well-made plays. Shaw disagreed with both the Scribeans and the naturalists who alike assumed that life was dull and undramatic, the former undertaking to "dramatize" it, the latter being prepared to forego drama in the interests of truth. Chesterton well described a Shavian play as an expanded paradox. And the paradox was not something Shaw imposed on his material to make it interesting. To him life was itself a mass of paradoxes. Shaw challenges the assumption of the naturalists that the facts can be understood by straightforward reasoning and realistic photography whereas paradox is taken to be the product of romantic fancy. He complains that "we never argue paradoxically on hard facts but always straightforwardly on assumptions that are partly romantic and partly mere commercial habits."

Quite unlike the method of the routine naturalists, Shaw's method resembled Ibsen's to the extent that it was to take the ordinary play of the nineteenth-century commercial stage and to give it a naturalistic twist. However, Shaw's naturalism was not Ibsen's any more than it was

Galsworthy's, nor did Shaw appropriate the same features of conventional drama. Ibsen used Dumas *fils* as his raw material for a personal kind of tragedy. Shaw used the more homely material of English farce and melodrama— characters, stories, ideas, stage tricks, settings—as the formal basis of a naturalistic comedy.

Such a thing as *Jitta's Atonement* shows his procedure very exactly. This play, which purports to be a translation from the German of Siegfried Trebitsch, is really related to Trebitsch's play exactly as the *Plays for Puritans* are related to Victorian melodrama. Only in the case of *Jitta* one can actually read the melodrama that Shaw started with. It is true to type in that all the human relationships and attitudes are the correct ones for the bourgeois theatre and the bourgeois imagination. Without altering the incidents, or even the sequence of scenes and speeches, Shaw re-writes the dialogue, "naturalizing" every motive and attitude. A Shavian character is not shocked when the Trebitsch character was. A Shavian character can adjust himself to a situation which the Trebitsch character, saved by the fall of the curtain, simply refused to accept. Trebitsch's play ends with a husband resolving to spend the rest of his lifetime punishing his wife for her unfaithfulness to him. In Shaw's play the husband realizes that a fit of anger cannot possibly be prolonged forever and that a *modus vivendi*, neither blissful nor desolating, has to be worked out.

Critics who see Shaw's relation to the ordinary Victorian theatre, or even to Gilbert and Wilde, are likely to avoid the errors of those who see only his relation to the Higher Theatre movement under whose auspices his plays

174

first appeared. There are some, of course, who see Shaw chiefly in relation to Molière, Jonson, and Aristophanes. One Shaw-worshipper compiled tables to show, diagrammatically as it were, that Shaw and Molière are at one in all major matters of thought and technique. The generality of scholarly commentators, no less obtuse, though very much less favorable to Shaw, get involved in hopelessly unhistorical categorizing and conclude with a distribution of prizes: first prize, usually, to Molière, second to Jonson, third to Aristophanes. Bernard Shaw also ran.

Indeed it is part of the regular critical routine nowadays to observe how inferior Shaw is to Molière. Very likely he is, though singularly poor arguments are usually advanced to convince us of the fact. The only serious argument I ever saw put forward is to the effect that while, to establish the critical and philosophic standpoint which is necessary to comedy, Molière took his stand on the general nature of men, Shaw stands on a very special philosophy of his own, and thus is a much narrower artist, a critic of but a segment or layer of life. Let us look into this.

Undoubtedly Shaw's comic sense is hand in glove with his philosophy. Consider for instance the conflict between vitality and system. The natural is assumed to be good, the artificial bad. Shaw is an eighteenth-century *philosophe* in his belief in natural goodness, the malleability of human life, the possible realization of the city of God on earth. Are these views too sanguine for comedy? One recalls what happened in the eighteenth century: all comedic conflicts were dissolved in tears of Reason and universal benevolence. When Shaw tells us that laughter

175

must be friendly and sympathetic, when he finds even so light a piece as *The Importance of Being Earnest* heartless, do we not begin to wonder whether his own art can belong to the same family as that of Jonson and Molière? Where in the Shavian canon shall we find such solid and instructive monsters as Morose or Harpagon? Even if Shaw *could* create such people his Rousseauistic philosophy would not let him.

We have seen how Shaw often places a model "vital" character in the midst of a group of reprehensible mechanized ones. Molière was often inclined to do the opposite: to make his protagonist the incarnation of the chief vice he is out to expose. Molière's method, given his genius, is obviously a much bolder confrontation of evil in man. No argument for verisimilitude (and the argument of realists and naturalists, Shaw included, is always all too much an argument for verisimilitude) can blind us to the solid advantages of comic abstraction. The techniques of the *commedia dell'arte* which Molière inherited were perfectly adapted to bring into high relief what he had to say about life. No comedy will ever be *better* than this, either as "truth" or "beauty."

Molière's monsters—Don Juan and Tartuffe, for instance—were hypocrites. Ben Jonson embodied human evil in maniacal humbugs. Shaw writes:

> It is not my object in the least to represent people as hypocrites and humbugs. It is conceit, not hypocrisy, that makes a man think he is guided by reasoned principles when he is really obeying his instincts.

176

The Shavian enterprise sounds rather slight, perhaps even trivial, beside Jonson's or Molière's. Undoubtedly Shaw lacks, almost totally lacks, something that they possess in abundance: a sense of horror. "Crime, like disease," he says in the preface to *Saint Joan*, "is not interesting." In context, this sentence makes a valuable point. In context or out, it is also a confession of limitation.

What could Shaw say in his own defence (beyond protesting that nineteenth-century melodrama and farce,[2] not Jonson and Molière, were his butt)? At best, one is at first inclined to think, Shaw can only tell us that his comedy is sociologically more up-to-date than Molière's. His satire is against the audience and not against the characters, against the system and not against individuals. And perhaps, in the beginning, that was all there was to Shavian comedy. Later, however, it became clear that there was more than socialism in Shavian satire. There was a whole view of life. Shaw the Rousseauist said (it is an avowal one may be forgiven for re-quoting): "It is quite useless to declare that all men are born free if you deny that they are born good." If men err it is not because they are natively depraved but because they are somehow misled. They know not what they do. There is compassion in Shaw's humor.

If there were nothing but compassion in it, of course, Shaw's critics would be right. In that case his comedy would collapse for lack of tension, his philosophy for lack of dialectic. Actually, however, Shaw finds as many obstacles to an ideal scheme of things as his harshest prede-

[2] "Man is a hypocrite and invariably affects to be better and wiser than he really is."—W. S. Gilbert's *The Mountebanks*.

177

cessors. It is something, no doubt, that men are not *naturally* depraved, but if they are often depraved *in fact*—however unnaturally—is not this problem enough? It is something, no doubt, that men are not hypocrites and humbugs, but if they are insufferably vain—is not this problem enough? It is something, no doubt, that there should be vital heroes to give us a glimpse of what life might be like, but if they are stabbed to death, crucified, burnt at the stake, can we be simple-minded progressives, warmhearted sentimentalists?

That Shaw's comedies are built upon flinty conflicts we have abundantly seen. But what view of man, what philosophy of comedy is implied? The human mind, he says, though not depraved, is unable to face reality except in the disguise of comforting illusions. "Men are for the most part so constituted that realities repel and illusions attract them." This is the human condition that underlies the comedy of conceit. The vital characters are those who are most free of illusions. The artificial systems are the illusions themselves—illusions which the world knows as philosophies, conventions, professional codes. Doubtless in his earliest plays Shaw too simply championed reality against illusion. In merely inverting melodrama, he was himself a melodramatist. But already in *Caesar* there are the complications we have noticed. In *John Bull* we learn that illusions actually help a certain kind of successful man. In *The Doctor's Dilemma* the heroine's illusion that the rascally Dubedat was not only a great artist but a king of men proves to be the noblest sentiment in the play. And in *Saint Joan* the fight is not between illusion and reality but between illusion and illusion, reality and reality. If in *Candida* disillusionment was, for Morell, a culmination and, for Shaw, a conclusion, in *Heartbreak House* it is scarcely more than a beginning. The characters in this play are readers of Bernard Shaw. They love removing veils. In fact under the pressure of their spiritual voyeurism the businessman Mangan breaks down and hysterically starts taking his clothes off. Later, the "hero" of *Too True To Be Good* is distressed by "the nakedness of the souls who until now have always disguised themselves from one another in beautiful impossible idealisms." Nakedness is not preferable to a beautiful impossible disguise. For Shaw was no longer naive enough to think that anyone knows the truth by simple commonsense and emancipation from current fallacies. He distinguishes not between mask and face but between good and bad masks:

> No frontier can be marked between drama and history or religion, or between acting and conduct, nor any distinction made between them that is not also the distinction between the masterpieces of the great dramatic poets and the commonplaces of our theatrical seasons.

Shaw's essay "The Illusions of Socialism" is the best general statement of the view of life that is concretely bodied forth in the plays. The opening sentences are:

> Do not suppose that I am going to write about the illusions of Socialism with the notion of saving anyone from them. Take from the activity of mankind that part of it which consists in the pur-

suit of illusions, and you take out the world's mainspring.

If life were a fight between people with illusions and people without them it would be a melodrama. One of the great sources of comedy is the fact that the elements are mixed. There is in each of us a constant interaction of reality and illusion. The paradox of the human mind is that even when it reaches reality it has arrived there along the road of illusion. In fact Shaw classifies as a necessary illusion "the guise in which reality must be presented before it can rouse a man's interest or hold his attention or even be consciously apprehended by him at all."

Now the necessity of illusions is a notion familiar to all readers of modern literature. On the stage the notion has been brilliantly used by Pirandello, and clumsily by Eugene O'Neill, for its pathos and horror. Shaw's use of it ought to be praised not because it is more cheerful and amusing (anyone can be an optimist even in these days) but because it is cheerful *and* pathetic, amusing *and* horrible. Shaw, as much as Marx or Hegel but after his own fashion, sees life as the interaction of opposites. Though one cannot have—one cannot bear—reality without illusions, one also cannot have illusions without stumbling occasionally upon realities. The superior man—whether man of action or seer or both—is the man who is free of the cruder illusions. Hence, the scale of relatively high and low Shavian characters is a necessary part of the comedy of illusion and reality. It is not a matter of putting on the stage clever people who spout Shavian epigrams. It is a matter of showing higher and lower products of the life force, people who can bear more or less of life without illusion. Obviously some of the finest Shavian characters will be the higher rather than the lower products of the Life Force, and this is something new, though surely not reprehensible, in comedy. Designating Shaw as "the only dramatist of genius now alive in Europe," Rémy de Gourmont added by way of explanation: "his dramas are the only ones which give intimations of a lofty and profoundly original life." To do this is no doubt to have given to comedy as personal a twist as Ibsen had given to tragedy. For the "lofty and original life" is not confined to such Utopian visions as the later plays of *Back to Methuselah* which indeed are neither comedy nor good drama of any sort. It is constantly shown in contrast to the corseted existence of the professional types. Shaw observes in *Man and Superman* that dramatists frequently announce that their heroes are geniuses and seldom give any evidence of the fact. This certainly could not be said of his line of men of action and thought or of his women. These people are not the disembodied supermen of *Back to Methuselah*. Though superior they are fleshed and blooded creatures of our world. In proportion as they have freed themselves from illusion, their convictions and their characters are supported, says Shaw, by the

> primal republican material—that sense of the sacredness of life which makes a man respect his fellow without regard to his social work or intellectual class, and recognizes the fool of Scripture only in those people who refuse to be bound by any relations except the personally luxurious

181

ones of love, admiration, and identity of political
opinion and religious creed.

This is the view of men one finds in Shaw's plays. Beside
Molière's, or any other man's, can one say that it is so
personal, so narrow, so superficial? I cannot think so. The
conflict between reality and illusion, vitality and artificial
system, naturalness and conceit, spontaneity and rationali-
zation is no peculiar ideological structure. It is the pri-
mordial antithesis of development and petrifaction,
growth and decay, life and death. And in Shavian comedy
it is presented in traditional forms, such as the contrast
of amateur and professional, ironist and impostor. Bernard Shaw, as we have seen, is conservative after his own
fashion. Although like every master of comedy he is
didactic and up to the chin in his own time, he is not a
propagandist in the sense that his people are either children of light or children of darkness or in the sense that
his plays have neat unambiguous theses. He stands for
society against anti-social conspiracies, he stands for style
against fashion, for man against the machinery of living,
and for life—"life with a blessing"—against any particular
"idea" whatsoever.

4. THE FOOL IN CHRIST

1

*For we are made a spectacle unto the world, and
to angels, and to men. We are fools for Christ's
sake.*

—*I Corinthians, IV, 9–10.*

WHAT IS THE SIGNIFICANCE OF BERNARD SHAW'S CAREER? TO
think of his life and personality is, unfortunately, to think
chiefly of the trivial anecdotes one has heard, anecdotes
which show Shaw to be many-sided, resourceful, well-
informed, brilliant, kind, generous, or, alternatively,
flippant, hasty, prejudiced, impudent and so forth. Shaw
as a person—a person who makes remarks, chops wood,
and occasionally sprains his ankle—is all too familiar to
us. He himself has confessed that his life is in most ways
unremarkable. In the thick skein of uneventful narrative
set before us by his biographers can one not discern a
scarlet thread of meaning?

In a sense what we are looking for is not biography at all. In a sense Shaw has no biography. Writing of himself in the third person—a symbolic act—he once told Mrs. Patrick Campbell:

> He is a mass of imagination with no heart. He is a writing and talking machine. . . . He cares for nothing really but his mission, as he calls it, and his work.

When George Sylvester Viereck questioned Shaw about his quiet way of life, Shaw replied:

> An author of my sort must keep in training like an athlete. How else could he wrestle with God as Jacob did with the angel?

We have to do here with a man who has scarcely been a private person at all, one who has accepted the challenge and example of Jesus to forego the family pleasures of *l'homme moyen sensuel* for a higher calling. Shaw said: "You cannot serve two divinities, God and the person you are married to."

In the modern world what happens to a man with a mission of this kind? What today is the upshot of a life-long wrestle with God? And, since no man goes so far as he who knows not whither he is going, it is fair to ask also: was Shaw's mission what he thought it was? If not, what was it?

In 1876 an Irishman, aged twenty, went to live in London. Another twenty years had to pass before London was fully aware of the fact that it possessed a new critic, a new novelist, a new thinker, a new wit, and—rarest of all—a new dramatist. In the first decade of the twentieth century Shaw's reputation swept across America and Central Europe. After the death of Anatole France in 1924 he was the surviving Great Man of European letters. A new play by Shaw was now a world event. Between 1923 and 1925 the part of Saint Joan was enacted by Winifred Lenihan in America, Sybil Thorndike in England, Ludmilla Pitoëff in Paris, Elisabeth Bergner in Berlin. On the occasion of his seventieth birthday a *New York Times* editorial declared Shaw "probably the most famous of living writers." Soon the fame won by plays and books was doubled by the fame won by his films. Shaw's opinions on everything were reported in the press almost weekly. Has any other writer ever been so famous? Has any other writer ever had half as much written about him during his lifetime? (Since about 1905 a considerable number of articles has appeared every single year. About forty whole books have been written about him.) Was there ever a success story like this in the whole history of literature? True, none of his books has sold like *Gone With the Wind,* none of his plays has run as long as *Tobacco Road.* But, even by the economic criterion, Shaw's career was 'sounder' than any merely popular writer's, for his books have gone on selling indefinitely and his plays have returned to the stage again and again. True, as a 'best-selling classic' Shaw does not rival Shakespeare or the Bible. But then it takes the death of its author to put the final seal of respectability upon a classic. And Shaw refuses to die.

If, as Freud says, the life of the artist is a quest for honor, riches, fame, love, and power, Shaw must be one of the most successful men who ever lived. Then why is he, rather obviously, a sad old man? Because he is sorry to leave a world which he has so brilliantly adorned? That is too shallow an explanation. Honor, riches, fame, the love of women, these he has been granted in abundance. Yet the striking thing about Shaw is his relative aloofness from all these worldly advantages. He talks about them all as if they belonged to somebody else whose name happened to be George Bernard Shaw. But Freud mentioned a fifth goal: power. And this Shaw has only had to the same extent as any other wealthy writer, and that is to a very small extent indeed. Not that Shaw wanted to be Prime Minister. The only time Shaw stood as candidate in a large-scale election his abstention from demagogy amounted to a Coriolanus-like repudiation of his electors. When the electors repudiated *him* they were returning a compliment. This was not the kind of power Shaw wanted. Crude personal ambition is something he scarcely understands. What he did feel was the consciousness of great spiritual resources within him, the consciousness of a mission, of, as he put it, being used by something larger than himself. When, therefore, people paid attention to the ego of Shaw and not to the message of Shaw, when they paid attention to the small and not to the large thing, that was the ultimate catastrophe. More plainly put, Shaw's aim has been to change our minds and save civilization; but we are still in the old ruts and civilization has gone from bad to worse. For Shaw this must be the cardinal fact of his career. "I have produced no permanent impression because nobody has ever believed me." Anyone who knows Shaw's aims and attitudes knows that this is as complete a confession of failure as the aging Carlyle's famous sentence: "They call me a great man now, but not one believes what I have told them." Three years after Carlyle's death Shaw wrote on behalf of the peaceful Fabians "that we had rather face a Civil War than such another century of suffering as this has been." And then came, of all things,—the twentieth century, the age of Wilhelm II, Tojo, and Hitler! In 1932 Shaw was again addressing the Fabians. He said: "For 48 years I have been addressing speeches to the Fabian Society and to other assemblies in this country. So far as I can make out, those speeches have not produced any effect whatsoever."

"What of it?" some will be content to say, reconciling themselves with cynical ease to the ways of the world. Why should Shaw think he can change civilization by thinking, writing, and talking? To think so, says one of his Marxist critics, is "the bourgeois illusion." Winston Churchill does not use the Marxist vocabulary but his essay on Shaw, in *Great Contemporaries,* conveys a similar contempt. He will accept Shaw only on condition that he does not ask to be taken seriously. He ignores Shaw's repeated assertion: "The real joke is that I am in earnest."

The fact that Shaw has been easy to brush off can be explained by the method which he has used to spread his fame, a method he expounded forty years ago with characteristic frankness:

> I may dodder and dote; I may potboil and plati-
> tudinize; I may become the butt and chopping-
> block of all the bright original spirits of the rising

187

generation; but my reputation shall not suffer; it
is built up fast and solid, like Shakespeare's, on
an impregnable basis of dogmatic iteration.

And again:

> In order to gain a hearing it was necessary for me
> to attain the footing of a privileged lunatic with
> the license of a jester. My method is to take the
> utmost trouble to find the right thing to say and
> then to say it with the utmost levity.

The lunatic jester was named "G.B.S.," a personage who
from the start was known to many more people than Bernard Shaw could ever hope to be, a Funny Man, whose
perversities were so outrageous that they could be forgiven only on the assumption that they were not intended,
whose views and artistic techniques seemed to be arrived
at by the simple expedient of inverting the customary.
Unfortunately Bernard Shaw proved a sorcerer's appren-
tice: he could not get rid of "G.B.S." The very method by
which Shaw made himself known prevented him from
being understood. The paradox of his career—for the
paradoxer is himself a paradox—is that he should have
had so much fame and so little tangible and positive influence.

The mask of clowning in Shaw's career has as its counterpart the mask of clowning, of farce and melodrama,
of *kitsch* and sheer entertainment, in his plays. Of this
second mask a great theatrical critic, Egon Friedell, re-
marked that it was clever of Shaw so to sugar his pill but
that it was even cleverer of the public to lick off the sugar

and leave the pill alone. In that battle with his audience which is a principal conflict in Shavian drama, in that battle with the public which is the main conflict in everything that Shaw writes or says, the audience, the public, has won. "I have solved practically all the pressing questions of our time," Shaw says, "but . . . they keep on being propounded as insoluble just as if I had never existed."

To gain an audience he invented a method and assumed a pose. They gained him his audience but prevented him from exerting the kind of influence he was interested in. "My reputation shall not suffer:" it was an idle vow. One can see exactly how Shaw's reputation fared both at the hands of the intelligentsia and of the general public.

With the intelligentsia Shaw scored a temporary success. As Edmund Wilson puts it:

> Here in this black arrowy figure, this lovely cultivated voice, is the spirit which for those of us who were young when Shaw had reached the high pitch of his power, permeated our minds for a time, stirring new intellectual appetites, exciting our sense of moral issues, sharpening the focus of our sight on the social relations of our world till we could see it as a vividly lit stage full of small distinct intensely conceived characters explaining their positions to each other. An explanation that burned like a poem.

Mr. Wilson is certainly right in locating Shaw's influence chiefly in the generation that was growing up in the early

189

years of this century. No one will ever be able to say how many minds Shaw changed at that time, how many young men and women, under his spell, began to question marriage, the family, education, science, religion and—above all—capitalism. The number must be much larger than that directly reached by more celebrated opinion-makers such as Marx, Darwin, or Freud.

And yet it was not what Shaw was after. Prodigious as it was, this influence was negative. Shaw was regarded as an iconoclastic publicist and no more. His name was linked with that of Wells or, at best, Anatole France. People were willing to go with Shaw when, in his biographer's words, he attacked the seven deadly sins of "respectability, conventional virtue, filial affection, modesty, sentiment, devotion to woman, romance." All this fell in with the anti-Victorian reaction. But what were the bright and original spirits of the rising generation to make of a declaration that "conscience is the most powerful of all the instincts and the love of God is the most powerful of all the passions"? At that point Bernard Shaw ceased to be useful to them. The religious ones suspected a hoax, the anti-religious ones feared that Shaw's arteries were hardening. Religious and anti-religious repudiated or ignored the positive content of Shavianism—and became the Lost Generation.

A *Nation* editorial of October 1909 already reflects new departures:

> The time has come . . . when the insolent Shavian advertising no longer fills us with astonishment or discovery, or disables our judgment

from a cool inspection of the wares advertised.
The youthful Athenians who darted most im-
petuously after his novelties are already hanker-
ing after some new thing. The deep young souls
who looked to him as an evangelist are beginning to see through him and despair.

The occasion of these patronizing remarks was the publication of Chesterton's brilliant book (still the best) on
Shaw which, despite Chesterton's avowed dislike of "time
snobbery," was an attempt to make Shaw sound dated.
In 1913 D. H. Lawrence wrote that there ought to be a
revolt against the generation of Shaw and Wells. In the
same year a young English critic, Dixon Scott, who was
soon after to be killed at Gallipoli, interpreted Shaw, in
one of the few really good essays ever written about him,
as essentially a child of London in the 'eighties. Shortly
after the First World War the leading poet of the new
generation, T. S. Eliot, was careful to put Shaw in his
place as an Edwardian, a quaint survivor from before the
flood. Several of the clever critics of this clever decade
wrote essays to prove Shaw an old fool.

What of the popular fame? Was it any kind of compensation for a bad literary reputation? During the first
decades "G.B.S." was a rather Dangerous Spirit, dis-
tinctly Mephistophelian, young, red-bearded, and aggres-
sive. No kind of philosopher can more easily be dismissed.
Eugene O'Neill's play *Ah, Wilderness* portrays the early
Shavian "influence" as a sort of measles which the more
literary high school boy must have and put behind him.
After the First World War, the great dividing line in

Shaw's career, "G.B.S." was regarded as rather 'cute,' a Santa Claus if not a Simple Simon. William Archer crowned his long series of attempts to discredit Shaw with a final blow: Shaw was a Grand Old Man. "Not taking me seriously," said Shaw, "is the Englishman's way of refusing to face facts." And by "the Englishman" Shaw has always meant Monsieur Tout-le-monde. "What is wrong with the prosaic Englishman is what is wrong with the prosaic men of all countries: stupidity."

The new "G.B.S." proved another spirit that could not be exorcised. And the new "G.B.S." was worse than the old, for fogies have even less influence than iconoclasts. "I see there is a tendency," Shaw—ever sensitive to the spirit of times—said in 1921, "to begin treating me like an archbishop. I fear in that case that I must be becoming a hopeless old twaddler." The old critics had at least feared and scorned Shaw. An admirer of the new sort wrote: "But I do not believe that we will thus scorn him or forget him when the irritation of his strictures on events that are close to our hearts or to our pride is removed." Unfortunately, for Shaw's purposes, irritation to our hearts and our pride was highly desirable, while praise for the irritator was neither here nor there. If the sheer rebelliousness of Mencken—whose first book of criticism (1905) happened to be the first book ever written about Shaw— was only a negative and distorted Shavianism, that is the only sort of Shavianism that has as yet had any currency at all. The people who have revered Shaw in his later years —revered him as patriarch, as senile prodigy—have not bothered to imbibe any of his teaching. This is best illustrated by the fact that Broadway, though always reluctant to stage anything but a new play, has revived old Shaw plays and made money with them, while his new plays have either been left alone or played to half-empty houses. It was not that Shaw's new plays were so obviously inferior to his old plays. They were in any case much better plays than most of those on Broadway. It was that Shaw was no longer welcome as a living force. He was a Classic, that is, the author of plays old and awesome enough to be innocuous.

When William Archer conferred the title of Grand Old Man, Shaw was not yet seventy. The wheel turned, and lo! an ancient of 75, 80, 85, 90. Diamond jubilees followed jubilees as the figure rose and rose. Now that Shaw is in his nineties—has not the phrase an odd ring to it?—some laugh with him and some laugh at him, some laugh sentimentally and some laugh superciliously. Few laugh in the true Shavian fashion—seriously. When a sphinx is both comic and talkative it is assumed that she has no secrets.

Shaw has a secret, though an open one. It is that his famous method, his pose of arrogance, was a deliberate strategy in an utterly altruistic struggle. It was precisely because Shaw was so unusually immune to the common frailties of vulgar ambition and rapacious egoism that he could adopt the manner of the literary exhibitionist without risk to his integrity. His campaign of self-promotion was not the campaign of a clever careerist who decides to secure at once by cunning what he will never secure later by genius. Shaw had artistic genius enough, and knew it. Only he was not primarily interested in artistic genius and artistic reputation. He wanted his pen to be his sword in a struggle that was more ethical than aesthetic. Wishing to change the world, he wished to speak to the public at large, not merely to his literary confreres. So he tried to put his genius at the service of his moral passion. He knew that this was to risk sacrificing altogether a high literary reputation (like, say, Henry James's); and the fact that his name is so often linked with the publicist Wells indicates that, for a time at least, Shaw has foregone that kind of reputation. The arrogant pose was an act of self-sacrifice. Shaw's modesty was offered up on the altar of a higher purpose. In order to be influential he consented to be notorious.

His failure was double. Willingly he forewent his literary reputation. Unwillingly he had to admit his lack of influence as a thinker. The term Artist-Philosopher which Shaw coined for himself is perhaps a concealed admission that both as artist and as philosopher he had failed to convince his audience.

2

If this were the whole story Shaw would of course be no more important than a hundred other men who have abandoned art for 'action' or propaganda without making any noticeable dent in the world's armour. Shaw's is a more complicated case. If he is today a sad old man it cannot be himself that he has found disappointing. His unhappiness is not that of a self-made man finding that success does not bring contentment. It is *us* he is disappointed in. It is modern civilization he grieves over. To the man who now proceeds to ask: but is not Shaw one of us? is he not an integral part of modern civilization? one would have to reply: his ideas are indeed typically modern, a sort of synthesis of all our romanticism and realism, our traditionalism and our revolutionism, yet he himself is not one of us. He is further apart from his contemporaries than any thinker since Nietzsche. Let us take another look at his career.

Shaw was born and bred a Protestant in the most fanatically Catholic city in the world. That is his situation in a nutshell. His home, far from being one of puritanic pressures like Samuel Butler's, was one of abnormally tepid relationships. From the beginning Shaw was encouraged to be independent. Practically the only thing his education taught him was how to stand alone. His keenest pleasures were those which the imagination could feast on without intrusion from people around him; when he speaks of his voluptuous youth he means he read novels, wandered round an art gallery, revelled in opera and melodrama. Since his schooling was as untyrannical as his home he was largely unaffected by it. The first time he felt the pressure of society was when he became a clerk. It was too much for him. He broke with his whole environment by going to seek his fortune in London. If he lived with his mother there, it was only to save money. Mother and son continued to see little of each other.

Shaw entered British society by the Bohemian gate. He never tried to become an established member of the upper, middle, or lower class. He remained "unassimilated." His first circle of acquaintance consisted largely of musicians, his later circle of writers and actors. Even his journalistic experience did not bring Shaw into overmuch contact with the general run of men. As book reviewer, art, drama, and music critic, he worked at home, at the gallery, the theatre, and the concert hall, not at the office. A brief connection with the telephone business convinced Shaw over again that he must never try to "earn an honest living."

Of course, from 1882 on, Shaw was a socialist, addressed mass audiences, served on committees, was elected borough councillor, stood as candidate for the London County Council. But how far all this work was from any mingling with the working class, the middle class, or any class except that of intellectuals is clear to anyone who studies the life of Shaw in particular or the history of the Fabian Socialists in general. The Fabian Society of the early years should be thought of less as one of the several branches of the British Labor movement than as one of the many societies for intellectuals which abounded in Victorian, and especially late-Victorian, England. One might almost say that the Fabians were nearer to the Aesthetes than to the Trade Unions. In some respects theirs was but another form of Bohemianism. "Instead of velvet jackets and a slap-dash joviality," as Dixon Scott put it, the young writers of the 'eighties "took to *saeva indignatio* and sandals," to "Jaeger and Ibsen and Esoteric Buddhism." "They became infidels," he adds, "atheists, anarchists, cosmogonists, vegetarians, antivivisectionists, anti-vaccinationists." Far from involving Shaw personally in ordinary British society, socialism helped to keep him out of it. And for good. For he married a wealthy Fabian in 1898, and in the twentieth century has barely pretended to be a part of our world at all. At best he descends upon us from his country house at Ayot

St. Lawrence like a prophet descending from mountain solitude.

If this version of Shaw's career seems fanciful, turn to the last page of the preface to *Immaturity*, the long essay which is the nearest approach to an autobiography that Shaw will ever write. Calling himself "a sojourner on this planet rather than a native of it," Shaw continues:

> Whether it be that I was born mad or a little too sane, my kingdom was not of this world: I was at home only in the realm of my imagination, and at my ease only with the mighty dead. Therefore I had to become an actor, and create for myself a fantastic personality fit and apt for dealing with men, and adaptable to the various parts I had to play as author, journalist, orator, politician, committeeman, man of the world and so forth. In this I succeeded later on only too well. In my boyhood I saw Charles Mathews act in a farce called *Cool as a Cucumber*. The hero was a young man just returned from a tour of the world, upon which he had been sent to cure him of an apparently hopeless bashfulness; and the fun lay in the cure having overshot the mark and transformed him into a monster of outrageous impudence. I am not sure that something of the kind did not happen to me; for when my imposture was at last accomplished, and I daily pulled the threads of the puppet who represented me in the public press, the applause that greeted it was

197

not unlike that which Mathews drew in *Cool as
a Cucumber*. . . . At the time of which I am
writing, however, I had not yet learned to act,
nor come to understand that my natural character was impossible on the great London stage.
When I had to come out of the realm of imagination into that of actuality I was still uncom-
fortable. I was outside society, outside politics,
outside sport, outside the church. If the term had
been invented then I should have been called
the Complete Outsider.

Shaw—a man with no country, no party, no class, no
coterie, no regular job—was certainly an Outsider. Nor,
as we have seen, was the ruse by which he sought to get
Inside by any means successful. The "fantastic personality" of "G.B.S." was not really "fit and apt for dealing with
men" at all. But Shaw makes a point in this passage in
1921 which he had not made twenty years earlier (in the
confession quoted above—p. 188—where his ruse is interpreted as *simply* a propagandist trick). The later passage
amounts to saying that the ruse also served as an adjustment, necessary for Shaw's peace of mind, to the alien
world. "I was . . . at my ease only with the mighty dead.
Therefore I had to become an actor and create for myself
a fantastic personality."

At this point Shaw's career is revealed to us as something more than a picturesque misadventure, and Shaw
as something more than a frustrated teacher or a frustrated man of action. Of course he *is* a frustrated teacher
to some extent. All teachers are. But he is not a man of

action at all. "I lacked both cruelty," he once said, "and the will to victory." He is an artist, and therefore, whatever his didactic urge, whatever the naturalistic ardor with which he seeks to portray the outer world, he gives expression to his own nature and tells the story of himself. In the art of persuasion one Hitler or one Hearst is worth a thousand Shaws. The fact that Shaw did not descend to the methods of the politician, let alone of the demagogue, would indicate that—in spite of himself—he was not fundamentally a propagandist. Why invent a fantastic personality like "G.B.S." when with the talents of a Bernard Shaw and a modicum of tact you might just as easily become the first editorial writer or columnist of the age? This is perhaps the one question about himself that Shaw could not answer.

Yet a kind of answer is to be found in the foreword to his Prefaces. When remarking that the good advice of the Gospels, Dickens, Plato, has never been heeded, Shaw says:

> You may well ask me why, with such examples before me, I took the trouble to write them. I can only reply that I do not know. There was no why about it: I had to: that was all.

A cryptic solution? To those who know their Shaw it recalls the statement in "The Sanity of Art": "We are afraid to look life in the face and see in it, not the fulfilment of a moral law or of the deductions of reason, but the satisfaction of a passion in us of which we can give no account whatever." To satisfy passions we do many things because we "have to"—there is "no why about it."

If the passion is a sufficiently high one the action is justi-fied.

Shaw's passions are high. In the preface to *Immaturity* a passage following the one cited above in which Shaw calls himself an Outsider explains that in a higher realm he was an Insider. This is the realm of the spirit.

> The moment music, painting, literature, or sci-ence came into question the positions were re-versed: it was I who was the Insider. I had the intellectual habit; and my natural combination of critical faculty with literary resource needed only a clear comprehension of life in the light of intelligible theory: in short, a religion, to set it in triumphant operation.

One thinks of John Tanner, the man of ideas who in this world of ours is rightly regarded as even more a gasbag than an iconoclast, but who in the realm of the spirit, as Don Juan Tenorio, is a true master.

Whatever his duties to us, Shaw had his duty to him-self. Whatever his function as a deliberate preacher Shaw also knew himself to be a *force* that had to act according to the inscrutable laws of its own nature. He was being used—for an unknown purpose—through the agency of a passion "of which we can give no account whatever." This passion led the man who thought of himself as a propagandist to what looks like the weakest and most un-promising of all propagandist media—the theatre. We have seen how Shaw's plays are much more successful as art than as propaganda. Shaw proved to be a very accom-plished playwright. But what attracted him to the theatre in the first place? He tells us jokingly that having accepted a critical brief for the New Drama he had to manufacture the evidence by writing "new" plays himself. And one knows that many of his plays had an "accidental" origin, were written for an occasion and on request. If, however, evidence were needed that Shaw turned to the theatre for other than accidental reasons one might find it precisely in the nature of the plays he supplied to those who requested them. Walkley asked for a play on love. Yeats asked for a play suitable to the Abbey Theatre. Archer asked for a play on death. Result: *Man and Superman, John Bull's Other Island, The Doctor's Dilemma*!

It has often been said that Shaw made a false start as an artist by writing five novels. "The novel," says Mr. Ronald Peacock, "with all its apparatus of description and report is a bore to him." On the other hand critics have often complained that his plays are too novelistic, that they contain too many descriptions and reports. Shaw's official biographer actually finds the essential technical feature of dramatic modernism to be "the employment of the technical methods of fiction." Yet the adoption of drama as his chosen medium was for Shaw much more than a matter of his own technical accomplishments. It was a matter of audience and his attitude to audience. To quote Mr. Peacock again:

> The audience of the novel is the individual; and the object of Shaw's criticism is society. In the theatre he catches three large groups who together make up the whole of mankind except its eccentrics: those interested in entertainment,

201

those interested in ideas, and those interested in art. He catches them, moreover, in their social agglomeration and cohesiveness—his address is to society, and there it is assembled before the stage.

The truth is really much more complicated. The drama was *not* the splendid platform and megaphone which Mr. Peacock suggests. Shaw adopted it not only (as he may have thought) as a pulpit but as a means of expression. His whole nature is histrionic. By this I mean, not that he is a charlatan, or insincere, but that acting is his means of communication, which is another way of saying that he communicates, not directly, but by impersonation. Such a relation to things and to other people is not peculiar to Shaw. It is the psychology of the born playwright and the born actor. (The playwright is an actor who cannot act, the actor a playwright who cannot write.) Anyone who has seen Shaw on the screen or heard him on the radio has experienced the theatrical magic of Shaw's presence and Shaw's performance. In an essay which ridiculed Shaw a good deal, Edmund Wilson wrote of his appearance at the Metropolitan Opera House: "He continues to stand for something which makes us see audience and theatre as we have never quite seen them before." Shaw's figure, his twinkling eyes, his lithe gait, his magnificent head combine, as with an actor, to express his spirit.

Since Shaw had no place in bourgeois society and was unwilling to enter what has been called its ghetto—Bohemia—the theatre was the one place for him. Had he been able to believe its dogmas he would have been willing to join Chesterton in the church. At one time he could say "The drum and trumpet for me" and take his stand in Hyde Park with other revolutionary orators; but the platform satisfied only a fragment of his nature, which was that of an artist. Rather than hope to make an art out of streetcorner oratory, he would pretend—so his unconscious decided—to make streetcorner oratory out of an art, the art of drama. Critics say that Shaw quite "frankly" regards the theatre as his platform. Frankness is not what is involved. When he himself writes in an encyclopedia: "Mr. Bernard Shaw . . . substituted the theatre for the platform . . . as his chief means of propaganda," Shaw is making his excuses. Having chosen art rather than propaganda as his profession, he tries to make up for it by making his art as propagandist as possible, or rather—which is a different thing—by *saying* that his art is as propagandist as possible. By saying this Shaw gives critics their most powerful weapon against him; he enables them to say that he is condemned out of his own mouth. Not that there is anything untrue in the statement that Shavian drama is didactic and public. But it is personal and expressive as well, a fact which Shaw has been at some pains to conceal.

It is the very peculiar mixture of the public and the private which the theatre affords that makes it so apt to his needs. A play is a public occasion like a political meeting; it is a celebration like a church service; it is a performance like a concert; and it is a work of art communicated by impersonations, by masks. The theatre is a magical world within a world, more satisfactory for

203

Shaw's purpose and temperament than any other. He has always been thoroughly at home in it, though by no means at home in the larger world. Yet no wonder that a militant extrovert like H. G. Wells ridiculed Shaw for believing that a "boxed-up affair" like the theatre could have any general importance. This criticism of course could only make Shaw redouble his efforts to make the theatre a platform. He had (if I am right) entered the theatre because it was a world apart. The paradox of Shaw's art is that he spends his energies in refusing to let the theatre *remain* a world apart. If his artist's nature made him a theatre critic instead of a statesman, his puritan conscience made him use his critical articles for attacks on the conventions of art, on the pure artist Shakespeare (whom he regrettably preferred to Karl Marx), and on defenses of reality. If his artist's nature drove him to the "unreality" of the theatre, his puritan's conscience drove him to take "reality" with him. From beginning to end Shaw's drama expresses his nature much more than it champions particular doctrines. It even mirrors Shaw's life rather closely in a series of self-portraits. It is not of course true, despite H. G. Wells, that *all* Shaw's characters are Shaw—at least not in any obvious or important way. Nor can one, as Mr. Harold Laski and others have hinted, simply look for a character who talks a lot, who believes in socialism or creative evolution, and stamp him as Shaw. In *Candida* for example there is actually more of Shaw's philosophy, more of Shaw's plight too, in the Pre-Raphaelite poet Marchbanks than in the platform-speaking socialist Morell. These two characters might perhaps be taken as two halves of Shaw's nature: his outer, glib, and confident half, at once socialist and social, and his spiritual, lonely, and artistic half, the half that puts him beyond the pale of society. The secret in the poet's heart is the secret of Shaw the Outsider who is the real Insider, the man who is strong enough to leave the homestead and live with himself and his vision.

In the later plays perhaps the most interesting self-portraits are Captain Shotover in *Heartbreak House* and King Magnus in *The Apple Cart*. Both portray Shaw's role in modern civilization and especially in England. In *Heartbreak House,* England is represented as a ship, with no captain, heading for the rocks. In a ship within this ship—a house in which the only room we see is got up like a ship's cabin—lives Shotover, half lunatic, half sage, an ex-sailor who had sold himself to the devil at Zanzibar. He is conducting researches with the aim of discovering a death ray ostensibly "to blow up the human race if it goes too far." Either we must learn to respect justice as such, Shaw had once said in an essay, or we must acquire power to kill each other instantaneously by merely thinking. *Responsibility,* our supreme desideratum, must be attained by whatever method—if not by a passion for justice, then by the passion of fear. It is significant that Shaw does not present Shotover as a noble character but as a senile eccentric. As poignantly as Nietzsche Shaw recognizes his own limitation. Although Shotover marries a young woman, in sadly ironic recognition of the Shavian union of artist man and mother woman, he does not discover the death ray any more than England learns to respect justice. The end is chaos and misunderstanding.

The Apple Cart was discussed flat-footedly at the time

of its first productions as a play advocating monarchy. This is wholly to misunderstand Shavian method. The situation of the play—a king confronting his Labor cabinet—is actually a fantasy which, like all Shavian fantasies, has very concrete implications. The king is a philosopher-king. In fact he is Shaw (even to his private life which includes a humdrum wife whom he prefers to his romantic lady friend Orinthia. The friend is to Magnus what Mrs. Pat Campbell may have been to Shaw. She flirts with him but is not his mistress). The problem of the play is not King George versus Ramsay MacDonald but the question: who knows better what is going on and who is better fitted to cope with the situation, Bernard Shaw the artist-philosopher or Ramsay MacDonald the prime minister? Their common enemy is Breakages Limited, that is, capitalism, the sinister power which the critics took no notice of because it is not personified on the stage. It lurks in the background. Now just as in Shotover Shaw does not make himself patriarchal, so in Magnus he does not make himself majestic. It is not clear that Magnus could really have won if he had gone to the polls, as he threatened, against the politicians. It is not clear that the philosopher *can* replace the prime minister. No basic problems are cleared up at the end. We are left with the not very encouraging title of the play.

But perhaps the completest picture of what I have called "Shaw's role in modern civilization" was provided in *John Bull's Other Island*. As in *Man and Superman* Shaw represents himself by two characters and, as in *Candida*, the two Shaws are brought up against a more masterful person, one who really assumes that he—in

Candida, it is *she*—has inherited the earth. In *Candida* the emphasis is chiefly psychological. In *John Bull's Other Island* it is chiefly philosophic, a matter of rival outlooks. The enemy is not a charming lady but—the Shavian Englishman, the Shavian professional man, the Shavian politician, Broadbent, the two syllables of whose name tell us nearly all we need to know of him. Shaw himself, I have suggested, is part Larry Doyle, part Father Keegan, that is, partly the worldly Irishman whose realism drives him to have his revenge on England by "succeeding" as an Englishman, partly the divinely mad priest who believes (Shaw has been quoting the line ever since) that "every jest is an earnest in the womb of time."

There is no passage in Shaw that more clearly shows what he is for and what he is against, there is no passage that more openly reveals his estrangement from our world, than this brief encounter between Keegan and Broadbent:

> BROADBENT: I find the world quite good enough for me: rather a jolly place in fact.
> KEEGAN: You are satisfied?
> BROADBENT: As a reasonable man, yes. I see no evils in the world—except of course, natural evils —that cannot be remedied by freedom, self-government, and English institutions. I think so, not because I am an Englishman, but as a matter of commonsense.
> KEEGAN: You feel at home in the world then?
> BROADBENT: Of course. Don't you?
> KEEGAN: [*from the very depths of his nature.*] No.

207

BROADBENT: Try phosphorus pills. I always take them when my brain is over-worked. I'll give you the address in Oxford Street.

At the end of the play, when Larry Doyle again expresses his contempt for dreaming—it is Shaw's own contempt for illusions, for idealism—and Broadbent tells us he has dreamt of heaven as a dreadful place, "a sort of pale blue satin," Keegan gives us *his* dream. It is Shaw's own ideal, which he hopes is no illusion:

> In my dreams it is a country where the State is the Church and the Church the people: three in one and one in three. It is a commonwealth in which work is play and play is life: three in one and one in three. It is a temple in which the priest is the worshipper and the worshipper the worshipped: three in one and one in three. It is a godhead in which all life is human and all humanity divine: three in one and one in three.

But Father Keegan is obviously even madder than Captain Shotover. He summarizes his own vision: "It is in short the dream of a madman." To which Shaw's Englishman retorts: "What a regular old Church and State Tory he is! He's a character: he'll be an attraction here. Really almost equal to Ruskin and Carlyle." To which Shaw's other half, Larry Doyle, adds: "Yes: and much good *they* did with all their talk!"

Shaw's dream of a better world, his impatience with dreams of a better world, his idealism and his anti-idealism, his knowledge of the world of "Englishmen" and his alienation from this world—all these are implicit in the last pages of *John Bull's Other Island*. These are not pages of the Bernard Shaw the public knows. They are pages of the man who once wrote haughtily: "My heart knows only its own bitterness." They are pages of one whom the poet A.E. called a "suffering sensitive soul."

3

We are now in a position to see what Shaw's career means over and above the well-attested fact that he wanted to be taken seriously and was not taken seriously. We can see that Shaw is a clear case of misunderstood genius. But, lest the story sound too much like that of the operatic "clown with a broken heart," we must see also that Shaw never relaxed into self-pity, that his celebrated gayety is precisely a prophylactic against such relaxation, that, alienated as he was, Shaw made a very special and subtle adjustment. He turned his alienation to artistic and moral profit. He is one of the few important modern artists who have not been dismayed by their own estrangement.

Our times suffer from sick conscience, and our geniuses suffer with the times. Modern writers are mainly of two types. The first, to use Flaubert's figure, wants to vomit at the thought of the horror of our epoch, which it nevertheless is not afraid to look at. The second looks in the other direction and calls loudly for literary Uplift, Patriotism, and something Wholesome. Shaw belonged to the first group. He vomited, but eventually emerged from the vomitorium with an incredibly "optimistic" smile on

209

his face. Had he decided to join the second group? No, but he had decided that vomiting did no good, that the facts had to be faced but that they had also to be changed, and that if one is alienated from one's environment one can recognize the fact and—work out a plan of campaign. "If you cannot get rid of the family skeleton," he said, "you may as well make it dance." Shaw's older contemporary Nietzsche had come to a similar conclusion but had followed up his affirmations of health by losing his reason. Shaw found a happier, though in some ways no less desperate, solution: he pretended to have no reason to lose. If modern life was as unreasonable as King Lear, Shaw would cast himself as the Fool. Trace the word *mad* through his plays and you will find that many of the finest characters and the finest actions have it applied to them.

Accordingly I do not think Shaw, despite his cheerful and moralistic manner, can find a place in the paradise of the middle-brows. To be sure, there are subterraneous realms which Shaw never enters. Yet, like Ibsen, Shaw has had "a strange, fairy-tale fate," strange because in some ways so close to his age, and in others so remote from it, strange because it was so hard for him to communicate. The problem of communication in the arts is never simple. Is not the artist one who tries to communicate the incommunicable? For the modern artist the problem, I think, is especially acute. One might discuss all the oddities and heterodoxies of the modern arts in this context. Suffice it here that Bernard Shaw resorted to some very bizarre shifts. Living in this queer, disgusting age he found he had to give the impression that his highest quality—a sort of delicate spirituality, purity, or holiness—was fooling when what he meant was that his fooling was holy. The devil's advocate was almost a sort of saint. The clown was something of a superman.

Unlike Nietzsche who finished few of his major works, Shaw has been able to give his very remarkable mind full expression. And to express his mind was to express his age. If the eighteen-eighties—the decade in which Shaw's outlook was formed—can be represented as quaint and limited, if they were anxious, negative years in which the Victorian ground began to tremble beneath men's feet, they were also youthful, positive years of regrouping and reaffirmation. The new literary generation congratulated itself upon its New Spirit. It was another Romantic Movement, or, more accurately perhaps, a renewal of the earlier Romantic Movement. The earlier movement had been, among other things, a time of new faiths, the chief of which were faith in Nature, Beauty, and Humanity. In the course of the nineteenth century these faiths were increasingly separated from each other and reduced to particular dogmatic systems and cults such as the Simple Life Movement, the Aesthetic Movement, the Comtist Religion of Humanity. Shaw tried to reunite the once united Romantic faiths. For him the chief meaning of Evolution, for instance, was the sacred unity of Nature: a factor which might help us to understand even his vegetarianism. The experience of Beauty in the arts—especially in music—was to Shaw tantamount to mystical experience of the divine. The religion of Humanity found expression in his political and vital economics.

The identity of the new generation became more distinct between 1890 and 1910 (Shaw's heyday) when several rather well-defined schools of opinion were formed. The fundamental question was: what was your attitude to modern life? The principal division of opinion was between the "tough" school that ranged from advocates of scientific enlightenment like Havelock Ellis to advocates of virile adventure like W. E. Henley and the "tender" school that ranged from advocates of art like Ernest Dowson to advocates of Orthodoxy like Francis Thompson. Again Shaw's answer was not Either/Or but Both/And. The scientific New Spirit was not new to him since it was nothing less than the spirit of the mid-century which had reached him in his late boyhood, the spirit of Darwin, Huxley, and Tyndall. Shaw never gave up his evolutionism or his free thinking. His socialism, his athleticism, his puritanism also put him on the side of the "tough" school. On the other hand Shaw was with the tenderminded in being utterly the man of feeling for whom music was the most complete of the arts, a veritable substitute for religion. And he could sympathize with both the aesthetes and the neo-catholics in their protest against scientism and in their yearning for larger, finer imaginative satisfactions and attachments. Think of the outstanding English opinion-makers of the time—Wilde and Kipling, Chesterton and Wells—and you will see that Shaw's view of life is an attempt to accept and integrate all their best intuitions.

But even in that generation of opinion-making and stand-taking the view of life was not all. Indeed one of the views of life—aestheticism—was precisely that views of life are much less important than artistic form. If Shaw stands head and shoulders above, say, Wells and Chesterton, and I think he does, it is partly because he found in the drama a form through which his gifts could reach full and large expression. Chesterton's limitation is that he never really mastered any of the finer or larger forms: he remained a bellettrist. Wells, highly gifted as a story teller, despised his own medium of the novel and degenerated into an endlessly repetitious publicist. Shaw is repetitious, too, to be sure. But whereas Shaw repeats his positions with a difference and in a context that lives by its literary form, so that one is never bored and never feels that one has plucked out the heart of his mystery, Wells simply lectures on and on. Not only in theory, like Shaw, but also in practice, unlike Shaw, Wells tried to have content without form. Talented as an artist, he had no respect for art, and his contempt for Shaw is identical with his more well-known contempt for Henry James.

At the same time as he had worked out his view of life Shaw had forged himself an instrument for its expression: his prose-style. In his early works one can trace rather exactly its genesis and development. Shaw's earliest utterances—including a great part of the novels—are not written in the manner that has become Shaw's hallmark. They are written in a rather impersonal and colorless mid-Victorian style, formal and periodic without the distinction of the formal and periodic style at even its half best. The change came when Shaw the socialist speaker and journalist began to write more nearly as he talked. It turned out that formal prose had merely held Shaw in check, had kept the whole Shavian substance out of his writing. Colloquialism opened the gates to his humor, his passion, his torrential Irish eloquence, his polemics, to everything in fact that forms a part of his prodigious dialectic skill.

Few of Shaw's early readers were much aware of his style (which pleased Shaw, who wanted his style to be merely a means to a didactic end). But since 1900 colloquial prose has become so much more colloquial than Shaw's that everyone today recognizes in his style many of the vestiges of the formal procedure. The modern reader is free to realize that Shavian prose, so far from being artless and "natural" in the naive sense, is a subtle combination of the old and the new: a happy cross between Macaulay and good modern journalism. If it happily combines the freedom and swiftness and simplicity of the colloquial style with the firmness and solidity and elaboration of the periodic style is it not partly because the colloquial surface is firmly underpinned by periodic structure? When Shaw's prose is faulty, which it sometimes is, it is never through excessive informality and looseness but always through the over-involvement of rhetoric.

Shaw's style has been praised by critics who like very little else about Shaw, and so we have come to see in his eloquence and verbal dexterity an isolated thing. (This was presumably the danger Shaw himself had in mind when he wrote on Dixon Scott.) Those who see nothing in Shaw but a master of prose are usually the same people who regard the plays and the prefaces (including under the latter head Shaw's non-dramatic works as a whole) as all one. The complaint is that, as with Wells, the voice goes on and on, the work of art prolonging the preface.

In point of fact nothing is more profoundly characteristic of Shaw's mind and art than the division of function between preface and play. What play of Shaw's gives a four-square presentation of the topics discussed in the preface? What preface of Shaw's is either a summary of the play or a prologue to it? The full-dress Shavian preface, written after the play is produced, is not an introduction but a series of after-thoughts on the play or—more often—a treatise on the subject out of which the play arose. There is no overlapping between play and preface. *Back to Methuselah* is a fable of Creative Evolution, its preface a refutation of Darwinism. *Pygmalion* is about human character; its preface is about phonetics. *Mrs. Warren* and *Blanco Posnet* are about prostitution and religion respectively; their prefaces are chiefly about censorship.

The relation between preface and play is oblique. The preface may be a general treatise—a short book—on Christianity, Education, Marriage, Democracy. In the plays Shaw accepts the limitations and realizes the peculiar potentialities of the theatre. While the preface to *The Doctor's Dilemma* thrashes out the whole question of private practice and presents proposals for reform, the play contains only one allusion to socialized medicine and is taken up rather with human destinies which are seriously affected by the medical profession. Many people have been disappointed by *Getting Married* and *Misalliance* because the play seems to cover only a tiny portion of the area discussed in the preface. The fact is that in his plays Shaw is less concerned with area than with depth, less with the general topic than with the lives of men.

Preface and play differ radically both in form and content. They differ also in their origin, in their function as the expression of Shaw's mind. The preface gives you a relatively detached account of a subject. In it you learn what Shaw thinks the correct and incorrect views, what he thinks should be done and what should not be done about it. They are the work of conscious and deliberate thought. They are direct advocacy. When he writes a play, however, we know that Shaw gives himself up to his unconscious as readily as any surrealist. He does not know what he is going to write until he has written it, and having written claims no greater sureness of interpretation than any other critic. Thus we sometimes find between play and preface not merely a difference but a discrepancy. What Shaw the *philosophe* states to be so is not always what Shaw the poet finds to be so. Hence the preface to *John Bull* is a fine swaggering analysis of imperialism throughout which we feel that the outlook is indeed hopeful with men like Shaw on the job; the play expresses frustration and pain and shows obstacles in the path of anti-imperialist reform which lie deeper than politics. Preface and play are similarly contrasted in *The Apple Cart*. In addition Shaw here tries to correct his play by touching up the character of the prime minister in the preface (as we found him liberally filling out the character of Napoleon in a stage-direction). The critics have usually been wrong in suggesting that Shaw needs stage directions and prefaces because he cannot express himself in terms of the drama itself. The original purpose of Shaw's copious apparatus was the very legitimate one of preparing the play for readers as well as (not instead of) theatre goers. The occasional discrepancy between apparatus and play is a discrepancy between Shaw's opinions, which are based partly on desire (all thinking is wishful, he says), and his visions of life, which being an artist's vision is uncompromising and cannot disregard the fly in the ointment.

Those who find this kind of discrepancy pervasive will obviously believe Shaw to be a Mass of Contradictions. To my mind the discrepancy is very occasional. Much as he may have failed as the propagandist he wanted to be, Shaw has succeeded as the artist he was prepared not to be. True to Shavian formula the force that moved Shaw without his knowing whence or why was wiser than his conscious intention. If one can see this, one can see that even the creation of the "fantastic personality" was not merely the mistake of a bad strategist. Shaw's creation of "G.B.S." was not solely the deliberate, Machiavellian creation he tells us about. It too was created by the Life Force, by the World's Will. By all means it is a mask. But then it is part of the Shavian philosophy that life offers us not a choice between face and mask but only a choice between one mask and another. The "natural character" which he calls "impossible on the great London stage," the stammering blushing young Protestant from Dublin, this also was a "role," though a bad one. Silly and self-defeating as "G.B.S." can be, he too has his divine spark. "Every jest is an earnest in the womb of time"—even the jests of a foolish-looking mask. By means of humor not only

217

could Shaw consciously evade punishment like a court jester. He could, perhaps unconsciously, express with a brave gesture the failure of so many of his pet ideas. Exaggerating this, Mr. Auden says that Shaw's humor is an admission that Shaw's ideas are not true. It is almost an admission, at any rate, that if his views aren't true, it doesn't—beyond a certain point—matter. In the end Shaw escapes from ideas, as Mr. Eliot says a first-rate mind should, and, in the defeat of his ideas, is a nobly tragic—or should one say comic?—figure. His levity, moreover, has its status and its value as a much-needed protest against the smug "spirit of gravity" which Nietzsche, another practitioner of *gaya scienza,* rightly found to be one of the ugliest diseases of our pseudo-scientific era. If man is not a moral animal, let us all shoot ourselves. If he *is* a moral animal, then pessimism is an irresponsible pose. Skeletons must be made to dance. "Supposing the world were only one of God's jokes, would you work any the less to make it a good joke instead of a bad one?"

If a teacher is one who helps others to learn, learning being something you do for yourself, a propagandist might be defined as one who wishes to save you the trouble of learning—you take his word for it. A failure as a propagandist, Shaw may prove not to have been a failure as a teacher. *John Bull's Other Island* does not solve the Irish problem. It does not, as many political plays have tried to do, send the audience rushing out to take action. Nor does it present a situation with the merely external truth ('objectivity') of naive naturalists. When Shaw feels the importance of a human situation he presents it truthfully—that is to say, in its manysidedness—

218

and with a passionate accuracy that betokens commitment without prejudice. This is teaching. Shaw's plays are not, though they seem to be, entertainments with propaganda awkwardly added. When they are faulty it is the 'entertainment' that is awkwardly added—added to the art, added to the didacticism, added as a sheer redundancy.

The fact that Shaw really wrote because he "had to" (and not to change the world) was fortunate in one respect: by not saving the world he saved his drama as art and, therefore, as teaching. Having obeyed the Life Force, having lived out his destiny, having worn the mask of the madman "G.B.S." without really knowing why, Shaw will leave us a rich legacy. We may learn in time not to despise even the mask, much less Bernard Shaw. The influence of propagandists is prodigious; that of teachers is lamentably small. Yet if we believe the influence of the latter to be entirely negligible we are cynics. Only if we find in it a solace and a hope are we men.

APPENDIX TO THE SECOND EDITION
(1957): SHAW AND THE ACTORS

IT IS PROBABLY ESTABLISHED BY NOW—IF SUCH THINGS
ever get to be established—that Bernard Shaw was an
artist. His plays have come to be accepted as plays. A
member of the youngest generation might be at a loss
to know how they could ever have failed to be so considered. The dramaturgy seems so much firmer and more
assured than that of these latter days; nor can it be
placed in the dreary pigeonhole of Naturalism or Social
Drama. "To combine a mirror-like exactness of character-
drawing with the wildest extravagances of humorous expression and grotesque situation"—Shaw described his
own art in defining that of Dickens. Do we realize even
today how far from Naturalism Shaw was? Contrasting
himself with Archer, he wrote in *The Saturday Review*:

> To me the play is only the means, the end being
> the expression of feeling by the arts of the actor,
> the poet, the musician. Anything that makes this

expression more vivid, whether it be versifica-
tion, or an orchestra, or a deliberately artificial
delivery of the lines, is so much to the good for
me, even though it may destroy all the verisimilitude of the scene.

I select this particular quotation from the many on Naturalism that I have copied into my notebooks because it
stresses the theatrical side of Shaw's art—a side which
will tend, perhaps, to be neglected as the memory of
Shaw's work with the actors in the theatre recedes. It
was even slighted in the first edition of this book; which
is my excuse for the appendix now.

The history of the modern drama begins with Shaw
the actor. As he records it in his foreword to Lillah Mc-
Carthy's autobiography:

. . . at the first performance of *A Doll's House*
in England, on a first floor in a Bloomsbury lodg-
ing house, Karl Marx's youngest daughter
played Nora Helmer, and I impersonated Krog-
stad at her request with a very vague notion of
what it was all about.

Yet the acting he stood for was not the kind most of us
associate with Ibsen:

In a generation which knew nothing of any sort
of acting but drawingroom acting, and which
considered a speech of more than twenty words
impossibly long, I went back to the classical
style and wrote long rhetorical speeches like
operatic solos, regarding my plays as musical

221

performances precisely as Shakespeare did. As a producer I went back to the forgotten heroic stage business and the exciting or impressive declamation I had learnt from oldtimers like Ristori, Salvini, and Barry Sullivan.

Shaw's piece on the actor John Hare (a contribution to *The Saturday Review*) is the classic analysis and destruction of the "cup-and-saucer" or "garden party" theatre of Naturalism. His pieces on the heroic acting of Forbes-Robertson recall Hazlitt's on the romantic acting of Edmund Kean: in both cases analysis is the handmaid of admiration and delight, and great acting is preserved for posterity in great words. Whoever would play Shaw's Caesar must remember that the character was created by the critic who wrote that Robertson "restored the perspectives of the stage with the character actor in his place in the middle distance and the classic actor sunlike above the horizon."

Garden parties are attended also by ladies. Shaw found the Victorian lady-actress even less acceptable than the Victorian gentleman-actor. The actress, just as obviously as the actor, embodies the established ideal of the society she belongs to. What the cover girl is to Main Street, the lady actress was to the upper middle class that dominated high theatre in Victorian London. Perhaps the quickest way of indicating her character for the modern reader is to say she resembled Dickens' anemic heroines. Shaw described her in *The Saturday Review* as "the brainless-susceptible woman" and called for a "clever-positive type" to replace her.

222

APPENDIX TO THE SECOND EDITION (1957)

He had met the clever-positive type in life. One of the leading actresses in this vein was Florence Farr, who was successively—improbable as it sounds—mistress to Shaw and Yeats; another was Henry James' friend, Elizabeth Robbins; a third, Janet Achurch, wife of a prominent Fabian. Perhaps, indeed, the only place where the theatres of Ibsen and Shaw truly meet is in these actresses. Victorian ladies couldn't act either Ibsen or Shaw; the post-Victorians might logically go, as Florence Farr did, from one to the other. We shall never know which helped Shaw more toward the creation of his own great female roles, Ibsen or the actresses who played him.

Yet there were better actresses than these. Shaw saw them; and formed his notion of what woman could be on the stage from seeing, in particular, two of them: Mrs. Patrick Campbell and Ellen Terry. Though Shaw the man knew Mrs. Campbell better—in all the ordinary senses of the verb to know—I should be inclined to think that Ellen Terry meant much more to Shaw the artist. Mrs. Campbell he only fell in love with; he was having the measles of the middle aged. Miss Terry he adored, as we very properly say, "from afar"; that is to say, from an aisle seat or a writing table. She was for him a loadstar, the *ewig weibliche*, the Idea of an Actress. If Mrs. Campbell "is" Orinthia in *The Apple Cart*, Miss Terry is not only Lady Cicely in *Captain Brassbound's Conversion*, she is the spirit of woman as it is found, mischievously or benignly, through all Shaw's *oeuvre*. She is also Shaw's Idea of an Actress—though this expression is too abstract to suggest the kind of inspiration which a creator of great roles for women can draw from a woman playing great

223

roles. When *Fanny's First Play* came out, everyone talked of *votes* for women; today, surely, we'd say: What *roles* for women!

To know something of the performers Shaw either saw or worked with, or both, is to learn something about the characters he created and also—as I shall now proceed to indicate—of the fullness of his interest in, and mastery of, the theatrical medium. That he did master that medium has been questioned not only by the generation that dismissed him as a "publicist, not an artist" but also by many theatre people since. I have heard a leading director describe Shaw as "dead on one side"; Edith Evans is reported to have said that he showed himself, in rehearsal, to be an "awful ham"; and *Misalliance* was said to have succeeded at The New York City Center not long ago because it was re-interpreted in a highly un-Shavian light.

It can surely be admitted that there are theatrical values which find no place in a Shavian play, but of what playwright could that not be said? Is Molière dead on one side because he didn't write *Phèdre* too? I can believe Dame Edith to be right—if all she means is that Shaw was not a *trained* actor and therefore was clumsy in his demonstrations. But still, if he got his meaning across to the actors? Surely it would be premature to assume that there are people who know how to do Shaw better than he did himself.

Admittedly, you can make a problematic artist palatable by removing the problem. The problem of acting Shaw is to render the long speeches; to cut them is mere evasion. As for jazzing Shaw up, he is extravagant enough in the first place. He freely acknowledged being mischievous to a fault; mischief is therefore an element to play down. Shaw's advice to actors and producers makes it quite clear that he saw the key to successful performance, not in gimmicks and "production ideas," but in the work of the actor. And, as one would expect of him, he made it his business to find out what that work was, and, having found out, proceeded to make suggestions for the actor's training. Those who have not followed Shaw into this field would probably not guess how far he went into it, what technical minutiae he found not unworthy of his attention.

Lillah McCarthy, the original Anne Whitefield and first wife of Granville-Barker, has printed the letters Shaw wrote her in the days when she worked with him in the theatre. They are a mine of theatrical wisdom. "What Raina wants is the extremity of style." "The transitions are very sudden, and come one after the other with fearful rapidity." "What is wrong is that you do not hold your part against him. You take his tone, you take his speed . . ." A letter on the climax in the last scene of *The Doctor's Dilemma* is too good not to quote at length:

> . . . you have softened it out of existence. What I call the climax is Jennifer's discovery that Ridgeon deliberately murdered Dubedat. The dramatic effect is built up rather deliberately, because there is first a misunderstanding, and then a discovery. When Ridgeon first says "I killed him," the audience knows that he means "I murdered him"; but Jennifer thinks that her

own frankness and sincerity have at last conquered his vanity, and that what he means is
"Yes, yes, I own up. I confess I was a duffer and
made a mess of the case." And on this she is de-
lighted and forgives him.

So far you seem to understand the scene clearly.
What I think you miss is the force of the revul-
sion of feeling when she makes the appalling
discovery that Louis was actually deliberately
murdered. The point may be a little difficult because I have not done it in my usual way with
a single stroke. She has to arrive at the truth by
arguing about the medicines, being a little stupid and off the track at first, because the truth is
so inconceivable and so wildly remote from her
first misunderstanding. But when the revelation
does come it really ought to be a blinding one.
It has to be done on the line "It is only dawning
on me, oh! oh! you MURDERED him." I think
you try to get this effect on the soft tack instead
of on the explosive one. That, of course, is often
a very good way of pulling off a big effect; but
in this case it misses fire. Also, the line goes
wrong. The repeated exclamation which is put
there to enable you to build up the final thunder-
clap becomes quite senseless. It does not belong
to the soft way of doing it.

Next time just try the effect of letting yourself
go on it for all you are worth, and keep up the

transport of horror and incredulous amazement until you get his reply to your threat to kill him, which will let you down easily.

The correspondence with Ellen Terry and Mrs. Campbell abounds in similar advice:

In playing Shakespeare, play *to* the lines, *through* the lines, *on* the lines, but never between the lines . . . Nothing short of a procession or a fight should ever make anything extraordinary as a silence during a Shakespearean performance.

For Prossy I want extreme snap in the execution: every consonant should have a ten pound gun hammer spring in it, also great rapidity and certainty of expression . . .

You are happy playing with worms. Barker [Harley Granville-Barker] loves worms. Worms never give any trouble, and in plays which can be *produced,* they make the best casts. (Darwin proved that the earth is made of worm casts.) But my plays must be acted and acted hard. They need a sort of bustle and crepitation of life which requires extraordinary energy and gives only glimpses and moments of the poetry underneath . . .

I missed the big bones of my play, its fortissimos, its allegros, its precipitous moments, its contrasts, and all its big bits. My orchestration was feeble on the cottage piano; and my cymbals were rather disappointing on the cups and saucers.

It will not have escaped notice that the drift of the passages I am quoting is the same: *towards* a grander style *by means of* a training as regular, exigent, and exhausting as that of an athlete. Some of this will strike the young actor today as old-fashioned, and I have found our actors eager to quote even less prepossessing things, such as—from *Our Theatre in the Nineties* *—"The right way to declaim Shakespeare is the sing-song way." Shaw's two essays on directing (listed below in the bibliography) show him, for better or worse, as a pre-Reinhardt man, with no awareness of (or interest in?) the claims of the modern Super-Director. The attitude he expresses to Barker as Director (Producer) in one of the above quotations is the severely sceptical one that many of us feel toward the Great Directors of today.

In some other respects, Shaw is "modern." In a great essay on acting that is supposed to be a review of something called *The Chili Widow,* Shaw proves himself the Irish Stanislavski, pointing to the key problem of maintaining "vigilant artistic sensitiveness throughout a performance," and suggesting that what the teacher can do for the actor is to awaken and cultivate his "artistic conscience." Technical exercises will not do the trick; we

* Not to confuse the inexpert in this field: the *Saturday Review* pieces are available complete as *Our Theatre in the Nineties.* A selection was issued earlier, and is cited elsewhere in this book, as *Dramatic Opinions.*

have to train the artistic sense; and one of the preliminary steps is to place the actor, somehow, in command of his own resources. Shaw put it this way:

> The defect of the old-fashioned systems of training for the stage was that they attempted to prescribe the conclusions of this constantly evolving artistic sense instead of cultivating it and leaving the artist to its guidance.

Even the matter of the sing-song delivery of verse is not clear-cut, for in the correspondence with Ellen Terry Shaw complains of "slow intonings and woolly execution." He thought verse should be spoken as verse; but he might very well have denounced what we call sing-song as "intoning."

The Both/And formula of the present book is applicable to this section of the subject too. In the matter of sing-song and verse speaking, Shaw, as usual, wants the best of both worlds—in this case, the traditional and modern methods of stage speech. His ideas on the education of actors, as we have just seen, are also both traditional and modern. Shaw's favorite actor Forbes-Robertson was once described as "the most natural actor of the age," and is always praised by Shaw as being "classic," "heroic," and so forth; our conclusion must be that his work was a straightforward case of Both/And, being a synthesis of grandeur and naturalness . . .

Shaw applied the Both/And principle to the relation of one theatre art to another. "I needed," he wrote (again in the foreword to Miss McCarthy's book) "the vigorous artificiality of the executive art of the Elizabethan stage to expose and bring back to nature the vapid artificiality of the Victorian play"—a statement which, in turn, is closely related to his Both/And theory of art in general, as summed up for *The Saturday Review:* "But vital art work comes always from a cross between art and life; art being of one sex only and quite sterile by itself."

Then there is that synthesis of acting and writing which is the produced, performed play. "The drama progresses," Shaw wrote to Janet Achurch, "by a series of experiments made on the public by actors and actresses with new plays." This remark illuminates Shaw's two-sided view of the theatre audience. First, the public is not to be pandered to, but experimented on; that side of the Shavian philosophy is well-enough known. The other side is expressed in the following remark in *The Saturday Review:* "It is dangerous to know that the average playgoer is a fool unless you also know that there is, somehow, hardly any surer way to failure than by treating him according to his folly." And, in actual fact a Shavian play, while characteristically making an enemy of the audience, does so chivalrously, that is, with respect for the enemy. The Shavian audience has it both ways: like a knight at a tournament, it enjoys the stimulant of combat combined with the compliment of being courteously treated. (The non-Shavian audience has it neither way: it is offered the non-stimulant of complaisant agreement and the non-compliment of flattery. Our playwrights nowadays aim to please, and succeed in being patronizing.)

Shaw had an understanding, at first instinctive, later highly developed, of the whole theatrical "dimension" of dramatic art. When an avant-garde ("Off Broadway") group launched his first play, he wrote, according to Archibald Henderson: "It was the existence of The Independent Theatre that made me finish that play, and by giving me the experience of its rehearsal and performance revealed the fact (to myself and others) that I possessed the gift of 'fingering' the stage." In his first full-dress Preface, he confessed that as he wrote he kept his "eye too much on the stage," and in *The Saturday Review* he provided an explanation of this perhaps excessive interest in performance: "as most modern plays have no thought, and are absolutely vulgar in purpose and feeling, I am mainly interested in their execution."

Finally, Shaw was himself (*pace* Dame Edith Evans) an actor, at least in the sense of being one of the most histrionic characters in the whole history of literature, taking a sweet and ebullient pleasure in his own performances, like all the old-time comedians. (In any case, it was the age, not of T. S. Eliot and Wallace Stevens and Julie Harris, but of Oscar Wilde and W. B. Yeats and Beerbohm Tree.) And Shaw had a soft spot for the actor, partly from being an actor himself, but even more because, like Shakespeare, he thought of all men and women as actors, and, like Hazlitt, he gave the professional player the credit for being the only person to make a public admission of the universal pretense. On reading Forbes-Robertson's autobiography, he wrote to the author:

> Reading this life of yours I perceive that as compared with our Lord Chief Justices, our front bench politicians, our medical baronets, our

archbishops, you, the actor, stand out with extraordinary distinction and loveableness because you are not a humbug. Instead of being the man who pretended to be Hamlet, you are precisely the man who never pretended to be anybody but Forbes-Robertson playing Hamlet. Beside the judge in his ermine and scarlet pretending to be justice, and the fashionable doctor pretending to be the omniscient master of life and death, and the priest with his apostolic succession and his bunch of keys of heaven and hell, you, whether as actor or painter, have the advantage of a celebrity that is not idolatry and a regard that is untainted by a secret abhorrence of the angry ape posing as a god. When Shakespeare wrote, All the world's a stage, he should have gone on like this:

All the world's a stage: trust not the man
That swears he's more than actor; for that lie
Waves like the devil's banner over murder,
Theft, rapine, etc., etc., etc.

BIBLIOGRAPHICAL NOTES

When you once get accustomed to my habit of mind, which I was born with and cannot help, you will not find me such bad company. But please do not think you can take in the work of my long lifetime at one reading. You must make it your practice to read all my works at least twice over every year for ten years or so.

—BERNARD SHAW

1. Shaw's Principal Works (plus some minor items of special interest)

1879–1883 The five novels: Immaturity, The Irrational Knot, Love among the Artists, Cashel Byron's Profession, The Unsocial Socialist.

1885–1892 Widowers' Houses.

1885 Starts book-reviewing for *The Pall Mall Gazette*.

1886–1887 Art Criticism for *The World*.

1888–1890 Music Criticism for *The Star* (later reprinted as "London Music in 1888–9 as heard by Corno di Bassetto").

1889 "Economic" and "Transition" in *Fabian Essays*, edited by G. Bernard Shaw.

1890–1894 Music Criticism for *The World* (later reprinted as "Music in London 1890–1894." 3 vols.).

1891 The Quintessence of Ibsenism.

233

1893   The Philanderer.
            Mrs. Warren's Profession.
            The Impossibilities of Anarchism (Fabian Tract 45).

1894   Arms and the Man.
            Candida.
            Socialism and Superior Brains (later, Fabian Tract 146).
            "The Religion of the Pianoforte," *Fortnightly Review*, February.
            "A Dramatic Realist to His Critics," *The New Review*, July.

1895   The Man of Destiny.
            The Sanity of Art.

1895–1898   Dramatic Criticism for *The Saturday Review* (later reprinted in part as *Dramatic Opinions*, later still in full as *Our Theatre in the Nineties*).

1896   You Never Can Tell.
            An Essay on Going to Church. (Originally in Arthur Symons' magazine *The Savoy*. Since 1905 separately published.)
            Socialism for Millionaires (later, Fabian Tract 107).

1897   The Devil's Disciple.
            "The Illusions of Socialism," in *Forecasts of the Coming Century*. U.S. title: *Hand and Brain*. Edited by Edward Carpenter. Had originally appeared in German in *Die Zeit*.

1898   Caesar and Cleopatra.
            The Perfect Wagnerite.
            "In the Days of My Youth," *Mainly about People*, September 17.

1899   Captain Brassbound's Conversion.

1900   Fabianism and the Empire.

1901   "Who I Am and What I Think," *Candid Friend*, May 18.

1901–1903   Man And Superman.

1904   John Bull's Other Island.
            The Commonsense of Municipal Trading.

234

BIBLIOGRAPHICAL NOTES

1905	Major Barbara.
1906	The Doctor's Dilemma.
1908	Getting Married.
1909	The Shewing-up of Blanco-Posnet.
1909–1910	Misalliance.
1910	Fanny's First Play.
	"Was ich der deutschen Kultur verdanke," in the first volume of the German edition of Shaw's works, translated by Siegfried Trebitsch.
1911–1912	Androcles and the Lion.
1912	Pygmalion.
	Overruled.
1913	The Case for Equality. (Originally a speech before the National Liberal Association, printed in *The Metropolitan*, December, 1913, reprinted in *The Socialism of Shaw*, edited by James Fuchs, 1926.)
1913–1916	Heartbreak House.
1914–1915	Commonsense about the War (later included in an ampler record: "What I really wrote about the War," 1930).
1916	"Introduction" to Leonard S. Woolf's *International Government*.
1917–1918	"What is to be done with doctors?" *The English Review*.
1918	"Schools and Schoolmasters," preface to *The Education Year Book*.
1921–1922	"Imprisonment," originally a preface to Lord Olivier's report on prison conditions, later the preface to Sidney and Beatrice Webb's *English Prisons under Local Government*, in 1946 separately published in New York as "The Crime of Imprisonment."
	This item, along with the two listed immediately above, and related correspondence, is to be found in Volume XXII of Shaw's Collected Works (Ayot St. Lawrence Edition).
1921	Back to Methuselah.
	Ruskin's Politics.

1922	"Make them do it well," *Collier's,* June 24. Originally a letter, this piece was reprinted in 1928 as "The Art of Rehearsal."
1923	Saint Joan.
1925	"On the History of Fabian Economics" and "On Guild Socialism," in E. R. Pease's important *History of the Fabian Society.*
1928	The Intelligent Woman's Guide to Socialism and Capitalism.
1929	The Apple Cart.
1932	Too True To Be Good.
	The Adventures of the Black Girl in Her Search for God.
1933	On the Rocks.
	Village Wooing.
	The Political Madhouse in America and Nearer Home.
	"In Praise of Guy Fawkes," in *Where Stands Socialism Today?*
1934	The Simpleton of the Unexpected Isles.
1936	The Millionairess.
	William Morris As I Knew Him. (Originally printed in May Morris's life of her father.)
1938	Geneva.
1939	In Good King Charles's Golden Days.
1944	Everybody's Political What's What.
1947	Buoyant Billions.
	"Barker's Wild Oats," *Harper's,* January.
1948	Farfetched Fables.
1949	Shakes vs. Shav.
	"Shaw's Rules for Directors," *Theatre Arts,* August.

2. What books of Shaw to look for

A. The fullest edition consulted in the preparation of the 1947 version of the present work was the splendid Ayot St. Lawrence Edition in 31 volumes. Today (1957) Shaw's British publisher, Constable & Co., has thirty-six volumes of an inexpensive Standard Edition on the market. Shaw's American publishers, Dodd, Mead,

BIBLIOGRAPHICAL NOTES

& Co., have apparently not found it possible to do anything like so well by their author: a *Selected Plays* in three volumes is at present their most substantial offering. But luckily a fair scattering of Shaw's works is available in popular editions: many plays, one play per volume, in Penguin Books; two volumes of plays in The Modern Library; *Plays and Players*, edited by A. C. Ward, in The World's Classics; and *Shaw on Music*, edited by Eric Bentley, in Doubleday Anchor Books.

B. Shaw's dramatic and musical criticism is not the only part of his periodical writing that has been reprinted in book-form. Attention is called to the following items:—

1. *The Socialism of Bernard Shaw*, edited by James Fuchs. New York, 1926. Includes several of Shaw's best Fabian Tracts and "The Case for Equality."
2. *Short Stories, Scraps, and Shavings*. New York, 1934. Includes "The Black Girl," "Don Giovanni Explains," a satire against millennial revolutionism called "Death of an Old Revolutionary Hero," and a rejected scene from *Back to Methuselah* portraying Chesterton.
3. *Bernard Shaw Gives Himself Away*. Newton, 1939. A limited edition of many of Shaw's autobiographical writings, such as "In the Days of My Youth," "Who I Am and What I Think" and the prefaces to *Immaturity* and *London Music*.
4. *Sixteen Self Sketches*. New York, 1949. Similar in content to the preceding item but lacking the two prefaces and adding some earlier pieces.
5. *Pen Portraits and Reviews*. In the Ayot St. Lawrence and Standard Editions. Contains important articles on Tolstoy, Wilde, Wells, Morris, Butler, Chesterton, Hyndman, Nietzsche, and others.

C. Since many libraries have a complete file of the Fabian Tracts, it may be of some use to list the numbers of Shaw's contributions (though this list is probably not complete): 2, 3, 6, 13, 40, 41, 43, 49, 70, 93, 107, 116, 142, 146, 226, 233. The last of these contains Shaw's encyclopedia articles on "Socialism" and "Fabianism" respectively: they are the concisest summaries of his political position.

For Shaw's critique of earlier Fabianism, see "Fabian Failures and Successes" in *The Fabian Quarterly*, April 1944, and his prefaces to the 1908 and 1931 reprints of *Fabian Essays*. The latter contains a proposal for a second set of Fabian Essays, but the closest we get to this is Beatrice Webb's Fabian Tract (No. 236) laying down the principles of "A New Reform Bill" and the volume of lectures *Where Stands Socialism Today?* (London, 1933) to which Shaw, Stafford Cripps, Hugh Dalton, Harold Laski, A. L. Rowse and others contributed.

3. The literature about Shaw

A. *Expository*

Duffin, H. C.: *The Quintessence of Bernard Shaw*. London, 1920 and 1939.

Fuller, Edmund: *George Bernard Shaw, Critic of Western Morale*. New York, 1950.

Irvine, William: *The Universe of GBS*. New York, 1949.

Rattray, R. F.: *Bernard Shaw, A Chronicle and an Introduction*. London, 1934 and 1951.

Ward, A. C.: *Bernard Shaw*. London, 1951.

B. *Critical* (see also Theatrical)

Bab, Julius: *Bernard Shaw*. Berlin, 1909 and 1926.

Eliot, T. S.: See (e.g.) "A Dialogue on Dramatic Poetry," in *Selected Essays*. Also: *The Dial*, October 1921 and May 1927, *The New Criterion*, April 1926.

Howe, P. P.: *Bernard Shaw*. London, 1915.

Joad, C. E. M.: *Shaw*. London, 1949.

Joad, C. E. M., ed.: *Shaw and Society*. London, 1953. Contributors: Kingsley Martin, Leonard S. Woolf, S. K. Ratcliffe, Benn W. Levy, Hugh Dalton.

Kronenberger, Louis, ed.: *George Bernard Shaw. A Critical Survey*. Cleveland and New York, 1953.

An anthology of Shaw criticism by Beerbohm, Huneker, Chesterton, Palmer, Howe, Dixon Scott, Philip Littell, Lewisohn, Nathan, Krutch, Edmund Wilson, Auden, Barzun, Pea-

BIBLIOGRAPHICAL NOTES

cock, Joad, Bentley, Stark Young, Spender, Pritchett, John Mason Brown, and Thomas Mann.

Mencken, H. L.: *George Bernard Shaw. His Plays.* Boston, 1905.

Skimpole, Herbert: *Bernard Shaw. The Man and His Work.* London, 1918.

Strauss, E.: *Bernard Shaw, Art, and Socialism.* London, 1942.

Turner, W. J.: "Bernard Shaw," in *Scrutinies,* collected by Edgell Rickword. London, 1928.

Winsten, S., ed.: *Bernard Shaw at 90.* New York, 1946.

> Contributors: Gilbert Murray, John Masefield, M. J. MacManus, Lord Passfield (Sidney Webb), Laurence Housman, J. B. Priestley, H. G. Wells, Max Beerbohm, C. E. M. Joad, James Bridie, Lord Dunsany, J. D. Bernal, W. R. Inge, E. J. Dent.

C. *Eulogy*

Braybrooke, Patrick: *The Genius of Bernard Shaw.* New York, 1925.
> *The Subtlety of George Bernard Shaw.* London, 1930.

Collis, J. S.: *Shaw.* London, 1925.

Hamon, Augustin: *Le Molière du XXe Siècle.* Paris, 1913.
> Translated as *The Twentieth-Century Molière.* New York, 1916.

D. *Diatribe*

Boyd, Ernest A.: "An Irish Protestant: Bernard Shaw," in *Appreciations and Depreciations.* New York, 1918.

Brinser, Ayers: *The Respectability of Mr. Bernard Shaw.* Cambridge, Mass., 1931.

Casseres, Benjamin de: *Mencken and Shaw.* New York, 1930.

Freeman, John: "George Bernard Shaw," in *The Moderns.* London, 1916.

Craig, Gordon: *Henry Irving.* New York, 1930.
> *Ellen Terry and Her Secret Self.* New York, 1931.

Jones, Henry Arthur: "Bernard Shaw as a Thinker," a series of five articles in *The English Review,* 1923–1924.
> *My Dear Wells.* New York, 1931.

239

Lawrence, D. H.: See (e.g.) *A propos of Lady Chatterley's Lover.* London, 1931. Hostile remarks about Shaw are scattered through Lawrence's works.

Le Mesurier, Mrs.: *The Socialist Woman's Guide to Intelligence.* London, 1929.

Turner, W. J.: see 3, A, above.

E. *Theatrical*

The largest collection of facts about the production of Shaw's plays is to be found in *The Theatrical Companion to Shaw: A Pictorial Record of the First Performances of the Plays of G.B.S. with Synopses, Casts and Detailed Notes* by Raymond Mander and Joe Mitcheson. New York, 1955. The dramatic critics' reviews are, of course, largely to be found in the files of newspapers and magazines. The following books of theatre reviews (among many others) include reviews of Shaw performances:

Agate, James: *Red Letter Nights.* London, 1944.

Beerbohm, Max: *Around Theatres.* New York, 1930 and 1954.

Bentley, Eric: *The Dramatic Event.* New York, 1954 and Boston, 1956.

Brown, John Mason: *Seeing Things.* New York, 1946.

MacCarthy, Desmond: *Shaw's Plays in Review.* New York, 1951.

Jacobsohn, Siegfried: *Das Jahr der Bühne.* 10 vols. Berlin, 1911–21.

Nathan, George Jean: *Theatre Book of the Year.* 9 vols. New York, 1942 ff.

Walkley, A. C.: *Drama and Life.* New York, 1907.

Young, Stark: *Immortal Shadows.* New York, 1948.

Ward, A. C., ed.: *Specimens of English Dramatic Criticism XVII to XX Centuries.* London and New York, 1945. Contains William Archer's review of *Arms and the Man.*

F. *Roman Catholic*

Chesterton, G. K.: *George Bernard Shaw.* London, 1909.
    Chesterton was not yet a member of the Church but even so . . .

Hackett, J. P.: *Shaw: George versus Bernard.* New York, 1937.

Walker, Leslie J.: *The Return to God.* London, 1933.

BIBLIOGRAPHICAL NOTES

A book about religion in general which began as a retort to Shaw.

G. *Rationalist*

McCabe, Joseph: *George Bernard Shaw.* New York, 1914.

Robertson, J. M.: *Mr. Shaw and the Maid.* London, 1926.

Wells, H. G.: *The Way the World Is Going.* New York, 1928. Chapter XXVIII.

Whitehead, George: *Bernard Shaw Explained.* London, 1925.

H. *Marxist*

Caudwell, Christopher: "George Bernard Shaw: a study of the bourgeois superman," in *Studies in a Dying Culture.* London, 1938.

Dobb, Maurice: "Bernard Shaw and Economics," *G.B.S. 90.*

Dutt, R. Palme: "Notes of the Month," July 1928, *Labour Monthly,* pp. 387–411.

Hyndman, H. M.: 1. See *Bernard Shaw and Karl Marx. A Symposium 1884–1889.* New York, 1930.
    2. See *The Clarion,* September, October, November, December, 1904.

Lunacharsky, A.: See *Isvestia,* July 31, 1931, or *Labour Monthly,* XIII, pp. 580–582.

Mirsky, Dmitri: *The Intelligentsia of Great Britain.* New York, 1935. Chapter II.

Trotsky, Leon: *Whither England?* New York, 1925. Chapter IV.

West, Alick: *George Bernard Shaw: A Good Man Fallen Among Fabians.* New York, 1950.

I. *Biographies and Correspondence*

i. *Biographies.*

Ervine, St. John: *Bernard Shaw. His Life, Works, and Friends.* New York, 1956.

Harris, Frank: *Bernard Shaw.* New York, 1931.
Valuable for material by Shaw himself, particularly his "sex credo" in Chapter XVII.

241

Henderson, Archibald: *George Bernard Shaw. His Life and Works.* Cincinnati, 1911.

Bernard Shaw, Playboy and Prophet. New York, 1932.

George Bernard Shaw. Man of the Century. New York, 1956.

Henderson's three books are the most informative of all works on Shaw.

Pearson, Hesketh: *G. B. S. A Full-Length Portrait.* New York, 1942. ii. *Correspondence.*

Campbell, Mrs. Patrick: *My Life and Some Letters.* London, 1922.

Dent, Alan, ed.: *Bernard Shaw and Mrs. Patrick Campbell. Their Correspondence.* New York, 1952.

St. John, Christopher, ed.: *Ellen Terry and Bernard Shaw. A Correspondence.* New York, 1931 and 1949.

McCarthy, Lillah: *Myself and My Friends.* London, 1933.

Though Miss McCarthy was not permitted to mention her ex-husband Harley Granville Barker she took all the more pleasure in displaying her friendship with Shaw who has contributed not only letters but a preface (called "An Aside").

Purdom, C. B., ed.: *Bernard Shaw's Letters to Granville Barker.* New York, 1956.

4. How To Find Out More

The Saturday Review of Literature published a complete list of all Shaw's separately published works (July 22, 1944). This list supersedes the one compiled by Geoffrey H. West as a supplement to *The Bookman's Journal,* 1928, and reprinted as a booklet, 1929. There are two Shaw bibliographies in full-length book form: X. Heydet's *Shaw-Kompendium* (Paris, 1936) and C. L. and V. M. Broad's *Dictionary to the Plays and Novels of Bernard Shaw* (New York, 1929). The former (in German) includes excerpts from Shaw criticism. The latter provides plot-summaries and an index of characters. Both contain many references to periodical material by and about Shaw. The *Dictionary* is full of inaccuracies. Of course even the two full-dress bibliographies are not complete even up to the dates

BIBLIOGRAPHICAL NOTES

when they were composed. For there is Shaw material spread through the magazines and newspapers of many countries. At this point one can only refer the reader to such things as the Indexes of *The Times* and *The New York Times* as well as to *The Reader's Guide to Periodical Literature*.

At the time of reprinting (1957) there are two Shaw Societies: The Shaw Society (London) * and The Shaw Society of America.** The former started to issue a Bulletin in 1946 and today issues *The Shavian* (a magazine) as well as a series of Shavian Tracts. The latter has been issuing *The Shaw Bulletin* since 1951.***

* Secretary: Eric Batson, 45 Steeplestone Close, London, N. 18.
** Secretary (1959): Benj. C. Rosset, 1014 Jennings St., Bronx 60, N.Y.
*** In 1959 *The Shaw Bulletin* became *The Shaw Review*. Editor, Dr. Stanley Weintraub, 221 Sparks Bldg., University Park, Pa.

KEY TO QUOTATIONS

The source of most of my quotations *about* Shaw by other authors can be pretty accurately conjectured from Section 3 of the above Bibliographical Notes. The source of many quotations from Shaw himself is often stated in the text, but there remain a number of unplaced ones which the reader may be curious about. They are identified here in the way that I thought would be helpful to most readers—which is not by page number in the case of works that have been issued in several differently paged editions.

Page
xviii.   *With the single.* "Blaming the Bard," in *Dramatic Opinions* and *Our Theatre in the Nineties* (henceforth *D.O.*)
xviii.   *I dare not claim. Everybody's Political What's What*, p. 47.
xix.   *As both he. The New York Times Book Review*, November 18, 1945.
xix.   *This has prevented.* Henderson's *Bernard Shaw Playboy and Prophet* (henceforth, "Henderson"), p. 608.
5.   *What the achievement. Fabian Essays*, p. 179.
5–6.   *Commodities produced. Fabian Tract*, No. 142, p. 9 (based on Fabian Essays, p. 17).
8.   *The line which. The Intelligent Woman's Guide*, Chapter 75.

KEY TO QUOTATIONS

12. *I am afraid.* "In Praise of Guy Fawkes," in *Where Stands Socialism Today?*

17. *The Labour Party.* Hamon's *Le Molière du XXᵉ siècle*, p. 47.

23. *You can conceive.* "In Praise of Guy Fawkes," *loc. cit.*

25. *The Inquisition was.* Preface to *Heartbreak House.*

25. *far more self-disciplined.* Preface to *Saint Joan.*

26. *Of course if you.* Undated pamphlet published in London, "Bernard Shaw and Fascism."

27. *The average citizen.* The *Intelligent W.G.*, Chapter 85.

28. *I do not believe.* Debate with Chesterton, *Do We Agree?*, published at Hartford, Connecticut, 1928.

29. *The cry of.* The *Intelligent W.G.*, Chapter 85.

30. *a post-communist. ibid.*

35–6. *What is the.* The *Socialism of Bernard Shaw*, ed. Fuchs, p. 83.

36. *only real tragedy.* "Epistle Dedicatory," *Man and Superman.*

37. *equality of income.* The *Intelligent W.G.*, Chapter 26.

37. *Society is like. ibid.*, Peroration.

38. *Marat killed by.* "Mr. Pinero's Past," *D.O.*

38–9. *A socialist state.* *Everybody's P.W.W.*, p. 252.

41. *The one danger.* "Commonsense About The War," in *What I Really Wrote About The War.*

41. *to convince men.* "The Impossibilities of Anarchism," *Fabian Tract* No. 45.

42. *You will never.* Preface to *Major Barbara.*

46. *In short we.* The 1911 version of Henderson's biography, *George Bernard Shaw His Life and Works*, p. 488.

50. *It is not.* Quoted by Rattray from *The Nation* (London), November 12, 1921.

50. *It is quite.* Preface to *Major Barbara.*

58. *It is an instinct.* "Michael and his Lost Angel," *D.O.*

61. *Natural Selection.* Interview with Shaw by George Sylvester Viereck, *Glimpses of the Great*, New York 1930.

65. *No. I believe.* Questionnaire in St. Martin's in the *Fields Review*, 1922.

65. *When you are.* Henderson, p. 521.

68.   *The true fall. The Nation* (London), December 1922.

68.   *Even when I.* "Bernard Shaw and a Critic," By H. C. Duffin, *Cornhill Magazine*, January 1924.

71.   *It is always. Everybody's P.W.W.*, p. 49.

72.   *Science is always.* Henderson, p. 673.

72.   *Impostor for. ibid.*, p. 676.

73.   *Compared with.* Viereck, *op. cit.*

74.   *In justice to.* "The Author's Apology," *D.O.*

76–7.   *Men do every.* "Michael and his Lost Angel," *D.O.*

77.   *Bourgeois morality.* "Bernard Shaw and a Critic," *loc. cit.*

77.   *a movement in.* "My Friend Fitzthunder," by Redbarn Wash [anagram for Bernard Shaw], *Today*, August 1888.

81–2.   *In school I. Everybody's P.W.W.*, p. 182.

85.   *The cruel.* "The Conflict between Science and Commonsense," *The Humane Review*, April 1900.

85.   *Property is.* Preface to *Immaturity*.

86.   *Our laws are.* Preface to *Major Barbara*.

90.   *I am by. The Intelligent W.G.*, Chapter 70.

92.   *I am prepared.* "Michael and his Lost Angel," *loc. cit.*

93.   *My plays are. The Table Talk of G.B.S.*, by Archibald Henderson, New York, 1923, p. 67.

94.   *The material of.* From symposium in *The Humanitarian*, May 1895.

96.   *I am as fond.* Preface to *Three Plays for Puritans*.

97.   *What power did.* "In The Days Of My Youth," *Mainly About People*, September 17, 1898.

97.   *If religion. ibid.*

97.   *religious music. Music in London*, Volume II, p. 275.

98.   *The bardolatry*, J. S. Collis's *Shaw*, p. 165.

99.   *Shakespeare survives.* "The Technical Novelty," in *The Quintessence of Ibsenism*.

99.   *I postulated.* "The Author's Apology," *D.O.*

99.   *I find myself.* "Keats," in *Pen Portraits and Reviews*, p. 192.

99.   *It was very. ibid.*, p. 245.

100.   *I deal with.* Preface to *The Sanity of Art*.

102.   *You will please.* Preface to *Widowers' Houses*.

103.   *And I claim. ibid.*

KEY TO QUOTATIONS

104–5. *You are an.* Henderson, p. 189.
107. *Nothing is.* "Toujours Shakespeare," *D.O.*
112. *that might not.* "Madame Sans Gêne," *D.O.*
143. *Absurdity is.* "Satan Saved At Last," *D.O.*
143. *My procedure.* Henderson's *Table Talk*, p. 63.
144. *My characters.* Preface to *Three Plays for Puritans.*
146. *Utterly unlike.* The Clarion, December 2, 1904.
146. *This is a.* "New Year Dramas," *D.O.*
159. *given Caesar.* The Academy, April 30, 1898.
160. *As a dramatist.* Preface to *The Sanity of Art.*
173. *we never argue.* Everybody's P.W.W., p. 121–2.
176. *It is not.* Henderson, p. 475.
179. *No frontier.* Preface to *Plays Pleasant.*
184. *He is a mass.* Mrs. Campbell's *My Life and Some Letters.*
184. *An author of.* Viereck, *op. cit.*
186. *I have produced.* Henderson, 1911 version, p. 202.
187. *that we had.* Fabian Tract, No. 2.
187. *For 48 years.* "In Praise of Guy Fawkes," *loc. cit.*
187. *The real joke.* "George Bernard Shaw," by Clarence Rook, *The Candid Friend*, November 1, 1896.
187–8. *I may dodder.* "Valedictory," *D.O.*
188. *In order to.* "George Bernard Shaw," by Clarence Rook, *loc. cit.*
189. *I have solved.* "In Praise of Guy Fawkes," *loc. cit.*
190. *conscience is.* The Christian Commonwealth, July 20, 1910.
192. *Not taking.* "In Praise of Guy Fawkes," *loc. cit.*
192. *What is wrong.* "Epistle Dedicatory," *Man and Superman.*
192. *I see there.* Preface to *Major Critical Essays.*
199. *I lacked both.* Preface to *Immaturity.*
203. *Mr. Bernard.* Chambers' Encyclopedia, reprinted in *Fabian Tract*, No. 233.
209. *My heart knows.* Collis, *op. cit.*, p. 181.
210. *If you cannot.* Preface to *Immaturity.*

INDEX

This is an index of art works, actual persons, and Shavian characters. These last are listed under whatever denomination is most familiar —thus "Barbara" and "George, Mrs.," not "Undershaft, Barbara" and "Collins, Mrs. George."

Achurch, Janet, 101, 223, 230

Adelphi, The, xv

Adventures of the Black Girl in Her Search for God, The, 62, 64

A.E. (George Russell), 209

Ah, Wilderness! 191

All's Well That Ends Well, 98

American Mercury, The, xvi

Anderson, Anthony, 110-111, 113, 157

Andrew Undershaft's Profession, 167

Antony, Mark, 114

Apollinaire, Guillaume, xvii

Apollodorus, 157, 160

Applecart, The, 117, 142, 152, 205, 216, 223

Archer, William, xi, 101-102, 113, 192, 193, 201, 220

Ariadne (Lady Utterword), 137, 138

Aristophanes, 175

Arnold, Matthew, 135

Aubrey, 142

Auden, W. H., xiii, 131, 218

"Auguries of Innocence," 64

Back to Methuselah, xiv, 50, 52-55, 58-60, 62, 64, 71, 83, 104, 121, 155, 162, 169, 181, 215

Bacon, Francis, 43

Bahr, Hermann, 14

Bakounin, 89

Baldwin, Lord, 26

Balzac, 149

Barbara, 67, 69, 136-137, 152, 166-168

Bax, E. Belfort, 33, 127

Bayard, 104

INDEX

Becque, Henry, 155

Beer, Max, 14-15, 31

Beethoven, 97

Bellamy, Edward, 19, 33

Belloc, Hilaire, 22

Bergner, Elisabeth, 185

Bergson, 54, 55, 119, 148

Bernal, J. D., 71, 83-84

Bernard Shaw: The Man and the Mask (Richard Burton), xx

Bernstein, Edouard, 13

Bismarck, 14

Blake, 64, 81

Blanche, 151, 167

Bluntschli, Captain, 150

Bohun, Walter, 144, 155

Brassbound, Captain, 111, 113, 114, 125

Bridie, James, 129

Brieux, 95

Broadbent, 158, 165-166, 207-208

Buffon, 61

Bulwer-Lytton, 112, 141

Bunyan, 96

Burgess, 167

Burgoyne, General, 109, 150

Burke, Edmund, 35

Butler, Samuel, 59, 61-62, 195

Caesar, 90, 107, 113-115, 139, 150, 157, 158, 159, 160-164, 165, 166

Caesar and Cleopatra, 14, 108, 111-115, 159, 163-165, 169, 172, 178

Campbell, Mrs. Patrick, 122, 124, 184, 223, 227

Candida, 110-111, 113, 114, 118, 121, 137, 152, 179, 204, 206-207

Candida, 110, 157, 167

Captain Brassbound's Conversion, 108, 111, 113, 223

Carlyle, 10, 33-35, 67, 187, 208

Cashel Byron's Profession, 105

Caudwell, Christopher, xiii

Chili Widow, The, 228

Chekhov, 132-133, 138, 139, 143

Cherry Orchard, The, 132

Chesterton, G. K., xiv, xx, 42, 160, 173, 191, 203, 212-213

Churchill, Winston, xii, 31, 187

Cicely, Lady, 111, 114, 125, 139, 150, 152, 167, 168, 223

Clandon, Mrs., 30

Clarion, The, 11

Cleopatra, 113-115

Cocteau, Jean, xvii

Cole, Margaret, 21

Communist Manifesto, The, 3

Congreve, 98

Conrad, Joseph, xvii

Constitution for the Socialist Commonwealth of Great Britain, A, 21-22

Cool as a Cucumber, 197

Corday, Charlotte, 38

Craig, Gordon, 161

Creative Evolution, 54

Crofts, Sir George, 103, 167

Cromwell, 96

Cusins, Adolphus, 149, 158, 166-167

Dante, xxii
Darwin, 59-61, 63, 74, 190, 212, 227
Daudet, Léon, xii
David, J. L., 161
Decay of Capitalist Civilization, The, 21
Dempsey, Father, 150
Dent, Edward, 97
Devil's Disciple, The, 108-111, 113, 121, 128, 133, 152
Dewey, John, 66
Dickens, 10, 144, 149, 151, 199, 220, 222
"Die Natur," 64
Die Zauberflöte, 97
Doctor's Dilemma, The, 83-84, 129, 178, 201, 215, 225
"Doctrine of the Brothers Barnabas, The," 118, 142
Doll's House, A, 95, 98, 117, 221
Don Giovanni, 131
"Don Giovanni Explains," 50
Don Juan, 51-53, 86, 200
"Don Juan in Hell," 50, 118, 127
Donne, John, xxiv
Doolittle, Alfred, 125-126
Dostoevsky, xxii, 76
Dowson, Ernest, 212
Doyle, Conan, 144
Doyle, Larry, 165, 166, 207-208
Dramatic Opinions, 98, 228

"Dramatic Realist to his Critics, A," 145
Drinkwater, Felix, 111
Dryden, 132
Dubedat, Louis, 30, 149, 227
Dudgeon, Dick, 109-110, 114, 125, 139, 150, 157
Dudgeon, Mrs., 144
Dumas *fils*, 174
Dunn, Bill, 155
Dunn, Ellie, 136-138, 141
Dunn, Mazzini, 147
Dutt, R. Palme, xiii

Eliot, T. S., xiv-xv, xvi-xvii, 170, 191, 218, 232
Eliza, 119-126, 168
Ellis, Havelock, 212
Enemy of the People, An, 14
Engels, 12
Ernst, Max, 14
Ervine, St. John, xiii
Essie, 109, 144
Evans, Edith, 225, 232
Everybody's Political What's What, xx, 27
Everyman, 132

Fabian Essays, 4, 16
Fabian Quarterly, 3
Fabian Tract No. 70, 3n
Fabius, 11
Farr, Florence, 223
Fanny's First Play, 224
Faust, 95
Fitzgerald, F. Scott, 148
Flaubert, xxiv, 209

INDEX

Forbes-Robertson, 98, 222, 229, 231-232
France, Anatole, 185, 190
Freud, 185, 190
Friedell, Egon, 188
Future of Political Science in America, The, 25

Galsworthy, 171, 173-174
Geneva, 41, 142
George III, 34
George V, 26, 206
George, Henry, 3, 32
George, Lloyd, 19
George, Mrs., (The Mayoress), 134, 136, 140, 141, 152, 168
Getting Married, 118, 120, 127-128, 130, 132, 133-136, 140, 142, 152, 215
Gilbert, W. S., 144, 155, 174, 177n
Gladstone, 107
Gloria, 30
Godwin, William, 2
Goethe, xxv, 33, 64
Gone With the Wind, 185
Gordon, General, 107
Gourmont, Rémy de, 181
Granville-Barker, 173, 225, 227, 228
Great Contemporaries, 187
Guinness, Nurse, 155

Hackett, J. P., xiv
Hallam, Sir Howard, 111
Hamlet, 95
Handel, 97

Harden, Maximilian, 14
Hare, John, 222, 223
Harris, Frank, xvi
Harris, Julie, 231
Hauptmann, Gerhart, 79
Hazlitt 222, 231
Hearst, W. R., 199
Heartbreak House, 132, 133, 136-142, 167, 179, 205
Hebbel, 148
Hegel, 148, 180
Henderson, Archibald, 231
Henley, W. E., 212
Hesione (Mrs. Hushabye), 137, 138
Higgins, Henry, 119-125
Higgins, Mrs., 121
Hitler, 23, 27, 30-31, 78, 79, 187, 199
Homer, xviii
Hook, Sidney, xiii
Hotchkiss, Sinjon, 130, 136, 148
Huneker, James, xi
Hushabye, Hector, 137
Huxley, T. H., 35, 61, 212
Hyndman, H. M., 7, 13, 19, 30, 55, 74, 104, 149, 154
Hypatia, 135, 167

Ibsen, xiii, xxv, 14, 48, 74, 98, 99, 106, 116-118, 143, 146, 173-174, 196, 210, 221, 223
"Illusions of Socialism, The," 30, 76, 179-182
Immaturity, 197, 200
Importance of Being Earnest, The, 176

251

"Impossibilities of Anarchism, The," 87-89
Imprisonment, 138
In Good King Charles's Golden Days, 118, 127
Inquisitor, The, 25, 171
Intelligent Woman's Guide, The, 4
Irving, Henry, 98, 107, 112, 161
"Isabella," 99

James, Henry, xii, xiii, xvi, xvii, 194, 213, 223
Jennifer, 152, 168, 225-226
Jesus, 42, 68, 115, 184
Jevons, Stanley, 4, 7, 33
Jitta's Atonement, 174
Joad, C. E. M., 53-55
Joan (Jeanne d'Arc), 25, 67, 68, 150, 152, 160, 161, 168-172
John Bull's Other Island, 86, 118, 165-166, 178, 201, 206-209, 216, 218
John the Baptist, xiii
Johnson, Samuel, 100, 100n
Jonson, Ben, 175-177
Joynes, J. L., 82
Judith, 110-111, 114, 125, 136, 157
Juggins, 155

Kafka, xii, xxii, 76
Kapital, 3
Kean, Edmund, 222
Keats, 81, 99

Keegan, Father, 86, 150, 158, 165, 166, 207-208
Kipling, 212
Knowles, Sheridan, 112
Knox, Margaret, 168
Kropotkin, xiv
Kruger, 19

La Parisienne, 155
Lamarck, 46, 61
L'Armour Médecin, 129
Laski, H. J., xvii, 204
Lavinia, 152, 168
Lawrence, D. H., xvi, 8, 191
Lawrence, Gertrude, 124
Lenihan, Winifred, 185
Lenin, xiii, xx, 10, 14
Lexy, 150
Lickcheese, 167
Life, xv
Light Shines in Darkness, The, 132
Lina, 135, 136, 140, 141, 152, 168
Lindbergh, Charles, 26
Louis XIV, 34
Lucius Septimius, 163, 166
Lunacharsky, A., xiii

Macaulay, 214
MacDonald, Ramsay, 10, 13, 26, 206
Machiavelli, 31
Madame Sans-Gêne, 112
Magnus, King, 149, 150, 158, 205, 206

INDEX

Major Barbara, 118, 166-167, 169

Malone, Hector, Sr., 154

Malraux, André, 77

Malthus, 63

Man and Superman, 21, 50-52, 54, 55-58, 64, 65, 72, 86, 115, 117, 121, 132, 152-157, 164, 166, 169, 181, 201, 206

Man of Destiny, The, 112, 159, 161

Mangan, Alfred, 137, 138, 147, 158, 179

Mann, Thomas, 48

Marat, 38

Marchbanks, Eugene, 110, 113, 157, 204

Marcus (-Hushabye, Hector), 137

Marx, xiii, 3, 5-7, 31, 32, 63, 74, 99, 104, 149, 180, 190, 204, 222

Mathews, Charles, 197-198

Matter, Life, and Value, 53

McCabe, Joseph, xiv

McCarthy, Lillah, 221, 225, 229

Meek, Private, 150

Mencken, H. L., xi, 192

Mendoza, 144, 154, 155

Meredith, 151

Michelangelo, xxiv

Midsummer Night's Dream, A, 95

Millionairess, The, 132

Milton, 96

Mirsky, D. S., xiii

Misalliance, 127, 132, 133, 135-136, 140, 142, 215, 224

Molière, 82, 102, 129, 145, 175-177, 182

Moore, George, xii

Morell, James Mavor, 110, 137, 150, 157, 179, 204

Morris, William, 33, 120

Mozart, 98, 131

Mrs. Daintry's Daughter, 101

Mrs. Warren's Profession, 94, 101, 103-105, 167

Murray, Gilbert, 149

Murry, J. Middleton, xv

Mussolini, 23, 26-27, 78

Nathan, G. J., xvi

Nation, The, 79, 190

Napoleon, 107, 112, 113, 158, 160-162, 216

New Republic, The, xvi, 79

New Statesman and Nation, The, 79

New York Times, The, 185

Newman, J. H., 35

Nietzsche, xv, 14, 31, 33, 41, 48, 56, 67, 74-75, 98, 195, 205, 210, 211, 218

Ninth Symphony, The, 97

Nora, 168

Nordau, Max, 74

Octavius, 156-157

Oken, Lorenz, 63

"On Going to Church," 69-70

On the Rocks, 142

O'Neill, Eugene, 180, 191

Origin of Species, The, 59

Orinthia, 206, 223

Othello, 96
Our Theatre in the Nineties, 228

Pascal, 47, 48
Pasteur, 83
Patient, The, 142
Paul, 68
Pavlov, 74, 121
Peacock, Ronald, 201-202
Peer Gynt, 95
"Perfect Wagnerite, The," 46, 50, 74
Pétain, 79
Phèdre, 224
Pilate, 68
Pirandello, 180
Pitoëff, Ludmilla, 185
Plato, 96, 120, 140, 199
Plays Pleasant and Unpleasant, 117
Political Madhouse in America and Nearer Home, The, 25
Posnet, Blanco, 65
Pound, Ezra, xii
Power of Darkness, The, 133
Prossy, 227
Proudhon, 5
Proust, xxii, 77
Pygmalion, 119-126, 127, 156, 166, 215

Quelch, Harry, 144
Quicherat, Jules, 168, 170
"Quintessence of Ibsenism, The," 46-49, 74, 117, 146

Raina, 225
Ramsden, Roebuck, 30, 154, 164, 165, 166
Rankin, 111
Reade, Charles, 95, 98
Rembrandt, 98
"Revolutionist's Handbook, The," 55
Rhinegold, 101
Ricardo, 4
Richard Wagner in Bayreuth, 74
Ridgeon, Sir Colenso, 225-226
Ristori, 222
Robertson, J. M., xiv, 170
Robbins, Elizabeth, 224
Robinson, E. A., xiii
Rousseau, 31-32, 48, 91
Rufio, 114, 163-164, 165
Ruskin, 33-35, 208

Saint Athanasius, 70
Saint Joan, xvii, 141, 148, 159, 168-172, 177, 178
Salt, Henry, 33
Salvemini, G., 25
Salvini, 222
"Sanity of Art, The," 46-49, 199
Sankey and Moody, 45
Sarcey, 119
Sardou, 112
Sartor Resartus, 34
Sartorius, 103
Saturday Review, The, 76, 144, 220, 222, 228, 230, 231
Savvy, 142
Schiller, 161, 170

254

INDEX

Schopenhauer, 48, 74

Schopenhauer als Erzieher, 74

Scott, Dixon, 99, 191, 196, 214

Scott, Walter, xviii

Scribe, 173

Sergius, 150

Shakespeare, xviii, xxii, 71, 76, 95-100, 112, 137, 143, 170, 185, 188, 204, 231, 232

Shaw: George versus Bernard (J. P. Hackett), xx

Shaw, Mrs. G. B., 168

Shewing-Up of Blanco Posnet, The, 133, 215

Shotover, Captain, 136-138, 140-141, 147, 158, 205, 206, 208

Simon, Sir John, 26

Simpleton of the Unexpected Isles, The, 138, 142

Skimpole, Herbert, 165

Socrates, 40

Stalin, 12, 14, 28, 31, 76

Stanislavski, 228

Stevens, Wallace, 231

Stevenson, R. L., 105

Straker, Henry, 154

Straker, Louisa, 155

Strife, 171

Strindberg, 106

Stuart-Glennie, 33

Sullivan, Barry, 222

Summerhays, Bentley, 136

Summerhays, Lord, 135

Sweetie, The, 142

Swindon, Major, 150

Synge, J. M., xvii

Tale of Two Cities, A, 109

Tallboys, Colonel, 150

Tanner, John, 1, 44, 55-57, 62, 149, 153, 156-157, 158, 164, 166, 200

Tarleton, John, 158, 167

Tennyson, 112

Terry, Ellen, 206, 223, 227

Thompson, Francis, 212

Thorndike, Sybil, 185

Three Plays for Puritans, 108-115, 117, 136, 149, 152, 156, 159, 166, 172, 174

Tobacco Road, 185

Tojo, 187

Tolstoy, xxv, 64, 67, 91, 96, 99, 132, 133, 143

Too True to be Good, 120, 142, 179

Trebitsch, Siegfried, 174

Tree, Beerbohm, 231

Trench, Harry, 103

Troilus and Cressida, 98

Trotsky, xiii

Turner, W. J., xv, xvi

Twain, Mark, 161, 170

Tyndall, John, 212

Uncle Tom's Cabin, 96

Undershaft, Andrew, 150, 158, 166-167

Undershaft, Stephen, 150

Unsocial Socialist, The, 104, 105

Utterword, Randall, 138

Viereck, G. S., 184

Violet, 154, 155

255

Vivie, 105-106, 167

Voltaire, xiii, xxv, 91

Wagner, 74

Waiter, The (William), 155

Walkley, A. B., 50, 201

War and Peace, 125

Warren, Mrs., 6, 103, 105-106, 167, 215

Webb, Beatrice, 5, 10, 18, 21, 66

Webb, Sidney, 9, 10, 34

"Webbs, the," xix, 9, 14-18, 20-21, 22, 24, 32, 57

Webster, John, 98, 99

Weismann, August, 61, 73, 74

Wells, H. G., xiv, xvi, 2, 11, 20, 71, 190, 191, 194, 204, 212-213, 214

What is Art? 96

Whitefield, Anne, 132, 154, 156-157, 164, 166, 167, 168, 225

Whitehead, A. N., 66

Widowers' Houses, 67, 101-102, 105, 106, 151

Wilde, Oscar, 174, 212, 231

Wilhelm II, ("the Kaiser"), 30, 31, 73, 187

Wilson, Edmund, xvi, xx, 3, 78, 169, 189, 202

Yeats, W. B., xiii, 201, 223, 231

You Never Can Tell, 155, 160

New Directions Paperbooks

Prince Ilango Adigal, *Shilappadikaram: The Ankle Bracelet*. NDP162.

Corrado Alvaro, *Revolt in Aspromonte*. NDP119.

Chairil Anwar, *Selected Poems*. WPS2.

Djuna Barnes, *Nightwood*. NDP98.

Charles Baudelaire, *Flowers of Evil*.† NDP71.

Eric Bentley, *Bernard Shaw*. NDP59.

Jorge Luis Borges, *Labyrinths*. NDP186.

Alain Bosquet, *Selected Poems*.† WPS4.

Kay Boyle, *Thirty Stories*. NDP62.

Breakthrough to Peace. (Anthology) NDP124.

William Bronk, *The World, the Worldless*. (SFR) NDP157.

Buddha, *The Dhammapada*. (Babbitt translation) NDP188.

Louis-Ferdinand Céline, *Journey to the End of the Night*. NDP84.

Blaise Cendrars, *Selected Writings*.† NDP203.

Bankim-chandra Chatterjee, *Krishnakanta's Will*. NDP120.

Jean Cocteau, *The Holy Terrors*. NDP212.
The Infernal Machine. NDP235.

Contemporary German Poetry.† (Anthology) NDP148.

Gregory Corso, *Happy Birthday of Death*. NDP86.
Long Live Man. NDP127.

Edward Dahlberg, *Because I Was Flesh*. NDP227.

Edward Dahlberg Reader. NDP246.

David Daiches, *Virginia Woolf*. (Revised) NDP96.

Robert Duncan, *Bending the Bow*. NDP255.

Richard Eberhart, *Selected Poems*. NDP198.

Russell Edson, *The Very Thing That Happens*. NDP137.

William Empson, *Seven Types of Ambiguity*. NDP204.
Some Versions of Pastoral. NDP92.

Lawrence Ferlinghetti, *A Coney Island of the Mind*. NDP74.
Her. NDP88.
Routines. NDP187.
Starting from San Francisco. NDP220.
Unfair Arguments with Existence. NDP143.

Ronald Firbank, *Two Novels*. NDP128.

Dudley Fitts, *Poems from the Greek Anthology*. NDP60.

F. Scott Fitzgerald, *The Crack-up*. NDP54.

Gustave Flaubert, *The Dictionary of Accepted Ideas*. NDP230.
Sentimental Education. NDP63.

M. K. Gandhi, *Gandhi on Non-Violence*. (ed. Thomas Merton) NDP197.

André Gide, *Dostoevsky*. NDP100.

Goethe, *Faust*, Part I. (MacIntyre translation) NDP70.

Albert J. Guerard, *Thomas Hardy*. NDP185.

James B. Hall, *Us He Devours* (SFR) NDP156.

Henry Hatfield, *Goethe*. NDP136.
Thomas Mann. (Revised Edition) NDP101.

John Hawkes, *The Cannibal*. NDP123.
The Lime Twig. NDP95.
Second Skin. NDP146.
The Beetle Leg. NDP239.
The Innocent Party. NDP238.

Hermann Hesse, *Siddhartha*. NDP65.

Edwin Honig, *García Lorca* (Rev.) NDP102.

Christopher Isherwood, *The Berlin Stories*. NDP134.

Henry James, *Stories of Writers and Artists*. NDP57.

Alfred Jarry, *Ubu Roi*. NDP105.

James Joyce, *Stephen Hero*. NDP133.

Franz Kafka, *Amerika*. NDP117.

Bob Kaufman, *Solitudes Crowded with Loneliness*. NDP199.

Hugh Kenner, *Wyndham Lewis*. NDP167.

Lincoln Kirstein, *Rhymes & More Rhymes of a Pfc*. NDP202.

P. Lal, translator, *Great Sanskrit Plays*. NDP142.

Tommaso Landolfi, *Gogol's Wife and Other Stories*. NDP155.

Lautréamont, *Maldoror*. NDP207.

Denise Levertov, *O Taste and See*. NDP149.
The Jacob's Ladder. NDP112.
The Sorrow Dance. NDP222.
With Eyes at the Back of Our Heads. NDP229.

Harry Levin, *James Joyce*. NDP87.

García Lorca, *Selected Poems*.† NDP114.
Three Tragedies. NDP52.
Five Plays. NDP232.

Carson McCullers, *The Member of the Wedding*. (Playscript) NDP153.

Thomas Merton, *Cables to the Ace*. NDP252.
Clement of Alexandria. Gift Edition. NDP173.
Emblems of a Season of Fury. NDP140.
Original Child Bomb. NDP174.
Raids on the Unspeakable. NDP213.
Selected Poems. NDP85.

Henry Miller, *Big Sur & Oranges of Hieronymus Bosch*. NDP161.
The Colossus of Maroussi. NDP75.
The Cosmological Eye. NDP109.
Henry Miller on Writing. NDP151.